GREAT SPEECHES
IN MINUTES

D0610478

GREAT SPEECHES
IN MINUTES

JACOB F. FIELD

Quercus

Contents

Introduction

Words empower people to take action, whether it is to galvanize society behind a political movement, to inspire people to fight for their freedom or to raise awareness of injustice and inequality. Throughout history, as well as in the contemporary world, significant and notable figures – be they admired or infamous – have deployed rhetoric to persuade people to join their cause.

Have you ever wondered how Alexander the Great sought to rouse his soldiers to join him in one final campaign, or thought about the words Elizabeth I might have used to rally the people of England behind her in the face of foreign invasion, or what Martin Luther King, Jr's last great speech was before his tragic assassination? *Great Speeches in Minutes* provides the answers and background to these questions, and many more. It presents 200 of the most epic and influential addresses ever given, delivered by speakers originating from every inhabited continent in the world.

The book is arranged chronologically as ten chapters, each with a focus on a different period in history. Beginning in the ancient world, the speeches span the centuries to the present day. Broad in their content, they cover a diverse range of subjects, from Buddha's first recorded sermon to Oprah Winfrey's optimism for a brighter future for the young girls of today. To help you find the speech you are looking for, three appendices list the entries by key lines alphabetically by speaker, and thematically. This means that you will be able to locate precisely the figure, rhetorical flourish or cause that is most important to you.

Each of the 200 entries in this book features a key extract from the speech in question, highlighting important and noteworthy sections of it. Alongside this is a succinct explanation of the historical, social and political context of the speech, including biographical information about the person who made it, as well as the impact his or her words had on those listening. Whether you want to master the art of rhetoric yourself or understand how great leaders and campaigners have held audiences spellbound before them, *Great Speeches in Minutes* is the perfect book.

Buddha

THE FIRST SERMON

Siddhārtha Gautama (c. sixth–fourth century BCE) was born in the northeast of the Indian subcontinent, possibly in Lumbini in Nepal. The son of a local ruler, he enjoyed a luxurious lifestyle sheltered from the harsh realities of existence until, at the age of 29, he looked outside his palace walls and realized death and sickness were part of life. He renounced his privilege and lived as an ascetic. Six years into his new life, after meditating for 49 days, Siddhārtha realized how humans could attain nirvana – freedom from the cycle of death and rebirth. It was through this enlightenment that he became the Buddha (Awakened One). Buddha gave his first recorded sermon at the deer park in the city of Sarnath, in northern India. In it, he set out the foundations of his philosophy, among them the Noble Eightfold Path towards achieving nirvana. For the rest of his life, he travelled the land teaching and gaining disciples and his followers formed communities of Buddhist monks, called *bhikkhus*. Buddhism spread across the Indian subcontinent and went on to become a major influence on religions such as Confucianism and Shintoism.

"Now this, oh *Bhikkhus*, is the noble truth concerning the way that leads to the destruction of sorrow. Verily! It is this noble eightfold path, which is to say: right views, right aspirations, right speech, right conduct, right livelihood, right effort, right mindfulness and right contemplation."

Sarnath, India, c. 5th century BCE

Pericles

FUNERAL ORATION

In 431 BCE, a war for dominance of Greece broke out between the Athenian Delian League and the Spartan Peloponnesian League. The Athenian leader was Pericles (c. 495–429 BCE), who had ruled the city since 461 BCE, rising to power as part of the democratic faction that stood in opposition to the aristocracy. After war broke out, Sparta and its allies invaded the countryside around Athens, forcing the Athenians to withdraw behind their walls. Some Athenians turned against Pericles, blaming him for the war and criticizing his refusal to engage the Spartans in open battle. As the first year of conflict ended, Athens held its annual public funeral for those who had died in conflict, and Pericles delivered the oration. He appealed to the people to remember the glory of their city, and praised the patriotic valour of those who had died in its defence. Although Pericles still enjoyed popular support, his political enemies removed him from power the year after his oration. In 429 BCE he regained his preeminent position but fell victim to a plague epidemic that was ravaging Athens at the time.

"For this offering of their lives, made in common by them all, they each of them individually received that renown that never grows old, and for a sepulchre, not so much that in which their bones have been deposited, but that noblest of shrines wherein their glory is laid up to be eternally remembered upon every occasion on which deed or story shall call for its commemoration. For heroes have the whole earth for their tomb, and in lands far from their own, where the column with its epitaph declares it, there is enshrined in every breast a record unwritten with no tablet to preserve it, except that of the heart. These take as your model and, judging happiness to be the fruit of freedom and freedom of valour, never decline the dangers of war... For it is only the love of honour that never grows old, and honour it is, not gain, as some would have it, that rejoices the heart of age and helplessness. ...And where the rewards for merit are greatest, there are found the best citizens."

Athens, Greece, 431 BCE

Cleon

ON THE PUNISHMENT OF THE MYTILENEANS

Following the death of Pericles (see page 10), the nobleman Cleon (d. 422 BCE) rose to lead Athens. He proposed a more active policy in the Peloponnesian War – instead of sheltering within the city walls, Athenians should aggressively attack their enemies by land and sea. In 428 BCE Cleon was tested when Mytilene, a city-state on the island of Lesbos and a former Athenian ally, revolted. The Mytilenean leaders hoped to seize all Lesbos, but before they could do so, an Athenian fleet arrived and put down the revolt by 427 BCE. That year, Cleon addressed the Athenian Assembly – the city's governing body – urging members to approve his proposal to put all the male citizens of Mytilene to death and enslave its women and children. Cleon's argument that any disloyalty to Athens should be crushed was initially accepted by the assembly but the next day, before his order could be enacted, it was rescinded. Even so, hundreds of Mytileneans were executed. Cleon continued his proactive policies but fell in battle against the Spartans in 422 BCE. Peace between Athens and Sparta followed, but it would prove to be merely temporary.

" No hope, therefore, that rhetoric may instil or money purchase, of the mercy due to human infirmity must be held out to the Mytileneans. Their offence was not involuntary, but of malice and deliberate, and mercy is only for unwilling offenders...

Do not, therefore, be traitors to yourselves, but recall as nearly as possible the moment of suffering and the supreme importance that you then attached to their reduction. And now pay them back in their turn, without yielding to present weakness or forgetting the peril that once hung over you. Punish them as they deserve, and teach your other allies by a striking example that the penalty of rebellion is death. "

Athens, Greece, 427 BCE

Alcibiades

IN SUPPORT OF THE ATHENIAN EXPEDITION

Many Athenians opposed the peace with Sparta that followed Cleon's death (see page 12). Chief among them was the politician Alcibiades (c. 450–404 BCE). The spark for further hostilities occurred on Sicily, where there were numerous Greek colonies. In 415 BCE, news reached Athens that one of its allies was under attack from Syracuse, a city-state linked to the Spartans. In a speech to the Athenian people, Alcibiades persuaded them to approve a military expedition to Sicily, under his command. Before departing Alcibiades was accused of mutilating religious statues around Athens. Though allowed to leave for Sicily, on arrival he received orders to return home to stand trial. En route, hearing he had already been condemned to death, Alcibiades defected to Sparta. In Sicily, the Athenians were defeated after two years of fighting, losing 200 ships and thousands of soldiers. Meanwhile, Alcibiades returned to the Athenian cause, enjoying some military victories and regaining political influence. His enemies forced him into exile and in 404 BCE he was murdered in the Anatolian city of Phrygia, possibly at the behest of the Spartans.

"Men do not rest content with parrying the attacks of a superior, but often strike the first blow to prevent the attack being made. And we cannot fix the exact point at which our empire shall stop. We have reached a position in which we must not be content with retaining, but must scheme to extend it, for, if we cease to rule others, we are in danger of being ruled ourselves.

…Understand that neither youth nor old age can do anything the one without the other, but that levity, sobriety and deliberate judgment are strongest when united, and that, by sinking into inaction, the city, like everything else, will wear itself out, and its skill in everything decay, while each fresh struggle will give it fresh experience, and make it more used to defend itself not in word but in deed."

Athens, Greece, 414 BCE

Gorgias

ENCOMIUM OF HELEN

During the fifth century BCE, the sophists emerged in the Hellenic world – itinerant intellectuals who, for a fee, instructed members of the public across a wide range of fields. One of the first sophists was Gorgias (c. 485–380 BCE), who specialized in rhetoric and philosophy.

Born in Leontini, a Greek colony in Sicily, Gorgias was sent to Athens as an emissary in around 427 BCE, winning fame as a public speaker. His signature piece of rhetoric was his encomium (or tribute) to Helen of Troy, a famed mythical beauty. In his speech, Gorgias used his linguistic skill to show that even though Helen's adultery with Paris had led to war between the Trojans and the Greeks, she could not be blamed if the affair was the work of fate or the gods. Furthermore, he argued that if Paris had used the power of speech to persuade Helen into their dalliance, she was likewise above reproach. Gorgias stayed in Greece until his death, reportedly nearing 100 years in age, travelling across the land instructing students and giving demonstrations.

"For it is the nature of things, not for the strong to be hindered by the weak, but for the weaker to be ruled and drawn by the stronger, and for the stronger to lead and the weaker to follow. God is a stronger force than man in might and in wit and in other ways. If, then, one must place blame on Fate and on a god, one must free Helen from disgrace.

…The effect of speech upon the condition of the soul is comparable to the power of drugs over the nature of bodies. For just as different drugs dispel different secretions from the body, and some bring an end to disease and others to life, so also in the case of speeches, some distress, others delight, some cause fear, others make the hearers bold and some drug and bewitch the soul with a kind of evil persuasion."

Athens, Greece, 427 BCE

Lysias

AGAINST ERATOSTHENES

Rhetoric was so valued in ancient Greece that professional speech writers were commonplace. They included Lysias (c. 445–380 BCE), who was born in Syracuse but settled in Athens in 412 BCE. When Athens was defeated in the Peloponnesian War in 404 BCE, the Thirty Tyrants rose to power. This group of oligarchs seized foreign residents and subjected political opponents to violent reprisal. Lysias fled the city, while his brother Polemarchus was arrested and forced to commit suicide by drinking hemlock. When democracy was restored in 403 BCE, Lysias returned to Athens and resumed his career as a speech writer. His most famous piece was an address against Eratosthenes, one of the Thirty Tyrants, accusing him of Polemarchus's murder. Lysias also claimed that the tyrants had arrested people not because they were any kind of threat to Athens, but because they wanted to seize Athenian property. The outcome of Lysias's speech and the fate of Eratosthenes are unknown. Lysias continued to live in Athens until his death in around 380 BCE, supporting himself by writing speeches for law courts.

"The crimes of Eratosthenes are not only too atrocious to describe, but too many to enumerate. No exaggeration can exceed, and within the time assigned for this discourse it is impossible fully to represent them. …Recall the cruel indignities that you suffered – how you were dragged from the tribunal and the altars, how no place, however sacred, could shelter you against their violence. Others, torn from their wives, their children, their parents, after putting an end to their miserable lives, were deprived of funeral rites. For these tyrants imagined their government so firmly established that even the vengeance of the gods was unable to shake it."

Athens, Greece, 403 BCE

Socrates

COMMENTS ON HIS SENTENCE

A founding figure of Western philosophy, the Athenian Socrates (c. 470–399 BCE) sought to answer the great questions of human existence, such as 'what is justice?', through debate and discussion. This Socratic method of examining hypotheses through critical argument and dialogue has become a mainstay of philosophical enquiry. Although none of Socrates's writings survive, his teachings were recorded by his students and followers, notably the great philosopher Plato. Socrates challenged the traditional mores of Athenian society, even critiquing democracy. In 399 BCE, he was tried for corrupting the minds of the youth of Athens, and for not believing in the city's gods. Instead of fleeing into exile, Socrates faced the charges. The jury found him guilty and sentenced him to death by drinking hemlock. Plato's account of the trial recorded Socrates's speech of defence and his address after his sentencing. Socrates's friends urged him to try and escape, but determined to obey the laws of Athens, he stayed and willingly drank the fatal poison.

"Wherefore, O judges, be of good cheer about death, and know this of a truth – that no evil can happen to a good man, either in life or after death… I am not angry with my accusers, or my condemners. They have done me no harm, although neither of them meant to do me any good.

…The hour of departure has arrived, and we go our ways – I to die, and you to live. Which is better God only knows."

Athens, Greece, 399 BCE

Isocrates

ON THE UNION OF GREECE TO RESIST PERSIA

The Persian Empire had twice invaded Greece during the first half of the fifth century BCE, but failed to conquer it. Persia continued to be involved in Greek affairs, such as during the Corinthian War (395–387 BCE), when it supported Athens and the other city-states attempting to prevent Sparta expanding its power. Just as it appeared Athens might triumph, Persia switched sides. The Persians then enforced a peace that gave them control of Cyprus and western Anatolia. For many Athenians, including Isocrates (436–338 BCE), such foreign interference in Greece was unacceptable. Born into a wealthy family that had made its fortune during the Peloponnesian War, Isocrates worked as a professional speech writer and opened a school of rhetoric. In 380 BCE, he urged the union of Greek city-states to keep the peace amongst them and to combat Persian hegemony. His Panhellenist dreams were never fulfilled. In 338 BCE, after the Kingdom of Macedon established dominance over much of Greece, Isocrates, wracked by despair, committed suicide by starving himself to death.

"For it is neither possible to enjoy a secure peace, unless we make war in concert against the foreign enemy, nor for the Greeks to be of one mind, until we consider both our advantages to come from one another, and our dangers to be against the same people.

…For who, either of those able to write poetry, or of those who understand how to speak, will not labour and study, wishing to leave behind him a memorial for all ages, at the same time of his own and of their valour?"

Athens, Greece, 380 BCE

Demosthenes

THE THIRD PHILIPPIC

Athenian statesman Demosthenes (384–322 BCE) honed his skill as an orator by practising in his underground study, shaving half his head so he could not leave. He overcame a speech impediment by speaking with a mouth full of pebbles. By his 30s, he was an influential voice in Athenian politics. During the mid-fourth century BCE, the northern Greek kingdom of Macedon began to eclipse Athens. A strident opponent of its expansion, Demosthenes publicly denounced the imperialist ambitions of the Macedonian king, Philip II, and demanded Athens oppose him. In 341 BCE, he delivered the third of his Philippics against him. Demosthenes's rhetoric was is vain; in 338 BCE Philip destroyed an Athenian-led coalition at the Battle of Chaeronea, giving Macedon dominance of Greece. This continued under Philip's successor Alexander the Great. Undeterred, Demosthenes continued to argue for Athenian independence until 322 BCE, when pressure from its Macedonian overlords forced civic authorities to condemn him to death. Before the sentence could be carried out, Demosthenes committed suicide by taking poison.

"As long as the vessel is safe, whether it be great or small, the mariner, the pilot, every man in turn should exert himself, and prevent its being overturned either by accident or design. But when the sea hath rolled over it, their efforts are vain. And we likewise, O Athenians, while we are safe, with a magnificent city, plentiful resources, lofty reputation – what must we do? Many of you, I dare say, have been longing to ask. Well then, I will tell you. I will move a resolution, pass it, if you please… let us prepare for our own defence, provide ourselves, I mean, with ships, money and troops – for surely, though all other people consent to be slaves, we at least ought to struggle for freedom."

Athens, Greece, 341 BCE

Aeschines

AGAINST CTESIPHON

Demosthenes's greatest opponent in Athens was Aeschines (389–314 BCE). He came from a humble background and, before entering politics, had worked as an actor and served in the army. At first Aeschines had opposed Philip II's expansionist policies (see page 24), but he came to realize that some kind of settlement with Macedon was inevitable. This led to a long and bitter feud between Demosthenes and Aeschines. When a minor Athenian politician called Ctesiphon proposed that Demosthenes be given a golden crown in honour of his service to the city-state, Aeschines brought a legal suit against him. In the trial, held in 330 BCE, Aeschines questioned Ctesiphon's morals and argued the offer of the crown was unlawful. Although Aeschines's speech contained many valid legal points, he was undone by a brilliant rebuttal from Demosthenes that took advantage of anti-Macedonian sentiment in Athens. Aeschines duly lost the case and went into a voluntary exile in Rhodes, where he opened a school of rhetoric. He died on the island of Samos, outliving his rival Demosthenes by eight years.

"He who is insensible to that natural affection that should engage his heart to those who are most intimate and near to him can never feel a greater regard to your welfare than to that of strangers. He who acts wickedly in private life cannot prove excellent in his public conduct. He who is base at home can never acquit himself with honour when sent to a strange country in a public character. For it is not the man but the scene that changes.

…It will be your part, Athenians, to put an end to this frequency of public honours, these precipitate grants of crowns, else they who obtain them will owe you no acknowledgement, nor shall the state receive the least advantage. For you never can make bad men better, and those of real merit must be cast into the utmost dejection."

Athens, Greece, 330 BCE

Alexander the Great

AT HYDASPES RIVER

In 336 BCE, Alexander (356–323 BCE) became King of Macedon, which his father Philip II had made the dominant power in Greece. Alexander outdid this achievement by conquering the Persian Empire, which he invaded in 334 BCE – despite often being outnumbered, Alexander never lost a battle. After taking Egypt in 332 BCE, he marched into Mesopotamia and within two years had overthrown the Persian emperor. In 326 BCE, Alexander turned his focus to the Indian subcontinent, advancing into the Indus Valley. After a hard-fought victory over a local king on the banks of the Hydaspes River, Alexander's army, exhausted and homesick, refused to go on. Alexander urged his men to match his ambition for glory, but he was unable to persuade them; the Macedonian army went no further east. Even so, Alexander had created a great empire, stretching from Greece to northwestern India. He did not rule it for long; in 323 BCE Alexander the Great died in Babylon – he was just 32 years old. His empire died with him, quickly descending into civil war and fragmenting.

> " O Macedonians and Grecian allies, stand firm! Glorious are the deeds of those who undergo labour and run the risk of danger. It is delightful to live a life of valour and to die leaving behind immortal glory. "

Hydaspes River, modern-day Pakistan, 326 BCE

Publius Cornelius Scipio

BEFORE THE BATTLE OF TICINUS

As the Roman Republic expanded from a small city-state to become a major power in the Mediterranean, its chief rival was the Carthaginian Empire, which ruled much of coastal North Africa and Iberia. In the First Punic War (264–241 BCE), Rome had defeated Carthage to gain Sicily, and then seized Corsica and Sardinia from them. Determined to take revenge, in 218 BCE the Carthaginian general Hannibal advanced into Italy. The invasion caught Roman authorities by surprise. Scipio (d. 211 BCE), the current consul (the senior elected office in the Roman Republic), was sent to defeat Hannibal. The two armies met on the banks of the Ticinus River, in northern Italy. Scipio appealed to his men to defend their homes against the foreign invaders, but was then caught out when Hannibal launched a cavalry charge while he was trying to organize his army. This left Scipio surrounded and he was only saved from death by his teenage son, later to win fame as Scipio Africanus (see page 34). Scipio the elder, who had been seriously wounded, retreated. The next year he was killed fighting Carthaginian forces in Spain.

"No, they are only semblances or rather ghosts of men, worn out with starvation, cold, filth and squalour, bruised and enfeebled amongst the rocks and precipices, and, what is more, their limbs are frostbitten, their thews and sinews cramped with cold, their frames shrunk and shrivelled with frost, their weapons battered and shivered, their horses lame and out of condition. This is the cavalry, this the infantry with whom you are going to fight. You will not have an enemy but only the last vestiges of an enemy to meet. My only fear is that when you have fought, it will appear to be the Alps that have conquered Hannibal. But perhaps it was right that it should be so, and that the gods, without any human aid, should begin and all but finish this war with a people and their general who have broken treaties, and that to us, who next to the gods have been sinned against, it should be left to complete what they began.

…There is no second army at our back to oppose the enemy if we fail to win, there are no more Alps to delay his advance while a fresh army can be raised for defence. Here it is, soldiers, that we have to resist, just as though we were fighting before the walls of Rome. Every one of you must remember that he is using his arms to protect not himself only, but also his wife and little children. Nor must his anxiety be confined to his home, he must realize, too, that the senate and people of Rome are watching our exploits today. What our strength and courage are now here, such will be the fortune of our city yonder and of the empire of Rome."

———————————————————————

Ticinus River, Italy, November 218 BCE

Hannibal Barca

BEFORE THE BATTLE OF THE TREBIA

The son of a Carthaginian general, Hannibal (247–c. 181 BCE) devoted his career to defeating Rome. In 218 BCE, he daringly marched an army from Spain into Italy via the Alps, beginning the Second Punic War. After his victory at the Battle of Ticinus, Hannibal faced a Roman army led by the consul Tiberius Sempronius Longus on the banks of the Trebia River. Having promised his men fortune and reminding them of the righteousness of their cause, Hannibal goaded Sempronius into a frontal assault. It was a trap: the general sent in reserves that included war elephants, cutting down the Roman army. Thanks to his brilliance, Hannibal enjoyed further triumphs at Lake Trasimene (217 BCE) and Cannae (216 BCE). Facing defeat, Rome adopted a new strategy of refusing to engage Hannibal in pitched battle. He became isolated, finding it difficult to gain supplies, and in 203 BCE was recalled to Carthage to fight off a Roman attack. He was defeated, and Carthage lost the Second Punic War. Exiled, Hannibal entered the service of rulers in the Middle East, and in around 183 BCE committed suicide when he learned he was on the verge of being handed over to Rome.

"Now the hour has come for you to enter upon rich and lucrative campaigns and to earn rewards that are worth the earning, after your long march over all those mountains and rivers, and through all those nations in arms. Here fortune has vouchsafed an end to your toils, here she will vouchsafe a reward worthy of all your past services.

…Wherever I turn my eyes I see nothing but courage and strength, a veteran infantry, a cavalry, regular and irregular alike, drawn from the noblest tribes, you, our most faithful and brave allies, you, Carthaginians, who are going to fight for your country, inspired by a most righteous indignation. We are taking the aggressive, we are descending in hostile array into Italy, prepared to fight more bravely and more fearlessly than our foe because he who attacks is animated by stronger hopes and greater courage than he who meets the attack."

Trebia River, Italy, December 218 BCE

Scipio Africanus

TO HIS MUTINOUS TROOPS

The man who vanquished Hannibal was Publius Cornelius Scipio (236–183 BCE), whose father (and namesake) had died fighting the Carthaginians in Spain. When Rome sent reinforcements to Spain in 210 BCE, Scipio volunteered to lead them. Given the command, he proved a brilliant and innovative general. In 206 BCE, Scipio fell ill. Hearing rumours their commander was on the verge of death, a Roman army of 8,000 camped at Sucro mutinied over arrears of pay. The seriousness of Scipio's condition had been exaggerated – he led an army to Sucro and surrounded the mutineers. Publicly upbraiding them, he beheaded the ringleaders, before completing his conquest of Spain. Scipio returned to Rome in triumph and was elected consul in 205 BCE. He invaded Carthage and, in 202 BCE, defeated Hannibal at the Battle of Zama, winning the Second Punic War for Rome. In honour of his achievement, he was rewarded with an additional surname, Africanus. Despite his successes, Africanus's rivals levelled baseless accusations of corruption against him – in disgust, he retired from political life to his country estate, where he died.

"Words and ideas alike fail me; I do not even know by what title I am to address you. Am I to call you Roman citizens – you who have revolted against your country? Can I call you soldiers when you have renounced the authority and auspices of your general, and broken the solemn obligations of your military oath? Your appearance, your features, your dress, your demeanour I recognize as those of my fellow countrymen, but I see that your actions, your language, your designs, your spirit and temper are those of your country's foes. …There is no doubt about it, soldiers, you were seized with madness. The bodily illness from which I suffered was not one whit more severe than the mental malady that overtook you. I shrink with horror from dwelling upon the credit men gave to rumours, the hopes they entertained, the ambitious schemes they formed. Let all be forgotten, if possible, or if not that, let silence at least draw a veil over all. I admit that my words have appeared stern and unfeeling to you, but how much more unfeeling, think you, has your conduct been than anything I have said? You imagine that it is right and proper for me to tolerate your actions, and yet you have not patience to hear them mentioned. Bad as they are however, I will not reproach you with them any longer. I only wish you may forget them as easily as I shall. As for the army as a body, if you sincerely repent of your wrongdoing you give me satisfaction enough and more than enough."

Sucro, Spain, 206 BCE

Cato the Elder

IN SUPPORT OF THE OPPIAN LAW

In 215 BCE, the year after Hannibal annihilated a Roman army at Cannae, a politician called Gaius Oppius passed a new law. His *lex oppia* regulated conspicuous consumption by women. They were forbidden from owning more than half an ounce of gold, wearing multicoloured clothes and travelling on animal-driven vehicles in and around cities and towns. This, and other sumptuary laws, aimed to limit extravagant spending so Rome could concentrate on defeating Carthage. In 195 BCE, six years after Rome had triumphed, there were proposals to abolish the *lex oppia*. These were opposed by the consul Cato (234–149 BCE), a commoner who had risen to high office through his ability as an orator and uncompromising morals. In his speech, Cato argued that the law was necessary to control the female desire to spend, as well as removing the stigma of wearing plain clothes since everyone had to dress modestly. Despite Cato's speech, the law was successfully repealed. For the rest of his life, Cato continued to be an influential and traditionalist figure, railing against the foreign ostentations he saw creeping into Roman society.

"That what is permitted to another should be forbidden to you may naturally create a feeling of shame or indignation, but when all are upon the same level as far as dress is concerned why should any one of you fear that you will not attract notice? The very last things to be ashamed of are thriftiness and poverty, but this law relieves you of both since you do not possess what it forbids you to possess.

…Depend upon it, as soon as a woman begins to be ashamed of what she ought not to be ashamed of, she will cease to feel shame at what she ought to be ashamed of. She who is in a position to do so will get what she wants with her own money, she who cannot do this will ask her husband. The husband is in a pitiable plight whether he yields or refuses. In the latter case he will see another giving what he refused to give. Now they are soliciting other women's husbands, and what is worse they are soliciting votes for the repeal of a law, and are getting them from some, against the interest of you and your property and your children. When once the law has ceased to fix a limit to your wife's expenses, you will never fix one. Do not imagine that things will be the same as they were before the law was made. It is safer for an evil-doer not to be prosecuted than for him to be tried and then acquitted, and luxury and extravagance would have been more tolerable had they never been interfered with than they will be now, just like wild beasts that have been irritated by their chains and then released."

———————————

Rome, Italy, 195 BCE

Gaius Memmius

ON A CORRUPT OLIGARCHY

During the second and first centuries BCE, there was rising social and political conflict within the Roman Republic between the commoners, known as the plebeians, and the aristocratic patrician class who dominated the Roman Senate. Representing the interests of the masses were officials called the tribunes of the plebs, who had the power to veto legislation they believed to be detrimental to the interests of the people. Gaius Memmius (d. 100 BCE) was elected tribune in 111 BCE. At the time, Rome was involved in a succession dispute in Numidia, an allied kingdom in North Africa. One of the claimants to the throne, Jugurtha, had sacked his rival's capital, killing several Roman citizens. Despite this, Jugurtha's supporters in Rome, including many senators and senior officials who he had bribed, continued to back him. For Memmius this was a brazen betrayal and he demanded the senate take action. Buoyed by his words and strong public support, Rome declared war, defeating Jugurtha by 106 BCE. Memmius went on to run for consul in 100 BCE, but was killed in violent rioting instigated by a political rival.

"The senate's dignity has been prostituted to a ruthless enemy, your sovereignty has been betrayed, your country has been offered for sale at home and abroad. Unless cognisance is taken of these outrages, unless the guilty are punished, what will remain except to pass our lives in submission to those who are guilty of these acts? For to do with impunity whatever one fancies is to be king. I am not urging you, Romans, to rejoice rather in the guilt than in the innocence of your fellow citizens, but you should not insist upon ruining the good by pardoning the wicked. Moreover, in a republic, it is far better to forget a kindness than an injury. The good man merely becomes less active in well doing when you neglect him, but the bad man grows more wicked."

Rome, Italy, c. 110 BCE

Marcus Tullius Cicero

FIRST CATILINE ORATION

One of Rome's greatest orators was Cicero (106–43 BCE), who served as a consul in 63 BCE. In winning the post, he defeated Catiline, a populist with radical plans to wipe out all debts. Near the end of Cicero's one-year term Catiline again failed to be elected consul. Stung by this loss, he planned to seize power by burning down parts of Rome, massacring his opponents and launching uprisings across Italy. Cicero became aware of the conspiracy, but many senators did not believe the seriousness of his plot. On 8th November, Cicero made the first of four orations against Catiline, addressing the Senate and persuading its members of the danger he posed to the republic. Catiline, who was in attendance, was shamed and fled Rome to join his supporters in the provinces. He was killed in 62 BCE, leading his men against republican forces. Cicero had triumphed. He was hailed as a saviour of Rome and given the title 'Father of the Fatherland' – the high-water mark of his political career. He went on to oppose Caesar's imperialist polices and, in 43 BCE, was proscribed a public enemy and executed.

"When, O Catiline, do you mean to cease abusing our patience? How long is that madness of yours still to mock us? When is there to be an end of that unbridled audacity of yours, swaggering about as it does now?

…O Catiline, be gone to your impious and nefarious war, to the great safety of the republic, to your own misfortune and injury and to the destruction of those who have joined themselves to you in every wickedness and atrocity. Then do you, O Jupiter, who were consecrated by Romulus with the same auspices as this city, whom we rightly call the stay of this city and empire, repel this man and his companions from your altars and from the other temples – from the houses and walls of the city – from the lives and fortunes of all the citizens. And overwhelm all the enemies of good men, the foes of the republic, the robbers of Italy, men bound together by a treaty and infamous alliance of crimes, dead and alive, with eternal punishments."

Rome, Italy, 63 BCE

Gaius Julius Caesar

BEFORE THE BATTLE OF PHARSALUS

Caesar (100–44 BCE) rose to power as a member of the Triumvirate, a political alliance comprised of him, Crassus and Pompey. After serving as consul in 59 BCE, Caesar began a hugely successful campaign against Gallic tribes to the north – by 50 BCE he had brought Gaul (most of modern-day France and Belgium) under Roman rule. Caesar's growing influence worried conservatives in the senate, including his erstwhile ally Pompey (Crassus had died in 53 BCE). When the war in Gaul ended, Caesar ignored orders to relinquish his command and crossed into Italy with his army in 49 BCE. This triggered a civil war between Caesar and his opponents that spread out from Italy across the Mediterranean; in 48 BCE Caesar faced Pompey at Pharsalus in Greece. Though outnumbered, Caesar inspired his men to win a victory that laid the foundations for his eventual triumph in the civil war in 45 BCE. The next year Caesar was proclaimed 'dictator in perpetuity', giving him unprecedented powers, but just a few weeks later he was assassinated by a group of senators seeking to restore the old system of government.

"Remember how you swore to each other in my presence that you would never leave the field except as conquerors.

…Before all else, in order that I may know that you are mindful of your promise to choose victory or death, throw down the walls of your camp as you go out to battle and fill up the ditch, so that we may have no place of refuge if we do not conquer, and so that the enemy may see that we have no camp and know that we are compelled to encamp in theirs."

Pharsalus, Greece, 9th August 48 BCE

Mark Antony

FUNERAL ORATION OVER CAESAR

After the assassination of Julius Caesar, his leading supporter Mark Antony (c. 83–30 BCE) addressed the crowds at his funeral. He reminded mourners of Caesar's great achievements and condemned his murderers. He then joined forces with Octavian, Caesar's great-nephew and adopted son, and another politician, called Lepidus, to form the Second Triumvirate. In 42 BCE they defeated the forces of the men who had plotted to kill Caesar and established a three-man dictatorship, dividing Roman territory amongst themselves. Mark Antony oversaw the eastern provinces, which included Egypt, a client-kingdom ruled by Cleopatra, Caesar's former lover. Despite being married to Octavian's sister, Mark Antony began an affair with Cleopatra. This strained the already fractious triumvirate (Lepidus had been expelled in 33 BCE) and led to civil war between Mark Antony and Octavian. By 30 BCE, Mark Antony had been defeated. Rather than be brought to Rome in chains, he and Cleopatra committed suicide. Octavian was now sole ruler of Rome; in 27 BCE, he adopted the title of Augustus, becoming the first Roman Emperor.

"It seems to me, fellow citizens, that this deed is not the work of human beings, but of some evil spirit. It becomes us to consider the present rather than the past, since the greatest danger approaches, if it is not already here, lest we be drawn into our former civil commotions and lose whatever remains of noble birth in the city. Let us, then, conduct this sacred one to the abode of the blest, chanting over him our accustomed hymn and lamentation.

...It is not fitting, citizens, that the funeral oration of so great a man should be pronounced by me alone, but rather by his whole country. ...Nobody... who found refuge with him was harmed, but he, whom you declared sacred and inviolable, was killed, although he did not extort these honours from you as a tyrant, and did not even ask for them."

Rome, Italy, 20th March 44 BCE

Jesus of Nazareth

THE SERMON ON THE MOUNT

A Jew born in Bethlehem, Jesus (c. 4 BCE–c. 33 CE) grew up in Nazareth; both places were in Judea, which became part of the Roman Empire in 6 CE. Jesus began his public ministry at around the age of 30, preaching, performing miracles and gathering disciples. His followers believed he was the Messiah – the Son of God sent to save humanity. The longest recorded continuous speech delivered by Jesus was the Sermon on the Mount, recorded in the Gospel of Matthew. This sermon encapsulated many of Jesus's moral teachings, starting with the Beatitudes, which recounted the blessings and rewards to those who were loving, merciful, peaceful and compassionate. Jesus then told his followers how to pray, reciting the words of the Lord's Prayer. Jesus continued his work, but faced suspicion and hostility from Jewish religious leaders and the Roman authorities. In Jerusalem, he was betrayed to the Roman governor of Judea and crucified. Christians believe that after dying on the cross, he rose again and ascended into Heaven. His teachings form the core tenets of Christianity, now the largest religion in the world.

"Blessed are the poor in spirit, for theirs is the kingdom of heaven. Blessed are they that mourn, for they shall be comforted. Blessed are the meek, for they shall inherit the earth. Blessed are they who do hunger and thirst after righteousness, for they shall be filled. Blessed are the merciful, for they shall obtain mercy. Blessed are the pure in heart, for they shall see God. Blessed are the peacemakers, for they shall be called the children of God. Blessed are they who are persecuted for righteousness' sake, for theirs is the kingdom of heaven. Blessed are you, when men shall revile you, and persecute you, and shall say all manner of evil against you falsely, for my sake. Rejoice, and be glad, for great is your reward in heaven."

Mount of Beatitudes, modern-day Israel, c. 28 CE

Calgacus

BEFORE THE BATTLE OF MONS GRAUPIUS

In 43 CE, Roman forces invaded Britain, adding much of the island to their empire. They faced fierce opposition from the local Celtic tribes, particularly the Caledonians, who lived in modern-day Scotland. In around 83 CE, the Roman governor of Britain, Gnaeus Julius Agricola, led an army north against the Caledonians, hoping to defeat them and bring their territory under imperial control. The leader of the alliance of Caledonian tribes was the chieftain Calgacus (b. 1st century CE). The two armies met at Mons Graupius in northeast Scotland. Before the battle, Calgacus is said to have warned his men of the dangers of Roman victory, reminding them that defeat would be catastrophic to their society. In all probability the speech was a work of fiction concocted by the historian Tacitus, who was Agricola's son-in-law and had joined the campaign. However, it has become emblematic of the rapacity of the Roman Empire. The Romans were victorious at Mons Graupius, but were unable to gain permanent control of Caledonian territory and eventually withdrew south.

"Now the furthest limits of Britain are thrown open. But there are no tribes beyond us, nothing indeed but waves and rocks, and the cruel Romans, from whose oppression escape is vainly sought by obedience and submission. Robbers of the world, having by their universal plunder exhausted the land, they rifle the deep. If the enemy be rich, they are rapacious, if he be poor, they lust for dominion, and neither the east nor the west has been able to satisfy them. Alone among men they covet with equal eagerness poverty and riches. To robbery, slaughter, plunder, they give the lying name of empire. They make a solitude and call it peace."

Mons Graupius, modern-day Scotland c. 83 CE

St Augustine of Hippo

SERMON ON THE LORD'S PRAYER

Born in modern-day Algeria, then part of the Roman Empire, St Augustine of Hippo (354–430 CE) studied and taught rhetoric in Carthage, Rome and Milan. He led a hedonistic, sometimes sinful life, before experiencing a spiritual awakening in 386. Ten years later, he became Bishop of Hippo in his homeland, a post he held for the rest of his life. Augustine became a persuasive defender of Christian doctrine and policies approved by the imperial regime and was well known throughout the Roman world. He campaigned against sects and teachings that had diverted from the official line. An incredibly prolific writer, he produced religious works such as *Confessions* and *The City of God*. More than five million words of Augustine's writings survive, including his sermon on the Lord's Prayer. In it, Augustine states the importance of the prayer to Christians, and how it expresses the trust that people must place in God. Following his death in 430, Augustine was canonized and remains one of history's most influential Christian theologians and philosophers.

"See how many brethren the only Son hath in His grace, sharing His inheritance with those for whom He suffered death. We had a father and mother on Earth, that we might be born to labours and to death, but we have found other parents, God our Father, and the Church our Mother, by whom we are born unto life eternal. Let us then consider, beloved, whose children we have begun to be and let us live so as becomes those who have such a Father. See how that our Creator had condescended to be our Father! We have heard whom we ought to call upon and with what hope of an eternal inheritance we have begun to have a Father in Heaven. Let us now hear what we must ask of Him. Of such a Father what shall we ask? Do we not ask rain of Him today, and yesterday, and the day before? This is no great thing to have asked of such a Father, and yet ye see with what sighings and with what great desire we ask for rain when death is feared – when that is feared which none can escape. For sooner or later every man must die, and we groan, and pray and travail in pain, and cry to God that we may die a little later. How much more ought we to cry to Him that we may come to that place where we shall never die!"

Hippo Regius (present-day Annaba, Algeria), 400 CE

The Prophet Muhammad

FAREWELL SERMON

When Muhammad (570–632 CE) was born, the population of his home city of Mecca and the rest of Arabia was predominantly polytheistic. A merchant for much of his early life, he spent hours in solitary prayer and reflection. When he was around 40 years old, the angel Gabriel visited Muhammad, convincing him there was only one true god (Allah), and that the only way to salvation was 'surrender' (*islam*) to Him. When Muhammad began to preach this message, gathering followers in Mecca, he fell subject to persecution and fled to Medina, where he continued to gain converts. Under his leadership, Medina conquered Mecca in 630, replacing pagan shrines with mosques. Then, in 632, Muhammad delivered his Farewell Sermon at Mount Arafat, just outside the city. He gave his people some final instructions and advice, and urged them to trust the teachings he had left them, later collected to form the Quran. The prophet died shortly after the sermon, and Islam rapidly spread out of Arabia, eventually becoming the second largest religion in the world.

"Behold! Everything pertaining to the Days of Ignorance is under my feet completely abolished…

…I have left among you the Book of Allah, and if you hold fast to it, you would never go astray."

Mecca, Saudi Arabia, 6th March 632 CE

St Bede the Venerable

SERMON ON ALL SAINTS

During the seventh century CE, missionaries converted England from paganism to Christianity. Religious houses were established across the country, particularly in isolated rural locations, so that monks could concentrate on spiritual matters. At the age of seven, Bede (c. 672–735 CE) received an education at the monastery of Monkwearmouth, in northeastern England, and by 685 he had moved to its sister foundation in nearby Jarrow. He spent the rest of his life living and working between these two sites. An ordained priest, Bede won renown as a prodigious and prolific scholar, writing and translating dozens of books across a wide range of subjects including nature, poetry and astronomy. His focus was on theology and history, and his 710 sermon argued that human sufferings were transient, and that a greater reward was to come. Bede's most acclaimed work was the *Ecclesiastical History of the English People*. It detailed the history of England from the first contact with the Romans in 55 BCE all the way up to the time the work was completed, around 731.

"For the ineffable and unbounded goodness of God has provided this also, that the time for labour and for agony should not be extended – not long, not enduring, but short, and, so to speak, momentary. That in this short and little life should be the pain and the labours, that in the life that is eternal should be the crown and the reward of merits, that the labours should quickly come to an end, but the reward of endurance should remain without end. That after the darkness of this world they should behold that most beautiful light, and should receive a blessedness greater than the bitterness of all passions, as the apostle beareth witness, when he saith, 'The sufferings of this present time are not worthy to be compared with the glory that shall be revealed in us'."

Monkwearmouth, England, c. 710

William the Conqueror

BEFORE THE BATTLE OF HASTINGS

The Duchy of Normandy, in northwestern France, was ruled by descendants of Norsemen who had raided the area. William (1028–87) inherited the duchy from his father in 1035, but because of his youth and illegitimacy, many nobles did not accept him. After a long and violent struggle, William – a shrewd, ambitious and effective leader – had consolidated his rule by 1047. He then set his sights on England, ruled by the Anglo-Saxons; its king, Edward the Confessor, whose mother was a Norman, was his distant cousin. When the childless Edward died in January 1066, he was succeeded by his brother-in-law Harold Godwinson. William challenged this, claiming Edward had promised him the throne. He invaded England, landing in Sussex with his army on 28th September. On 14th October the Normans met Harold's Anglo-Saxons near Hastings. William exhorted his men to victory and, emboldened, they won the day. Harold was killed in the fighting, allowing William to seize control of the country, ruling it (and Normandy) until his death in 1087.

"Normans! Bravest of nations! I have no doubt of your courage, and none of your victory, which never by any chance or obstacle escaped your efforts. If indeed you had, once only, failed to conquer, there might be a need now to inflame your courage by exhortation. But your native spirit does not require to be roused… Raise your standards, my brave men, and set neither measure nor limit to your merited rage. May the lightning of your glory be seen and the thunders of your onset heard from east to west, and be ye the avengers of noble blood."

Hastings, England, 14th October 1066

Pope Urban II
AT THE COUNCIL OF CLERMONT

The crusading movement began in 1095. For two centuries, Europeans fought a series of campaigns aimed at winning and defending Christian control of the Holy Land. The Crusades were initiated by Byzantine Emperor Alexios I's appeal to Pope Urban II (1035–99) for help against the Muslim Seljuk Turks, who had won control of most of Anatolia and were advancing towards the Holy Land. Born in France as Otho de Lagery, Urban had been pope since 1088. In November 1095, he preached to the Council of Clermont. Urban appealed to Christians to fight the Seljuks, promising them removal of sins if they fell in battle. He then travelled across France repeating his message, which was spread across the rest of Europe by other preachers. Motivated by promises of heavenly rewards (as well, doubtless, as the prospect of earthly glory and profit), thousands took the cross. On 15th July 1099, a crusader army captured Jerusalem, establishing a Christian kingdom in the Holy Land. Pope Urban died a fortnight later in Rome, too soon for news of the conquest to reach him.

"On this account I, or rather the Lord, beseech you as Christ's heralds to publish this everywhere and to persuade all people of whatever rank, foot soldiers and knights, poor and rich, to carry aid promptly to those Christians and to banish that vile race from the lands of our friends. I say this to those who are present, it is meant also for those who are absent. Moreover, Christ commands it. All who die by the way, whether by land or by sea, or in battle against the pagans, shall have immediate remission of sins. This I grant them through the power of God with which I am invested."

Clermont, France, 27th November 1095

St Bernard of Clairvaux

WHY ANOTHER CRUSADE?

In 1144 the County of Edessa, a Crusader state located across modern-day Turkey and Syria, was conquered by Zengi, a Muslim Turkish ruler. This threatened Christian control of the Holy Land, and motivated Pope Eugene III to announce the Second Crusade. The person chosen to rally Europe behind this crusade was the French abbot Bernard of Clairvaux (1090–1153). He was a Cistercian, an order of monks who lived an austere life of manual labour and prayer, and had established and led the monastery at Clairvaux since 1115. In addition, Bernard was a patron and promoter of the Knights Templar, a military order founded in 1119 to protect Christians in the Holy Land, which grew to become incredibly wealthy and influential. On Palm Sunday 1146, Bernard preached before an assembly at the central French town of Vézelay, where he urged Christians to renew their crusading spirit. Despite being led by the kings of France and Germany, the Second Crusade was a failure. Its defeat in 1149 greatly disheartened Bernard. He died four years later at Clairvaux, and was canonized in 1174.

"If it were announced to you that the enemy had invaded your cities, your castles, your lands, had ravished your wives and your daughters, and profaned your temples – which among you would not fly to arms? Well, then, all these calamities, and calamities still greater, have fallen upon your brethren, upon the family of Jesus Christ, which is yours. Why do you hesitate to repair so many evils – to revenge so many outrages? Will you allow the infidels to contemplate in peace the ravages they have committed on Christian people? Remember that their triumph will be a subject for grief to all ages and an eternal opprobrium upon the generation that has endured it. Yes, the living God has charged me to announce to you that He will punish them who shall not have defended Him against His enemies. Fly then to arms. Let a holy rage animate you in the fight, and let the Christian world resound with these words of the prophet, 'Cursed be he who does not stain his sword with blood!'

...Christian warriors, He who gave His life for you, today demands yours in return. These are combats worthy of you, combats in which it is glorious to conquer and advantageous to die. Illustrious knights, generous defenders of the Cross, remember the example of your fathers who conquered Jerusalem, and whose names are inscribed in Heaven. Abandon then the things that perish, to gather unfading palms, and conquer a Kingdom that has no end."

———————————————

Vézelay, France, 31st March 1146

Saladin

THE RECOVERY OF JERUSALEM

Salāh ad-Dīn Yūsuf ibn Ayyūb (c. 1137–93), better known as Saladin, was a Muslim of Kurdish origin born in modern-day Iraq. From the mid-12th century, Muslim powers made gains against the Christian presence in the Holy Land. Saladin built his empire in the Middle East by unifying Muslims under his leadership. They conquered Egypt in 1171, before adding Syria and territory in Yemen, Arabia and Mesopotamia. Saladin then turned his attention to the Crusader states. Following a string of victories, in 1187 Saladin annihilated a Crusader army at the Battle of Hattin, leaving him in control of most of the Holy Land. He then declared his next step would be to capture Jerusalem; that September, his army laid siege to the city, which was holy to Muslims as well as Jews and Christians, and after less than two weeks, it peacefully surrendered to him. The loss of Jerusalem led to the Third Crusade, which failed to recover the city. Saladin died in 1193. Although his empire quickly disintegrated, the Christians never gained permanent control of Jerusalem again, and were forced out of the Holy Land by 1291.

" If God blesses us by enabling us to drive His enemies out of Jerusalem, how fortunate and happy we would be! For Jerusalem has been controlled by the enemy for 91 years, during which time God has received nothing from us here in the way of adoration… The zeal of the Muslim rulers to deliver it languished. Time passed, and so did many in different generations, while the Franks succeeded in rooting themselves strongly there. Now God has reserved the merit of its recovery for one house, the house of the sons of Ayyub, in order to unite all hearts in appreciation of its members. "

Jerusalem, present-day Israel,
September 1187

John Ball

'WHEN ADAM DELVED AND EVE SPAN'

During the mid-14th century the Black Death struck Europe, killing millions. When survivors demanded higher wages many states responded with laws that set maximum earnings. In England such legislation led to resentment amongst the labouring population, who also faced high taxes. Authorities clamped down on anyone who challenged the traditional hierarchy, including John Ball (c. 1338–81), a radical priest frequently imprisoned for his sermons on social equality. In May 1381 the Peasants' Revolt started when protests against a poll tax in Essex spread out across England. Ball, incarcerated in Kent at the time, was freed by local rebels and marched on London with them. On 12th June, he preached before a huge crowd gathered at Blackheath, outside London. Inspired by his words, rebels then entered the capital and forced King Richard II to agree to their demands. Richard's regime quickly went back on these promises, forcing the rebels to disperse and killing their ringleaders. Ball was captured and tried for treason; found guilty, he was hung, drawn and quartered.

"When Adam delved and Eve span,
Who was then the gentleman?
From the beginning all men by nature
were created alike, and our bondage
or servitude came in by the unjust
oppression of naughty men.

…And therefore I exhort you
to consider that now the time is come,
appointed to us by God, in which ye may,
if ye will, cast off the yoke of bondage,
and recover liberty."

London, England, 12th June 1381

Joan of Arc

RECANTATION AT HER TRIAL

The Hundred Years' War, fought between England and France, started in 1337. By the 1420s, France was facing defeat until help came from an unexpected source, Joan of Arc (c. 1412–31). Born to a peasant family, Joan had left home as a teenager in 1428, driven by voices compelling her to assist Charles VII of France. With his support, and wearing men's clothes, Joan travelled to Orléans, a strategically vital city beseiged by the English. Her arrival inspired the French to break the siege in May 1429. Encouraged, the French went on to win a series of victories. In May 1430, Joan was captured by soldiers from Burgundy, an independent duchy allied to England, and handed over to the English. The English tried her for heresy, subjecting her to imprisonment, interrogations and threats of torture. On 24th May 1431, Joan publicly recanted, saving herself from death. Just a few days later, on reversing her abjuration, she was burnt as a heretic. Despite her death, France would defeat England in 1453. Joan was canonized in 1920 and has grown to become her country's national heroine.

"I confess that I have most grievously sinned in falsely pretending to have had revelations and apparitions from God, His angels, St Catherine and St Margaret, in seducing others, in believing foolishly and lightly, in making superstitious divinations, in blaspheming God and His Saints, in breaking the divine law, Holy Scripture, and the caaon laws, in wearing a dissolute, ill-shaped and immodest dress against the decency of nature, and hair cropped round like a man's, against all the modesty of womankind. Also in bearing arms most presumptuously, in cruelly desiring the shedding of human blood, in declaring that I did all these things by the command of God, His angels and the said saints, and that to do so was good and not to err, in being seditious and idolatrous, adoring and calling up evil spirits. I confess also that I have been schismatic and in many ways have erred from the path."

Rouen, France, 24th May 1431

Emperor Constantine XI

FINAL STAND AT CONSTANTINOPLE

At its peak, in the sixth century, the Byzantine Empire dominated the Mediterranean, ruling much of the region from its capital, Constantinople. By the 15th century, Byzantium's power had receded in the face of domestic instability and foreign attacks, particularly from the Ottoman Empire, a Muslim dynasty that had started as a small kingdom in Anatolia. A triple ring of stone walls had protected Constantinople during two Ottoman sieges in 1411 and 1422, but in 1453 Sultan Mehmed II made a third attempt, arriving with a great fleet, artillery and 75,000 soldiers. Constantine XI Palaiologos (1404–53) had a garrison of just 8,000. The siege began on 6th April. The Byzantines initially repelled Ottoman attacks, but on 29th May Mehmed launched a massed frontal assault. Constantine, personally overseeing the defence, reminded his men of the importance of the city to Christendom and the dire consequences of failure. Shortly afterwards, he was cut down leading a counterattack – so died the last Byzantine emperor. The Ottomans then conquered the city, which Mehmed made his capital, renaming it Istanbul.

"Yet now too, my brothers, feel no cowardice, even if small parts of our fortifications have collapsed from the explosions and engine missiles, as you can see, we made all possible, necessary repairs. We are placing all hope in the irresistible glory of God. Some have faith in armament, others in cavalry, might and numbers, but we believe in the name of our Lord, our God and Saviour, and second, in our arms and strength granted to us by divine power.

…Now he wants to enslave her and throw the yoke upon the Mistress of Cities, our holy churches, where the Holy Trinity was worshipped, where the Holy Ghost was glorified in hymns, where angels were heard praising in chant the deity of and the incarnation of God's word, he wants to turn into shrines of his blasphemy, shrines of the mad and false Prophet, Muhammad, as well as into stables for his horses and camels. Consider then, my brother and comrades in arms, how the commemoration of our death, our memory, fame and freedom can be rendered eternal."

Constantinople (present-day Istanbul, Turkey), 29th May 1453

Hernán Cortés

ADDRESS TO THE CONQUISTADORS

After Christopher Columbus's 1492 voyage across the Atlantic, Spain established an empire in the New World, initially concentrated in the Caribbean. Thousands emigrated there in search of fame and fortune, including Hernán Cortés (1485–1547), who settled in Hispaniola in 1504 before moving to Cuba in 1511, securing lands, money and offices. In 1518, the governor of Cuba named him to lead the exploration and colonization of Mexico. Cortés paid for ships and soldiers and was about to depart when the governor changed his mind. Fuelled by ambition, Cortés disobeyed an order to stay in Cuba and set out for Mexico. Before leaving, he told his men of the labour and glory that awaited them. Despite commanding a force of just 500, Cortés overthrew the Aztec Empire, sacking their great capital at Tenochtitlan, and conquering Mexico by 1521. The Spanish crown named him governor of the territory, but he lost the position after a series of arguments with other colonial officials and an unsuccessful expedition to Honduras. Cortés never recovered his status and died in Spain, in 1547.

"I hold out to you a glorious prize, but it is to be won by incessant toil. Great things are achieved only by great exertions and glory was never the reward of sloth. If I have laboured hard and staked my all on this undertaking, it is for the love of that renown, which is the noblest recompense of man. But, if any among you covet riches more, be but true to me, as I will be true to you and to the occasion, and I will make you masters of such as our countrymen have never dreamed of! You are few in number, but strong in resolution. If this does not falter, doubt not but that the Almighty, who has never deserted the Spaniard in his contest with the infidel, will shield you, though encompassed by a cloud of enemies. For your cause is a just cause, and you are to fight under the banner of the Cross. Go forward then, with alacrity and confidence, and carry to a glorious issue the work so auspiciously begun."

Cape San Antonio, Cuba, February 1519

Martin Luther

'I STAND HERE AND CAN SAY NO MORE'

The Reformation challenged core teachings of Catholicism. It was initiated by Martin Luther (1483–1546), a German monk who taught theology at the University of Wittenberg. In 1517, Luther posted The Ninety-Five Theses, publicly disputing the sale of indulgences, certificates that reduced punishment for sins. He went on to question other Catholic practices and beliefs, arguing that many were not mentioned in the Bible and were thus invalid. He claimed people were saved by their faith alone, that only God granted salvation and that the Pope was not infallible. These views led to Luther's excommunication from the Catholic Church in January 1521. He was then summoned by Emperor Charles V to the Diet of Worms, the imperial council of the Holy Roman Empire, to explain himself to secular authorities. At Worms, Luther steadfastly refused to recant and was thus declared an outlaw. Despite this, he carried on writing and preaching, establishing the Lutheran Church. His work laid the foundations for Protestantism, radically altering Europe's religious and political landscape.

"I cannot submit my faith either to the pope or to the council, because it is as clear as noonday that they have fallen into error and even into glaring inconsistency with themselves. If, then, I am not convinced by proof from Holy Scripture, or by cogent reasons, if I am not satisfied by the very text I have cited, and if my judgment is not in this way brought into subjection to God's word, I neither can nor will retract anything. For it cannot be right for a Christian to speak against his conscience. I stand here and can say no more. God help me. Amen."

Worms, modern-day Germany, 18th April 1521

Huldrych Zwingli

ON MERCENARY SOLDIERS

Switzerland, which during the 16th century was a loose confederation of largely independent states, was a major centre of Protestantism. It was the birthplace of the religious leader Huldrych Zwingli (1484–1531), who had been ordained a Catholic priest and was a chaplain in the Swiss Army. He took up a position as a pastor in Zürich, and found himself increasingly drawn to the reformed faith, challenging Catholic orthodoxy. During the 1520s, Zwingli led the religious reformation of Zürich, and Protestantism spread to other areas of Switzerland. To defend the Swiss Reformation, Zwingli allied Zürich with other Protestant states, leading to a brief armed standoff against Catholic states in 1529. In addition to his religious views, Zwingli was a critic of the mercenary system that saw many of his countrymen fight for other European states, as well as being an advocate for Swiss unity, giving a sermon in 1530 crystallizing many of his thoughts on the subjects. The next year open war broke out in Switzerland; Zwingli was killed leading Zürich's army against Catholic forces at the Battle of Kappel.

"Those who, for truth, religion, justice and native country, venture their lives in war, are true men, and their cause is sacred. But as for those bloodthirsty, mercenary soldiers who take the field for gain, of whom the world is now full, and those wars that princes carry on, from day to day, out of lust of power, filling the earth with bloodshed, I, for my part, not only cannot approve them, but I believe there is nothing more wicked and criminal, and have the opinion that such men deserve to be branded as highwaymen, and that they are unworthy of the name of Christians.

...How are we to deliver ourselves from these evils, and return again to union? I answer, by abstaining from selfishness. For, if this base passion did not reign among us, the confederacy were more a union of brothers than of confederates. If one rejoins to this, selfishness is implanted in the human heart, from whence it cannot be eradicated, for God alone can know and change the heart, then I answer, do earnestly that which lies in your power. Where you find it punishable, punish it, and let it not grow."

———————

Switzerland, 1530

John Knox

ON A KING'S APPOINTMENT BY GOD

By the mid-16th century, Protestant ideas were gaining traction in Scotland, although supporters of the Reformation were persecuted by the country's pro-French Catholic rulers, with many executed, imprisoned or exiled. One of the reformers forced to leave the country was former Catholic priest John Knox (c. 1514–72). Fleeing Scotland in 1549, Knox went to live in England, then Frankfurt and Geneva, where he met the famed reformer John Calvin, who would become a major theological influence. Knox returned to his homeland in 1559, at the invitation of Protestant nobles who the next year seized control of the country from the Catholic Mary, Queen of Scots. With Protestantism in the ascendancy, Knox set about founding the reformed Church of Scotland, establishing many of its central principles and doctrines. He spent the rest of his life living and working in Edinburgh, where he delivered this sermon in 1565, stating that people had both the right and a responsibility to challenge monarchs if they did not rule according to God's commandments.

"The sword of God is not committed to the hand of man, to use as it pleases him, but only to punish vice and maintain virtue, that men may live in such society as is acceptable before God. And this is the true and only cause why God has appointed powers in this earth.
For such is the furious rage of man's corrupt nature, that, unless severe punishment were appointed and put in execution upon malefactors, better it were that man should live among brutes and wild beasts than among men.

...Kings then have not an absolute power, to do in their government what pleases them, but their power is limited by God's word. So that if they strike where God has not commanded, they are but murderers, and if they spare where God has commanded to strike, they and their throne are criminal and guilty of the wickedness that abounds upon the face of the earth, for lack of punishment.
...Wouldst thou, O Scotland, have a king to reign over thee in justice, equity and mercy?"

Edinburgh, Scotland, 19th August 1565

Elizabeth I

ADDRESS AT TILBURY

Elizabeth I (1533–1603) ascended the English throne in 1558. Her decision to keep the Church of England separate from Rome led to her eventual excommunication by the pope and rising tension between her and Philip II of Spain, Europe's greatest Catholic monarch. Philip was angered at English raids on his shipping as well as their support for Dutch rebels fighting for independence from Spain. Elizabeth's sanctioning of the execution of her cousin Mary, Queen of Scots, the main Catholic claimant to the English throne, was the final straw – in May 1588 the Spanish Armada set sail for the English Channel. With invasion imminent, an English force gathered at Tilbury in Essex in August. Wearing a white gown and silver armour, Elizabeth addressed her men, extolling them to stand firm against the foreign threat. As it happened, they were not called into action. A combination of English naval attacks and storms forced the Armada to return home. England had survived and the Tilbury Address formed a central part of the image of Elizabeth as the 'Virgin Queen' devoted solely to her people.

"My loving people. . . I have always so behaved myself that, under God, I have placed my chiefest strength and safe guard in the loyal hearts and good will of my subjects, and therefore I am come amongst you, as you see, at this time, not for my recreation and disport, but being resolved, in the midst and heat of the battle, to live or die amongst you all, to lay down my life for my God and for my kingdom and for my people, my honour, and my blood, even in the dust. I know I have the body of a weak and feeble woman, but I have the heart and stomach of a king, and a king of England too, and think foul scorn that... any prince of Europe should dare to invade the borders of my realm."

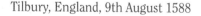

Tilbury, England, 9th August 1588

Elizabeth I

ON HER LOVE FOR HER SUBJECTS

As well as facing down challenges from abroad, Elizabeth I of England maintained the loyalty of the majority of the country by pursuing pragmatic policies that placed obedience to her first. She had a fractious relationship with Parliament, which had to approve royal taxation. This was problematic, because the finances of the Elizabethan regime were precarious, and Elizabeth often had to ask Parliament for money. The 1590s were challenging; the country was engaged in costly wars with Spain and Catholic rebels in Ireland, and there were frequent poor harvests. In addition, Elizabeth had begun to grant monopolies over certain products to her favourites, leading to price rises. As such, when Parliament gathered at the end of 1601, many of its members were dissatisfied. Seeking to placate them in her address of 30th November, Elizabeth promised reform, stating this would be her final parliament and expressing her love for her subjects. Just 16 months later, Elizabeth died, and was succeeded by her first-cousin-twice-removed, James VI of Scotland, whose English title was James I.

"Of myself I must say this, I never was any greedy scraping grasper, nor a strict fast-holding prince, nor yet a waster. My heart was never set upon any worldly goods, but only for my subjects' good. What you do bestow on me, I will not hoard up, but receive it to bestow on you again. Yea, mine own properties I account yours, to be expended for your good, and your eyes shall see the bestowing of it for your welfare...

For it is not my desire to live or reign longer, than my life and reign shall be for your good. And though you have had and may have many mightier and wiser princes sitting in this seat, yet you never had, nor shall have any that will love you better."

London, England, 30th November 1601

Walter Raleigh

LAST WORDS ON THE SCAFFOLD

One of the most famed figures of the Elizabethan era was Walter Raleigh (c. 1554–1618). Born in Devon, England, he fought for the Protestants in the French Wars of Religion and against Catholic rebels in Ireland. By the 1580s he had come to the attention of Elizabeth I, who gave him a knighthood, land, offices and monopolies. She also granted him the right to explore and colonize the New World. In 1595, Raleigh led an expedition to South America to locate El Dorado, the fabled city of gold, but he returned without finding it. After Elizabeth died, Raleigh was accused of plotting to overthrow her successor James I and convicted of treason in 1603. He escaped execution but was confined to the Tower of London until 1616, when he was released and allowed to lead another attempt to find El Dorado – this, too, failed. On the voyage, Raleigh had attacked a Spanish settlement, despite promising to be peaceful. When he returned home, under pressure from the Spanish, James ordered Raleigh's execution, and before he was beheaded in Westminster he gave a final statement.

"I thank my God heartily that He hath brought me into the light to die, and not suffered me to die in the dark prison of the Tower, where I have suffered a great deal of adversity and a long sickness. And I thank God that my fever hath not taken me at this time, as I prayed God it might not.

…And now I entreat you all to join with me in prayer, that the great God of Heaven, whom I have grievously offended, being a man full of all vanity, and having lived a sinful life, in all sinful callings, having been a soldier, a captain, a sea captain and a courtier, which are all places of wickedness and vice, that God, I say, would forgive me, cast away my sins from me, and receive me into everlasting life. So I take my leave of you all, making my peace with God.**"**

London, England, 29th October 1618

Charles I

SPEECH BEFORE HIS EXECUTION

During the mid-17th century, no one was more responsible for plunging his kingdoms into years of civil war than Charles I of England (1600–49). Ascending the throne in 1625, he clashed with Parliament in his attempts to impose his authority. Charles's conservative religious views were unpalatable to many hard-line Protestants. In Scotland, they led to an uprising in 1639, which defeated royal forces. War in England broke out in 1642, after Charles failed to secure a settlement with Parliament. By 1646, Parliament had triumphed and Charles gave himself up to Scottish forces. Imprisoned, he conducted secret negotiations with Scottish Presbyterians, promising he would impose their religious policies in England in return for military support, and civil war restarted in February 1648. The Parliamentarians were again victorious. This time, Charles was tried for high treason and found guilty on 27th January 1649. His execution took place three days later; in his last speech before his beheading Charles insisted he had acted within his rights as king and in the interests of his subjects.

"But I think it is my duty to God first and to my country for to clear myself both as an honest man and a good king, and a good Christian. I shall begin first with my innocence. In troth I think it not very needful for me to insist long upon this, for all the world knows that I never did begin a war with the two houses of Parliament. And I call God to witness, to whom I must shortly make an account, that I never did intend for to encroach upon their privileges.

…I tell you, and I pray God it be not laid to your charge that I am the martyr of the people.

…I have a good cause, and I have a gracious God… I go from a corruptible, to an incorruptible crown, where no disturbance can be, no disturbance in the world."

London, England, 30th January 1649

Oliver Cromwell

DISMISSAL OF THE RUMP PARLIAMENT

During the English Civil War, Oliver Cromwell (1599–1658) rose from obscurity to become the most important Parliamentarian leader. Despite Parliament's military victory in 1646, there were disputes about what to do with Charles I. Some Parliamentarians wanted to allow Charles to remain on the throne with limited powers, whilst others sought to abolish the monarchy. In 1648, soldiers marched on Parliament and removed members who wanted to settle with Charles. The remainder, or 'Rump', with Cromwell's support, oversaw Charles's execution. Cromwell then set about putting down resistance in Ireland and Scotland. He grew frustrated at the Rump's failure to establish a new constitution and on 20th April 1653 upbraided them, criticizing their vacillations and dissensions, before calling on soldiers to clear the chamber. He appointed new members of parliament and a new constitution was issued that December, which named Cromwell 'Lord Protector'. Cromwell died in 1658, creating a power vacuum that was filled by Charles I's exiled son Charles II, who in 1660 was restored to the throne.

"It is high time for me to put an end to your sitting in this place, which you have dishonoured by your contempt of all virtue, and defiled by your practice of every vice. Ye are a factious crew, and enemies to all good government. Ye are a pack of mercenary wretches and would, like Esau, sell your country for a mess of pottage and, like Judas, betray your God for a few pieces of money. …In the name of God, go!"

London, England, 20th April 1653

Patrick Henry

'GIVE ME LIBERTY, OR GIVE ME DEATH!'

By the mid-18th century, there were 13 British colonies on the Atlantic coast of North America. Although they had locally elected assemblies, they could not vote for Members of Parliament in Britain. Therefore, when Westminster passed the Stamp Act in 1765, a direct tax on printed materials in the colonies, many decried it as illegal taxation without representation. One of the most vocal critics of the British was Patrick Henry (1736–99), the son of a Scottish immigrant, who was a member of Virginia's House of Burgesses. Tensions with the British continued to rise, and Henry urged the colonies to prepare for war. On 23rd March 1775, he spoke in Richmond, Virginia, in front of a crowd that included Thomas Jefferson and George Washington. His words galvanized the audience, who chanted, 'To Arms! To Arms!' and the Virginian government vowed to mobilize its militia if war started. For most of the American Revolutionary War, Henry was Governor of Virginia, also serving in the post after the fighting ended, from 1784–86.

"Sir, we have done everything that could be done to avert the storm that is now coming on. We have petitioned, we have remonstrated, we have supplicated, we have prostrated ourselves before the throne and have implored its interposition to arrest the tyrannical hands of the ministry and Parliament. Our petitions have been slighted, our remonstrances have produced additional violence and insult, our supplications have been disregarded and we have been spurned, with contempt, from the foot of the throne! In vain, after these things, may we indulge the fond hope of peace and reconciliation. There is no longer any room for hope. If we wish to be free, if we mean to preserve inviolate those inestimable privileges for which we have been so long contending, if we mean not basely to abandon the noble struggle in which we have been so long engaged, and which we have pledged ourselves never to abandon until the glorious object of our contest shall be obtained, we must fight!

…Is life so dear, or peace so sweet, as to be purchased at the price of chains and slavery? Forbid it, Almighty God! I know not what course others may take, but as for me, give me liberty or give me death!"

Richmond, Virginia, modern-day USA, 23rd March 1775

John Wesley

'IF ADAM HAD NOT FALLEN'

The founder of Methodism was John Wesley (1703–91), who was ordained a Church of England priest in 1728. The next year, with his brother Charles, he formed a religious study and prayer group in Oxford that also carried out charitable works. Critics derisively nicknamed them 'Methodists' because of their pious and methodical activities, but Wesley would positively reappropriate the name for the religious movement he started. In 1738, Wesley had a spiritual awakening, realizing that everyone could be saved through God's grace. He publicly advocated a closer individual relationship with God and promoted small societies where people could discuss their faith. He often preached in the open air and sermons, such as this one delivered in 1782, inspired thousands to join his movement. Wesley intended for Methodism to be a reformist movement within the Church of England, but after he died, in 1791, it officially split off. The Methodists grew to become one of the largest Protestant denominations, with churches across the world and over 40 million members.

"First, mankind in general has gained, by the fall of Adam, a capacity of attaining more holiness and happiness on earth than it would have been possible for them to attain if Adam had not fallen. For if Adam had not fallen, Christ had not died. Nothing can be more clear than this, nothing more undeniable. The more thoroughly we consider the point, the more deeply shall we be convinced of it. Unless all the partakers of human nature had received that deadly wound in Adam, it would not have been needful for the Son of God to take our nature upon him.

…He made man in his own image, a spirit endued with understanding and liberty. Man, abusing that liberty, produced evil, brought sin and pain into the world. This God permitted, in order to a fuller manifestation of his wisdom, justice and mercy, by bestowing on all who would receive it an infinitely greater happiness than they could possibly have attained if Adam had not fallen.

…The plan he had laid before the foundation of the world, he created the parent of all mankind in his own image and he permitted all men to be made sinners, by the disobedience of that one man, that, by the obedience of one, all who receive the free gift may be infinitely holier and happier to all eternity."

England, 1782

Benjamin Franklin

TO THE CONSTITUTIONAL CONVENTION

Few Founding Fathers of the United States were more influential and accomplished than Benjamin Franklin (1706–90). Born in Boston, he settled in Philadelphia, becoming a successful publisher and winning political offices, as well as pursuing scientific research. When the American Revolutionary War started, Franklin was highly respected in the 13 British colonies, helping to draft the Declaration of Independence. His most important role in the war was as a diplomat: he negotiated the crucial Franco-American alliance while ambassador in Paris and represented the United States in the peace talks with Britain that ended the war in 1783. Franklin returned to Philadelphia in 1785, attending the Constitutional Convention held there two years later. At 81 years of age, he was the oldest delegate, and played a minor role in the debates that shaped the political structure of the new nation. However, on the last day of the convention he championed the endorsement of the constitution that had been drafted and died in 1790, one year after it had been formally ratified.

"For when you assemble a number of men to have the advantage of their joint wisdom, you inevitably assemble with those men, all their prejudices, their passions, their errors of opinion, their local interests and their selfish views. From such an assembly can a perfect production be expected? ...On the whole, I cannot help expressing a wish that every member of the convention who may still have objections to it, would with me, on this occasion doubt a little of his own infallibility, and to make manifest our unanimity, put his name to this instrument."

Philadelphia, Pennsylvania, USA, September 1787

George Washington

FIRST INAUGURAL ADDRESS

A Virginian from a prosperous landowning family, George Washington (1732–99) won renown during the 1750s as an officer in the Seven Years' War. He came to find British interference in American affairs oppressive, adding his voice to the growing criticism of its rule. When conflict broke out in 1775, he was selected as commander-in-chief of the American military forces. By 1781 he had secured, with French support, the surrender of the last major British army at Yorktown, forcing peace talks. Once the Constitution was ratified, he was the natural choice to be the first president, and was inaugurated on 30th April 1789, pledging in his address to preserve liberty and fulfil the trust placed in him. Over the next eight years (he won a second term in 1793) Washington skilfully guided the republic, remaining nonpartisan during increasingly rancorous party politics. Refusing to serve a third term, he retired to his Virginia plantation, where he died in 1799. Regarded as one of the greatest American presidents, Washington was bestowed with the honour of having the nation's capital named after him.

" I dwell on this prospect with every satisfaction that an
ardent love for my country can inspire: since there is
no truth more thoroughly established, than that
there exists in the economy and course of nature,
an indissoluble union between virtue and
happiness, between duty and advantage,
between the genuine maxims of an honest
and magnanimous policy, and the solid
rewards of public prosperity and felicity;
since we ought to be no less persuaded that the
propitious smiles of Heaven, can never be expected
on a nation that disregards the eternal rules of order
and right, which Heaven itself has ordained; and since
the preservation of the sacred fire of liberty, and the
destiny of the Republican model of government,
are justly considered as deeply, perhaps as
finally staked, on the experiment entrusted
to the hands of the American people. "

Washington, DC, USA, 30th April 1789

William Wilberforce

ABOLITION SPEECH TO PARLIAMENT

The transatlantic slave trade saw Africans transported to the Americas where they primarily laboured in mines and on plantations. Many of the raw materials they produced, such as cotton, were exported to Europe. Slavery became vital to the British economy but, from the late 18th century, an increasingly vocal antislavery campaign began there. The leading abolitionist was the reforming politician William Wilberforce (1759–1833), an evangelical Christian elected to Parliament in 1780. On 12th May 1789, he addressed the House of Commons and condemned the slave trade, describing its brutal nature, and proposing 12 resolutions against it. Opponents of abolition delayed proceedings, however, to ensure the resolutions were not voted on. In 1791, Wilberforce introduced a bill to abolish the slave trade, but it was defeated. The abolitionist movement continued to gather supporters and, in 1807, legislation was passed that prohibited the slave trade within the British Empire. Wilberforce died in July 1833, the month before a law wholly abolishing the institution of slavery was passed by Parliament.

"I mean not to accuse anyone, but to take the shame upon myself, in common, indeed, with the whole Parliament of Great Britain, for having suffered this horrid trade to be carried on under their authority. We are all guilty. We ought all to plead guilty, and not to exculpate ourselves by throwing the blame on others. I therefore deprecate every kind of reflection against the various descriptions of people who are more immediately involved in this wretched business.

…As soon as ever I had arrived thus far in my investigation of the slave trade, I confess to you, so enormous so dreadful, so irremediable did its wickedness appear that my own mind was completely made up for the abolition. A trade founded in iniquity, and carried on as this was, must be abolished, let the policy be what it might. Let the consequences be what they would, I from this time determined that I would never rest until I had effected its abolition."

London, England, 12th May 1789

Maximilien Robespierre

ON THE ENEMIES OF THE NATION

The French Revolution replaced absolute monarchy with a democratic republic. With France facing internal disorder, economic crisis and foreign invasion, the Committee of Public Safety was established in April 1793 to safeguard the republic. It was dominated by the Montagnards, the radical faction of the Jacobins, a leading force of the revolution. At the end of July, Montagnard Maximilien Robespierre (1758–94) was elected to the committee – a lawyer and politician who believed that the revolution must be defended at any cost. In September, he helped initiate the Reign of Terror, aiming to purge France of potential opposition: 17,000 people were executed and 250,000 imprisoned. Wanting to reform society, Robespierre introduced a decimal calendar and instituted the Cult of the Supreme Being, a deist civic religion intended to replace Christianity. In May 1794, he addressed France's National Convention, warning them they must remain vigilant. Many of its members had grown tired of the violence and feared being targeted by Robespierre – that July the Convention ordered his arrest; he was captured and guillotined.

"They will perish, all of the tyrants armed against the French people! They will perish, all the factions that rely upon their power in order to destroy our freedom. You will not make peace, but you will give it to the world, taking it from the hands of crime… The destiny of the republic is not yet fixed, and the vigilance of the people's representatives is more than ever necessary.

…The moment in which we find ourselves is favourable, but it is perhaps unique. In the state of equilibrium in which things are, it is easy to consolidate liberty, and it is easy to lose it. If France were to be governed for a few months by a corrupted legislature, freedom would be lost. Victory would fall to the factions and immorality.

…I saw the French people rise up from degradation and servitude to the heights of glory and freedom. I saw the chains broken and the guilty thrones that weigh upon the earth near to being overthrown by triumphant hands.

…Accomplish, citizens, accomplish your sublime destiny. You have placed us in the vanguard to bear up under the first efforts of the enemies of liberty. We will be worthy of this honour, and with our blood we will trace the route of immortality. May you constantly deploy that unquenchable energy, which you need to put down the monsters of the universe that conspire against you, and to then enjoy in peace the benedictions of the people and of the fruits of your virtues."

Paris, France, 26th May 1794

Thomas Jefferson

FIRST INAUGURAL ADDRESS

A central question in American politics had always been the relationship between the states and the federal government. This issue divided the early republic, with the Federalists supporting centralization of power and the Democratic-Republicans favouring strong states' rights. One of the founders of the Democratic-Republicans was Thomas Jefferson (1743–1826), a Virginian landowner and principal author of the 1776 Declaration of Independence. He served as secretary of state under Washington from 1790 to 1793. In March 1801, Jefferson was inaugurated as president and used his address to state that Americans should remain united despite their political differences, and that they should work together to build a strong nation. In 1803, he concluded the Louisiana Purchase with Napoleon's France, adding 828,000 square miles of territory to the United States. This helped him win a second term, after which he retired from office. Jefferson lived another 17 years, devoting himself to intellectual interests and founding the University of Virginia.

"We have called by different names brethren of the same principle. We are all Republicans, we are all Federalists… Let us, then, with courage and confidence pursue our own Federal and Republican principles, our attachment to union and representative government. Kindly separated by nature and a wide ocean from the exterminating havoc of one-quarter of the globe. Too high-minded to endure the degradations of the others. Possessing a chosen country, with room enough for our descendants to the thousandth and thousandth generation. Entertaining a due sense of our equal right to the use of our own faculties, to the acquisitions of our own industry, to honour and confidence from our fellow citizens, resulting not from birth, but from our actions and their sense of them. Enlightened by a benign religion, professed, indeed, and practised in various forms, yet all of them inculcating honesty, truth, temperance, gratitude and the love of man. Acknowledging and adoring an overruling Providence, which by all its dispensations proves that it delights in the happiness of man here and his greater happiness hereafter, with all these blessings, what more is necessary to make us a happy and a prosperous people? Still one thing more, fellow citizens. A wise and frugal government, which shall restrain men from injuring one another, shall leave them otherwise free to regulate their own pursuits of industry and improvement, and shall not take from the mouth of labour the bread it has earned. This is the sum of good government, and this is necessary to close the circle of our felicities."

Washington, DC, USA, 4th March 1801

Toussaint L'Ouverture

FINAL PROCLAMATION

France gained the western third of the Caribbean island of Hispaniola from Spain in 1659, naming the territory Saint-Domingue. Subjected to brutal discipline, African slaves labouring on the island's sugar crops revolted in 1791, led by former slave Toussaint Bréda (c. 1743–1803). Adopting the surname L'Ouverture (The Opening), Toussaint fought the French until 1794, when they abolished slavery. He then advanced into the Spanish part of Hispaniola and freed the slaves there, too. In January 1801, L'Ouverture issued a constitution making Saint-Domingue autonomous and naming himself governor-for-life. This put him at odds with France's leader, Napoleon, who was determined to restore slavery. At the end of the year, L'Ouverture rallied his people in advance of a French invasion force. He retreated into the mountainous interior but surrendered after three months of fighting. L'Ouverture was arrested and sent to France, where he died in 1803. His supporters eventually defeated the French, and in 1804 proclaimed their independence as the Republic of Haiti (from the indigenous name for the island).

"I am a soldier and I don't fear men. I fear only God. If I must die, I will die like a soldier of honour who has nothing to reproach himself for… Brave military personnel, generals, officers, noncommissioned officers and soldiers, do not listen to the evil ones who ask nothing better than to do you harm in order to have a pretext to dishonour you. Attached to the soil of this country, unite yourselves with your chief to render it fruitful and to preserve it in its current state of prosperity. Ever on the path of honour, I will show you the route you must follow. You are soldiers. You must be faithful observers of the subordination and military virtues, and must vanquish or die at your posts."

Modern-day Haiti, 20th December 1801

James Mackintosh

A PLEA FOR FREE SPEECH

The French Revolution was much debated in Britain, attracting significant controversy. One of its most eloquent supporters was James Mackintosh (1765–1832), a Scotsman living in London, who won fame by publishing a book defending the revolution in 1791. Although he was a trained doctor, Mackintosh decided to forgo medicine in favour of law, qualifying as a barrister in 1795.

Mackintosh had a successful legal practice, and in his most famous case represented Jean Gabriel Peltier, a French journalist who had fled to England and published articles highly critical of Napoleon, even encouraging his assassination. As a result, Peltier was sued for libel by the French government in 1803 and defended by Mackintosh, whose appeal for the right to free speech resonated in Britain and across Europe. Peltier was found guilty, but the case was ultimately dropped without judgment being delivered. After the trial, Mackintosh was knighted and appointed as a judge in India.

"One asylum of free discussion is still inviolate. There is still one spot in Europe where man can freely exercise his reason on the most important concerns of society, where he can boldly publish his judgment on the acts of the proudest and most powerful tyrants. The Press of England is still free. It is guarded by the free constitution of our forefathers. It is guarded by the heart and arms of Englishmen, and I trust I may venture to say that if it be to fall, it will fall only under the ruins of the British Empire. It is an awful consideration, gentlemen. Every other monument of European liberty has perished. That ancient fabric that has been gradually reared by the wisdom and virtue of our fathers still stands. It stands, thanks be to God, solid and entire, but it stands alone, and it stands amid ruins."

London, England, February 1803

Robert Emmet

SPEECH FROM THE DOCK

In 1798, there was an uprising in Ireland against British rule, which had begun in the late 12th century. Largely organized by the Society of United Irishmen, a group seeking to establish an independent republic in Ireland, the rebellion was put down. In 1800, the Acts of Union were passed, which merged Great Britain and Ireland to form the United Kingdom. Irish nationalists vowed to continue their struggle, amongst them Robert Emmet (1778–1803), who had fled Ireland in 1799 to escape arrest. He travelled through Europe seeking support for another insurrection, before returning to Dublin in 1802. Emmet began secretly manufacturing and stockpiling armaments, but an explosion at a weapons depot in July 1803 forced him to announce the rebellion peremptorily. A disaster, it was put down by British forces; Emmet fled once more, but was captured on 25th August. He was tried for treason the next month and found guilty. Before sentencing, he addressed the court, his words becoming a clarion call for the republican cause. After his execution the next day, he achieved posthumous glory as a martyr for Irish freedom.

"My country was my idol. To it I sacrificed every selfish, every endearing sentiment, and for it I now offer myself, O God! No, my lords, I acted as an Irishman, determined on delivering my country from the yoke of a foreign and unrelenting tyranny, and from the more galling yoke of a domestic faction, its joint partner and perpetrator in the patricide, whose reward is the ignominy of existing with an exterior of splendour and a consciousness of depravity. It was the wish of my heart to extricate my country from this doubly riveted despotism. I wish to place her independence beyond the reach of any power on earth. I wish to exalt her to that proud station in the world that Providence had destined her to fill.

...Let no man write my epitaph, for as no man who knows my motives dare now vindicate them, let not prejudice or ignorance asperse them. Let them, and me, rest in obscurity and peace, and my name remain uninscribed, until other times and other men can do justice to my character. When my country takes her place among the nations of the earth, then, and not until then, let my epitaph be written."

Dublin, Ireland, 19th September 1803

Sagoyewatha (Red Jacket)

ON RELIGIOUS TOLERANCE

Native American peoples fought on both sides of the American Revolutionary War. The Seneca, who lived close to the Canadian border in New York state, allied with Britain. One of their clan chiefs, famed for his oratory, was Sagoyewatha (c. 1750–1830), also known as Red Jacket for the scarlet coat he wore.

Once the British were defeated, they deserted their erstwhile Native American allies, ceding the rights to their territory to the United States, which was eager to claim the land. Sagoyewatha was a leading figure in negotiations with the US government, heading a delegation to Washington in 1792, and helping to negotiate a peace settlement. Ultimately the Seneca were forced to give up much of their land, but Sagoyewatha objected to white influence on their customs, particularly in religious matters. When a Christian missionary requested his permission to seek converts in his land, Sagoyewatha denied him, defending the right of his people to their own religions.

"Brother, our seats were once large, and yours were very small. You have now become a great people, and we have scarcely a place left to spread our blankets. You have got our country, but are not satisfied. You want to force your religion upon us.

…Brother, the Great Spirit has made us all, but he has made a great difference between his white and red children. He has given us a different complexion, and different customs. To you he has given the arts, to these he has not opened our eyes. We know these things to be true. Since he has made so great a difference between us in other things, why may we not conclude that he has given us a different religion according to our understanding. The Great Spirit does right. He knows what is best for his children. We are satisfied. Brother, we do not wish to destroy your religion, or take it from you, we only want to enjoy our own."

New York State, USA, Summer 1805

Napoleon Bonaparte

FAREWELL TO THE OLD GUARD

In 1792, France entered a series of wars against other European powers, which sought to restore the monarchy overthrown in the French Revolution. The fighting gave Napoleon Bonaparte (1769–1821), a young artillery lieutenant, the chance to advance his career. Promoted to general in 1793, he won a series of victories in battle that made him a powerful and prominent figure. In 1799, he seized power in a coup, and in 1804 named himself emperor of the French. In 1812, Napoleon took the disastrous decision to invade Russia. He was forced to retreat with his army in tatters, and Europe's great powers formed a grand alliance against him, advancing into France. Forced to abdicate in April 1814, Napoleon went into exile on the Mediterranean island of Elba. Before leaving, he made a speech bidding farewell to his Old Guard, the elite veteran force he personally commanded. Napoleon spent less than a year on Elba, escaping in February 1815 and taking control of France – however, after defeat at Waterloo in June he stepped down a second time, and was exiled to the remote Atlantic island of Saint Helena, where he died in 1821.

" Soldiers of my Old Guard, I bid you farewell.
For 20 years I have constantly accompanied
you on the road to honour and glory.
In these latter times, as in the days of our
prosperity, you have invariably been models
of courage and fidelity. With men such as you,
our cause could not be lost, but the war
would have been interminable. It would
have been civil war, and that would have
entailed deeper misfortunes on France.
I have sacrificed all of my interests
to those of the country. I go, but you, my
friends, will continue to serve France.
Her happiness was my only thought.
It will still be the object of my wishes.
Do not regret my fate. If I have consented
to survive, it is to serve your glory. I intend to
write the history of the great achievements we
have performed together. Adieu, my friends.
Would I could press you all to my heart. "

Fontainebleau, France, 20th April 1814

Simón Bolívar

ADDRESS AT THE CONGRESS OF ANGOSTURA

In 1808, Spanish colonial government in South America faced the challenge of local juntas declaring their independence. Fighting between rebels and imperial forces was widespread by 1810. The leading figure of the independence movement, Simón Bolívar (1783–1830) led a series of campaigns to liberate New Granada (modern-day Colombia) and Venezuela from Spanish rule. In 1819, a congress of pro-independence delegates was held at Angostura, Venezuela; Bolívar addressed them on the first day, extolling the justness of their cause. At this meeting, the independent republic of Gran Colombia was proclaimed (modern-day Colombia, Ecuador, Panama and Venezuela, along with parts of Brazil, Guyana and Peru), with Bolívar as president. He ejected the last Spanish soldiers from the republic before helping to liberate Peru in 1824 and Bolivia (named after him) in 1825. While Bolívar was away fighting, internal tensions arose in Gran Colombia, and it began to fragment. Realizing the dissolution of the state was imminent, Bolívar resigned as president in April 1830.

"We have been ruled more by deceit than by force, and we have been degraded more by vice than by superstition. Slavery is the daughter of darkness. An ignorant people is a blind instrument of its own destruction. Ambition and intrigue abuse the credulity and experience of men lacking all political, economic and civic knowledge. They adopt pure illusion as reality, they take license for liberty, treachery for patriotism and vengeance for justice. If a people, perverted by their training, succeed in achieving their liberty, they will soon lose it, for it would be of no avail to endeavour to explain to them that happiness consists in the practice of virtue, that the rule of law is more powerful than the rule of tyrants, because, as the laws are more inflexible, every one should submit to their beneficent austerity, that proper morals, and not force, are the bases of law, and that to practise justice is to practise liberty.

…Precisely because no form of government is so weak as the democratic, its framework must be firmer, and its institutions must be studied to determine their degree of stability… unless this is done, we will have to reckon with an ungovernable, tumultuous and anarchic society, not with a social order where happiness, peace and justice prevail."

Angostura, Venezuela, 15th February 1819

José de San Martín

FAREWELL ADDRESS TO THE PERUVIAN PEOPLE

While Simón Bolívar was overseeing the liberation of northern South America from Spanish rule (see page 112), leading the effort in the centre and south of the continent was José de San Martín (1778–1850). Born in modern-day Argentina, he moved to Spain with his family in 1783. He joined the Spanish army as a cadet at the age of 11 and rose to become a lieutenant colonel, but resigned his commission in 1811 to return to South America. He arrived in Buenos Aires in 1812 and offered his services to the United Provinces of the Rio de la Plata (later, Argentina). He was a highly effective military leader and organizer, winning several victories in Argentinian territory before helping to liberate Chile in 1818 and Peru in 1821. San Martín was made 'protector' of Peru that July, although many Peruvians believed he wanted to become its dictator or king. Frustrated by these suspicions, San Martín resigned after two months. As he left Peru, he bade farewell to its people – he did not return to Argentina, but spent the rest of his life in Europe, dying in France in 1850.

"My promises to the people for whom I have waged war have been fulfilled – to accomplish their independence and leave the choice of their rulers to their own will. The presence of an unfortunate soldier, however disinterested he may be, is not desirable in newly constituted states. On the other hand, I am tired of having it said that I wish to make myself king. In short, I shall always be ready to make the ultimate sacrifice for the liberty of the country, but as in the character of a simple private citizen and in no other. As for my conduct in public office, my compatriots, as is usually the case, will divide their opinions, their children will render true judgment. Peruvians, I leave you with your national representation established. If you place your entire confidence in it, count on succes. If not, anarchy will destroy you. May Heaven preside over your destinies and may you reach the summit of happiness and peace."

Lima, Peru, 20th September 1822

James Monroe

THE MONROE DOCTRINE

The Monroe Doctrine has been a central tenet of American foreign policy for two centuries. It is named after James Monroe (1758–1831), a Virginian who fought in the Revolutionary War, served as both senator and governor for his home state and as ambassador to France and the United Kingdom. He was appointed secretary of state in 1811, holding the position for nearly six years. Monroe went on to win two presidential elections, enjoying a landslide victory in 1816, and effectively running unopposed in 1820. His presidency was the height of the Era of Good Feelings, a period in domestic American politics characterized by national unity and lack of partisan rancour.

On 2nd December 1823, Madison gave his penultimate State of the Union Address to Congress, where he declared that the United States would not become involved in internal European affairs and that no further European colonialism or interference in the New World would be permitted. After Monroe's second term ended in 1825 he retired, living for another six years.

"The citizens of the United States cherish sentiments the most friendly in favour of the liberty and happiness of their fellow men on that side of the Atlantic. In the wars of the European powers in matters relating to themselves we have never taken any part, nor does it comport with our policy so to do. It is only when our rights are invaded or seriously menaced that we resent injuries or make preparation for our defence. With the movements in this hemisphere we are of necessity more immediately connected, and by causes which must be obvious to all enlightened and impartial observers.

…We owe it, therefore, to candour and to the amicable relations existing between the United States and those powers to declare that we should consider any attempt on their part to extend their system to any portion of this hemisphere as dangerous to our peace and safety. With the existing colonies or dependencies of any European power we have not interfered and shall not interfere, but with the governments who have declared their independence and maintained it, and whose independence we have, on great consideration and on just principles, acknowledged, we could not view any interposition for the purpose of oppressing them, or controlling in any other manner their destiny, by any European power in any other light than as the manifestation of an unfriendly disposition towards the United States."

Washington DC, USA, 2nd December 1823

Maria W. Stewart

'WHY SIT YE HERE AND DIE?'

Born into a free African-American family in Connecticut, Maria Stewart (1803–79) was orphaned at the age of five and received no formal education as a child, supporting herself by working as a domestic servant. After moving to Boston, she married a prosperous widower in 1826, but he died three years later and Stewart was defrauded of her inheritance, meaning she had to work once more as a servant. Experiencing a religious conversion in 1830, she became active in the Boston abolitionist movement, at first by writing pamphlets and articles. From April 1832, she began a series of lectures on religious and political issues, addressing crowds comprised of men and women, blacks and whites. She called for African Americans to organize against slavery and racism and extolled the importance of women's rights and education. Stewart was a trailblazer. She was the first African-American woman to lecture in public, but faced racist and sexist attacks for doing so and gave her final lecture in September 1833. She continued to publish and remained active in the abolitionist movement until her death in 1879.

"Why sit ye here and die?
If we say we will go to a foreign land,
the famine and the pestilence are
there, and there we shall die. If we sit
here, we shall die. Come let us plead
our cause before the whites. If they
save us alive, we shall live, and if
they kill us, we shall but die."

Boston, Massachusetts, USA, 21st September 1832

Elizabeth Cady Stanton

'WE NOW DEMAND OUR RIGHT TO VOTE'

The Seneca Falls Convention marked the starting point of the 'first wave' of feminism in the United States. Held from 18–19th July 1848 in upstate New York and attended by 300 people, it was organized by two prominent slavery abolitionists, Lucretia Coffin Mott and Elizabeth Cady Stanton (1815–1902). At the meeting, Stanton issued the Declaration of Sentiments, which set out the subordinate status of women in society and the unjust laws they were subject to. She then delivered the keynote address of the conference, urging her listeners to campaign for gender equality, including equal suffrage. Together with her close friend Susan B. Anthony, Stanton played an influential role in the growing American women's rights movement, organizing conventions, making public addresses and publishing pamphlets and articles. She later became involved in pro-temperance activism but the main focus of her campaigning was winning the vote for women. Stanton remained an indefatigable and energetic voice for women until her death at the age of 86, in 1902.

"We are assembled to protest against a form of government existing without the consent of the governed, to declare our right to be free as man is free, to be represented in the government which we are taxed to support, to have such disgraceful laws as give man the power to chastise and imprison his wife, to take the wages which she earns, the property which she inherits, and, in case of separation, the children of her love, laws which make her the mere dependent on his bounty. It is to protest against such unjust laws as these that we are assembled today, and to have them, if possible, forever erased from our statute books, deeming them a shame and a disgrace to a Christian republic in the 19th century. We have met to uplift woman's fallen divinity upon an even pedestal with man's. And, strange as it may seem to many, we now demand our right to vote according to the declaration of the government under which we live. This right no one pretends to deny.

…We do not expect our path will be strewn with the flowers of popular applause, but over the thorns of bigotry and prejudice will be our way, and on our banners will beat the dark storm clouds of opposition from those who have entrenched themselves behind the stormy bulwarks of custom and authority, and who have fortified their position by every means, holy and unholy. But we will steadfastly abide the result. Unmoved we will bear it aloft. Undauntedly we will unfurl it to the gale, for we know that the storm cannot rend from it a shred, that the electric flash will but more clearly show to us the glorious words inscribed upon it, Equality of Rights."

Seneca Falls, New York, USA, 19th July 1848

Victor Hugo

'A DAY WILL COME'

Author of *The Hunchback of Notre-Dame* and *Les Misérables*, Victor Hugo (1802–85) is one of France's greatest writers. The son of a general, he was a conservative royalist in his youth, but became more liberal and politically active over time. Following the 1848 revolution that overthrew the French monarchy, Hugo was elected to the National Assembly, where he proposed universal suffrage and an end to the death penalty. He also became involved in the International Peace Congress, a global movement to provide a forum to discuss how to forge harmony between nations. In 1849, Hugo presided over the congress's meeting in Paris, optimistically calling forth a vision of a world without conflict, and proposing a 'United States of Europe'. Hugo's liberalism caused him to flee into exile when Emperor Napoleon III seized power in 1851 and he did not return until after the French Republic was restored in 1870. Although he was hailed as a national hero, ill health and the death of family members and loved ones reduced his ability to play a major public role, and he died in 1885.

"A day will come when you, France, you, Russia, you, Italy, you, England, you, Germany, all of you, nations of the Continent, will, without losing your distinctive qualities and your glorious individuality, be blended into a superior unity, and constitute an European fraternity… A day will come when the only battlefield will be the market open to commerce and the mind opening to new ideas. A day will come when bullets and bombshells will be replaced by votes, by the universal suffrage of nations, by the venerable arbitration of a great Sovereign Senate, which will be to Europe what the Parliament is to England, what the Diet is to Germany, what the Legislative Assembly is to France. A day will come when a cannon will be exhibited in public museums, just as an instrument of torture is now, and people will be astonished how such a thing could have been. A day will come when those two immense groups, the United States of America and the United States of Europe shall be seen placed in presence of each other, extending the hand of fellowship across the ocean, exchanging their produce, their commerce, their industry, their arts, their genius, clearing the earth, peopling the deserts, improving creation under the eye of the Creator, and uniting, for the good of all, these two irresistible and infinite powers, the fraternity of men and the power of God."

Paris, France, 22nd August 1849

Sojourner Truth

'AIN'T I A WOMAN?'

Born into slavery in New York state as Isabella Baumfree, Sojourner Truth (c. 1797–1883) was bought and sold several times, often being beaten and abused by her masters, before escaping to freedom in 1827. Following a series of religious visions, she was inspired to change her name and converted to Methodism, beginning her ministry as a travelling preacher. At the time, the United States was divided over the issue of slavery. Whilst it was generally unpopular and illegal in northern states, in the South it was firmly entrenched, as slave labour was the foundation of its plantation economy. Truth became a central figure in abolitionist campaigning, often attracting huge crowds. She was also involved in the burgeoning women's rights movement. In 1851, she attended the Women's Rights Convention in Akron, Ohio, delivering an extempore speech that challenged the majority white audience to consider the rights of black women. Her refrain of 'Ain't I a Woman?' became a clarion call for those fighting for racial and gender equality, a struggle that Truth participated in until her death in 1883.

"That man over there says that women need to be helped into carriages and lifted over ditches, and to have the best place everywhere. Nobody ever helps me into carriages, or over mud puddles, or gives me any best place! And ain't I a woman? Look at me! Look at my arm! I have ploughed and planted and gathered into barns, and no man could head me! And ain't I a woman? I could work as much and eat as much as a man, when I could get it, and bear the lash as well! And ain't I a woman? I have borne 13 children, and seen most all sold off to slavery, and when I cried out with my mother's grief, none but Jesus heard me! And ain't I a woman?"

Akron, Ohio, USA, 29th May 1851

Frederick Douglass

'WHAT TO THE SLAVE IS YOUR FOURTH OF JULY?'

For the first 20 years of his life, Frederick Douglass (c. 1818–95) was a slave in Maryland before escaping to New York City to find freedom. He then settled in Massachusetts, where he joined the abolitionist movement, winning renown as an orator and writing an autobiography in 1845. Taking such a public role placed him at risk of being recaptured by his former master. To avoid this, Douglass went on a two-year lecture tour of the United Kingdom, where supporters raised money to buy his freedom. Returning to the United States in 1847, Douglass founded an abolitionist newspaper, the *North Star*, became involved in the women's rights movement and continued campaigning and lecturing. In 1852, he addressed a women's anti-slavery society in Rochester, New York. As it was the day after Independence Day, he used the speech to question if white Americans could take pride in their nation whilst slavery still existed. Douglass went on to become an important advisor to Abraham Lincoln during the American Civil War, to serve as ambassador to Haiti and to play a pivotal role in the battle for equality.

"What, to the American slave, is your Fourth of July? …The existence of slavery in this country brands your republicanism as a sham, your humanity as a base pretence and your Christianity as a lie. It destroys your moral power abroad, it corrupts your politicians at home. It saps the foundation of religion, it makes your name a hissing, and a byword to a mocking earth. It is the antagonistic force in your government, the only thing that seriously disturbs and endangers your Union. It fetters your progress, it is the enemy of improvement, the deadly foe of education. It fosters pride, it breeds insolence. It promotes vice, it shelters crime, it is a curse to the earth that supports it, and yet, you cling to it, as if it were the sheet anchor of all your hopes. Oh! Be warned! Be warned! A horrible reptile is coiled up in your nation's bosom. The venomous creature is nursing at the tender breast of your youthful republic. For the love of God, tear away and fling from you the hideous monster, and let the weight of 20 millions crush and destroy it forever!"

Rochester, New York, USA, 5th July 1852

John Brown

'SO LET IT BE DONE'

The United States had been split by the issue of slavery since its inception. By the mid-19th century, slavery had gradually been abolished in the North and there was a growing movement to do away with it nationwide. One of the most famed abolitionists was John Brown (1800–59), who believed that militant action was necessary. He planned to instigate a mass slave uprising in the South, the prelude to which would be seizing the armoury at Harpers Ferry, Virginia (now in West Virginia). Brown launched his raid on 16th October, accompanied by 21 supporters. He captured the armoury, but was forced to surrender to government troops after two days of fighting. Brown was captured, tried and found guilty of murder, slave insurrection and treason. Brown spoke with eloquence throughout his trial, and in his final address, having been condemned to death, he re-stated his belief in the righteousness of his cause. Brown was hanged a month later. Although his raid had been unsuccessful, it did much to further drive the wedge between northern and southern states that would erupt into civil war less than two years later.

"This court acknowledges, as I suppose, the validity of the law of God. I see a book kissed here which I suppose to be the Bible, or at least the New Testament. That teaches me that all things whatsoever I would that men should do to me, I should do even so to them. It teaches me, further, to remember them that are in bonds, as bound with them. I endeavoured to act up to that instruction. I say I am yet too young to understand that God is any respecter of persons. I believe that to have interfered as I have done, as I have always freely admitted I have done, on behalf of His despised poor was not wrong, but right. Now, if it is deemed necessary that I should forfeit my life for the furtherance of the ends of justice, and mingle my blood further with the blood of my children and with the blood of millions in this slave country whose rights are disregarded by wicked, cruel and unjust enactments, I submit. So let it be done!"

Charles Town, modern-day West Virginia, USA, 2nd November 1859

Giuseppe Garibaldi

'TO ARMS, THEN, ALL OF YOU'

In the early 19th century, a movement to unify Italy, then fragmented into different states and territories, gathered pace. One particular uprising occurred in Piedmont, northwest Italy, in 1835, and was joined by Giuseppe Garibaldi (1807–82), then a captain in the merchant navy. When the insurrection failed, Garibaldi fled to France, and then South America. Returning to Italy in 1848, he re-joined the unification campaign, fighting against the Austrian Empire that ruled much of northern Italy. Garibaldi supported the king of Sardinia, aiming to unify Italy under him. In 1859, he fought against Austrian forces and the next year raised a volunteer army of 1,000, known as the Red Shirts, which formed the nucleus of an army that conquered Sicily and most of southern Italy. Before returning home, Garibaldi addressed his victorious band in Naples, bidding them to continue their struggle. He heeded his own words, taking up his sword in 1863 and 1866 in campaigns to unify more Italian territory under Sardinian rule. In 1871, all of Italy was finally joined together into a single kingdom. Garibaldi died 11 years later, a popular hero in his homeland and beyond.

"To arms, then, all of you! All of you! And the oppressors and the mighty shall disappear like dust. You, too, women, cast away all the cowards from your embraces. They will give you only cowards for children, and you who are the daughters of the land of beauty must bear children who are noble and brave. Let timid doctrinaires depart from among us to carry their servility and their miserable fears elsewhere. This people is its own master. It wishes to be the brother of other peoples, but to look on the insolent with a proud glance, not to grovel before them imploring its own freedom. It will no longer follow in the trail of men whose hearts are foul. No! No! No!"

Naples, Italy, September 1860

Otto von Bismarck

'IRON AND BLOOD'

Until the mid-19th century, Germany was divided into several states, the largest and most powerful of which was Prussia. Many wanted to unify these territories into a single nation, but an attempt to do so through protest and political reform in 1848–49 failed. The main architect of German unification was the Prussian politician Otto von Bismarck (1815–98), an aristocrat and statesman who was appointed minister president of the kingdom on 23rd September 1862. One week after his appointment, Bismarck addressed the Budget Committee, telling them military strength was vital to the success of the nation. Despite parliamentary opposition, Bismarck increased the size of the army, helping Prussia to defeat Austria in 1866. Bismarck's masterstroke was provoking France to declare war on Prussia in 1870, correctly believing it would unite all of the German states. After Prussia soundly defeated France in 1871, the Prussian king was proclaimed Kaiser of a united German Empire. Bismarck was selected as the first imperial chancellor, serving in the post until 1890.

"It is not by speeches and majority resolutions that the great questions of the time are decided – that was the big mistake of 1848 and 1849 – but by iron and blood."

Berlin, modern-day Germany, 30th September 1862

Abraham Lincoln

GETTYSBURG ADDRESS

The inauguration of Abraham Lincoln (1809–65) as president in 1861 precipitated the American Civil War, a struggle between the United States and the Confederacy, a group of southern states who wished to secede so they could continue the practice of slavery. Lincoln, an outspoken abolitionist, had risen to fame in Illinois as a lawyer and local politician. He was an able and inspirational wartime president, providing the Union with strong and decisive leadership. A major turning point of the war was the Battle of Gettysburg, fought in July 1863 in Pennsylvania, where the Union repelled a major Confederate attack. Four months later, Lincoln spoke at the dedication of a military cemetery on the site of the battlefield, vowing to honour the memory of the fallen by winning victory and preserving the Union. Lincoln was re-elected president in 1864, and oversaw the final defeat of the South in April 1865. Tragically, just five days after the final Confederate army had surrendered, Lincoln was assassinated, preventing him overseeing the reconstruction of a nation shattered by four years of brutal warfare.

Fourscore and seven years ago our fathers brought forth, on this continent, a new nation, conceived in liberty, and dedicated to the proposition that all men are created equal. Now we are engaged in a great civil war, testing whether that nation, or any nation so conceived, and so dedicated, can long endure. We are met on a great battlefield of that war. We have come to dedicate a portion of that field, as a final resting place for those who here gave their lives, that that nation might live.

…The world will little note, nor long remember what we say here, but it can never forget what they did here. It is for us the living, rather, to be dedicated here to the unfinished work, which they who fought here have thus far so nobly advanced. It is rather for us to be here, dedicated to the great task remaining before us, that from these honoured dead we take increased devotion to that cause for which they here gave the last full measure of devotion, that we here highly resolve that these dead shall not have died in vain, that this nation, under God, shall have a new birth of freedom, and that government of the people, by the people, for the people, shall not perish from the earth.

Gettysburg, Pennsylvania, USA, 19th November 1863

John A. Macdonald

'THIS PEACEFUL REVOLUTION'

By the mid-19th century, the British colonies in mainland North America were divided into separate provinces, the most important of which was the Province of Canada, created in 1841. A movement arose to create a confederation that would deliver a strong central government whilst allowing individual provinces control over their own affairs. Supporters included Scottish-born John A. Macdonald (1815–91), joint premier of the Province of Canada. In 1864, an agreement for confederation was reached after meetings between delegates from the Province of Canada, Nova Scotia and New Brunswick but it required approval from each province's legislature. The next year Macdonald made a speech extolling unification that was central to the proposal being approved in the Province of Canada. Nova Scotia and New Brunswick also gave their backing, making way for the 1867 British North America Act that created the Dominion of Canada. Macdonald was the first prime minister of this new nation, serving until 1873, before winning re-election in 1878 and dying in office in 1891.

"We should feel sincerely grateful to beneficent Providence that we have had the opportunity vouchsafed us of calmly considering this great constitutional change, this peaceful revolution. That we have not been hurried into it, like the United States, by the exigencies of war. That we have not had a violent revolutionary period forced on us, as in other nations, by hostile action from without, or by domestic dissensions within. …It is our privilege and happiness to be in such a position, and we cannot be too grateful for the blessings thus conferred upon us. …At the risk of repeating myself, I would say, it was only by a happy concurrence of circumstances, that we were enabled to bring this great question to its present position. If we do not take advantage of the time, if we show ourselves unequal to the occasion, it may never return, and we shall hereafter bitterly and unavailingly regret having failed to embrace the happy opportunity now offered of founding a great nation under the fostering care of Great Britain, and our Sovereign Lady, Queen Victoria."

Quebec City, modern-day Quebec, Canada, 6th February 1865

Thomas Carlyle

ON BEING A DILIGENT STUDENT

The son of a stonemason, Thomas Carlyle (1795–1881) was born in Ecclefechan, a village in southwestern Scotland, and began studying at the University of Edinburgh shortly before his 14th birthday. Although his father wanted him to become a minister, Carlyle never qualified as one, working as a teacher and journalist instead. He published a novel and wrote about German literature and philosophy, translating many works into English. In 1834, Carlyle left Scotland for London, where he began writing a history of the French Revolution – it proved a major success, establishing Carlyle's reputation and stabilizing his precarious finances. His career then went from strength to strength. He wrote widely on history and contemporary society and gave highly popular lecture tours. In April 1866, he was installed as rector of the University of Edinburgh, and gave a speech urging the student body to approach their studies with the utmost diligence. That month Jane, Carlyle's wife for four decades, died; the grief caused him to withdraw from public life and curtail his writing over the last 16 years of his life.

"Advices, I believe, to young men, as to all men, are very seldom much valued. There is a great deal of advising, and very little faithful performing, and talk that does not end in any kind of action is better suppressed altogether. I would not, therefore, go much into advising, but there is one advice I must give you. In fact, it is the summary of all advices, and doubtless you have heard it a thousand times, but I must nevertheless let you hear it the thousand-and-first time, for it is most intensely true, whether you will believe it at present or not. Namely, that above all things the interest of your whole life depends on your being diligent, now while it is called today, in this place where you have come to get education! Diligent: that includes in it all virtues that a student can have. I mean it to include all those qualities of conduct that lead on to the acquirement of real instruction and improvement in such a place."

Edinburgh, Scotland, 2nd April 1866

Benjamin Disraeli

ON ONE-NATION CONSERVATISM

Following a dispute over the repeal of the Corn Laws in Great Britain in 1846, the Conservative Party split, and would not win a majority for another 28 years. Responsible for their resurgence was Benjamin Disraeli (1804–81), who had been elected an MP in 1837. Under the Earl of Derby, the Conservatives formed minority governments in 1852, 1858–59, and 1866–68, with Disraeli acting as chancellor of the exchequer. He oversaw the passage of the 1867 Reform Act, which doubled the size of the electorate. When Derby retired as prime minister in February 1868, Disraeli replaced him for the rest of the year, but then suffered electoral defeat at the hands of William Gladstone's Liberals. While in opposition, Disraeli made a speech setting out some of the principles of 'one-nation conservatism', which aimed to appeal to all levels of society by combining tradition with social reform and pride in empire. The Conservatives were victorious in the 1874 general election and Disraeli served as prime minister for the next six years – his political vision remains an important influence on his party to the present day.

"Gentlemen, the Tory party, unless it is a national party, is nothing. It is not a confederacy of nobles, it is not a democratic multitude. It is a party formed from all the numerous classes in the realm – classes alike and equal before the law, but whose different conditions and different aims give vigour and variety to our national life.

…Now, I have always been of the opinion that the Tory party has three great objects. The first is to maintain the institutions of the country, not from any sentiment of political superstition, but because we believe that they embody the principles upon which a community like England can alone safely rest. The principles of liberty, of order, of law and of religion ought not to be entrusted to individual opinion or to the caprice and passion of multitudes, but should be embodied in a form of permanence and power.

…Gentlemen, there is another and second great object of the Tory party. If the first is to maintain the institutions of the country, the second is, in my opinion, to uphold the empire of England.

…Gentlemen, another great object of the Tory party, and one not inferior to the maintenance of the empire, or the upholding of our institutions, is the elevation of the condition of the people."

London, England, 24th June 1872

Susan B. Anthony

ON A 'CITIZEN'S RIGHT TO VOTE'

Born into a Quaker family in Massachusetts, USA, Susan B. Anthony (1820–1906) became involved in the women's rights movement after meeting Elizabeth Cady Stanton in 1851. She devoted her energy to activism, lecturing and helping to organize women's rights associations. Although she wanted wholesale reform of women's status, she focused on securing female suffrage. In 1872, she decided to test if the recently passed 14th Amendment, which stated all American citizens had the right to equal protection under the law, would allow women to vote. That November she cast a ballot in the presidential elections and was arrested. Before her trial she embarked on a speaking tour asking the public if she had truly committed a crime. According to the courts, she had: Anthony was found guilty of breaking electoral law and fined $100 (she refused to pay). The verdict did nothing to dampen Anthony's dedication. She continued to travel and organize, giving her final speech just one month before her death. Fourteen years later, the 19th Amendment was passed, guaranteeing the right of American women to vote.

"There is an old saying that 'A rose by any other name would smell as sweet'. And I submit if the deprivation by law of the right of ownership of one's own person, wages, property, children, the denial of the right of an individual to sue and be sued in the courts is not a condition of servitude most bitter and absolute, though under the sacred name of marriage.

…And it is upon this conclusion of the citizen's constitutional right to vote that our National Woman Suffrage association has based its argument and action for the last four years. We no longer petition legislature nor Congress to give us the right to vote. We appeal to the women everywhere to assume their too-long neglected citizen's right to vote. We appeal to the inspectors of elections everywhere to receive the votes of all United States citizens as it is their duty to do. We appeal to United States commissioners and marshals to arrest the inspectors who reject the names and votes of United States citizens, as it is their duty to do, and leave alone those who, like our eighth-ward inspectors, perform their duties faithfully and well."

Monroe County, New York, USA, 3rd April 1873

Chief Joseph

'I WILL FIGHT NO MORE FOREVER'

The westward expansion of the United States displaced many Native Americans. Amongst them were the Nez Perce of the Pacific Northwest, who in 1877 were forced to relocate to Idaho. Hinmatóowyalahtǫit (1840–1904), also known by his Christian name Joseph, was the chief of a Nez Perce band from the Wallowa Valley, northeastern Oregon. As they were about to depart, he learned three of his men had killed some white settlers. Knowing this would bring reprisals from the US Army, Chief Joseph decided to lead his people to safety in Canada. Vastly outnumbered and suffering numerous casualties, they fought their way to within 40 miles of the frontier before being surrounded. Chief Joseph surrendered, making a speech pledging peace. His band was held in a prisoner-of-war camp in Kansas for eight months before resettlement in a reservation in Oklahoma, where many died of disease. In 1885, Chief Joseph and his followers were permitted to return to the Pacific Northwest, but were not allowed to resettle their ancestral lands. Instead they moved to a reservation in central Washington state, where Chief Joseph died in 1904.

"The old men are all dead. It is the young men who say yes or no. He who led on the young men is dead. It is cold, and we have no blankets. The little children are freezing to death. My people, some of them, have run away to the hills, and have no blankets, no food. No one knows where they are, perhaps freezing to death. I want to have time to look for my children, and see how many of them I can find. Maybe I shall find them among the dead. Hear me, my chiefs! I am tired. My heart is sick and sad. From where the sun now stands, I will fight no more forever."

Montana, USA, 5th October 1877

William Gladstone

'INSPIRED BY THE LOVE OF FREEDOM'

Known as the 'Grand Old Man', William Gladstone (1809–98) became leader of the British Liberal Party in 1867. They won the 1868 general election and Gladstone oversaw a tranche of reforms as prime minister, before his government was ousted by Benjamin Disraeli's Conservatives in 1874. Gladstone retired as leader, but re-emerged to protest Disraeli's inaction in the face of Ottoman atrocities in Bulgaria. With a general election looming in 1880, and standing for the Scottish seat of Midlothian, Gladstone unleashed a rhetorical campaign criticizing Conservative policy at home and abroad. It helped sweep the Liberals to power, with Gladstone returning as prime minister until resigning in 1885. A year later, and in support of Irish home rule, Gladstone allied with Irish MPs to run government for a third time, but his ministry fell after five months, following the defeat of legislation that would have given Ireland self-government. At the age of 82, Gladstone was elected prime minister for a fourth time in 1892, but resigned after two years, having seen his second attempt at passing an Irish home rule bill fail.

"The foreign policy of England should always be inspired by the love of freedom. There should be a sympathy with freedom, a desire to give it scope, founded not upon visionary ideas, but upon the long experience of many generations within the shores of this happy isle, that in freedom you lay the firmest foundations both of loyalty and order, the firmest foundations for the development of individual character, and the best provision for the happiness of the nation at large."

West Calder, Scotland, 27th November 1879

Swami Vivekananda

'THE DEATH KNELL OF ALL FANATICISM'

On 1st May 1893, the World's Columbian Exposition opened in Chicago, bringing together art and technology from around the globe. It ran for six months, and was attended by more than 25 million visitors. The gathering marked an opportunity for transnational meetings, the largest of which was the Parliament of World Religions, an interfaith dialogue that began on 11th September. Attended by representatives from different religions, it was opened by an address from the Hindu mystic and spiritual leader Swami Vivekananda (1863–1902). Born into a prosperous family in Bengal, Vivekananda had studied religion and philosophy and was a monk and social reformer. He travelled to Chicago as a spokesman for Hinduism and his speech extolling unity between different faiths was received by a standing ovation. Vivekananda lectured across the United States and the United Kingdom, introducing Hindu spiritualism and Indian philosophy to the West. On returning to India in 1897, he founded the Ramakrishna Mission, a religious organization also involved in educational and charitable activities.

"It fills my heart with unspeakable joy to rise in response to the warm and cordial welcome that you have given me. I thank you in the name of the most ancient order of monks in the world. I thank you in the name of the mother of religions and I thank you in the name of the millions and millions of Hindu people of all classes and sects.

…I am proud to belong to a religion that has taught the world both tolerance and universal acceptance. We believe not only in universal tolerance, but we accept all religions as true.

…Sectarianism, bigotry and its horrible descendant, fanaticism, have long possessed this beautiful earth. They have filled the earth with violence, drenched it often and often with human blood, destroyed civilization and sent whole nations to despair. Had it not been for these horrible demons, human society would be far more advanced than it is now.

But their time is come. And I fervently hope that the bell that tolled this morning in honour of this convention may be the death knell of all fanaticism, of all persecutions with the sword or with the pen, and of all uncharitable feelings between persons wending their way to the same goal."

Chicago, Illinois, USA, 11th September 1893

Booker T. Washington

'CAST DOWN YOUR BUCKET'

After the American Civil War, constitutional amendments abolished slavery, guaranteed equal citizenship rights and protection before the law and forbade race-based discrimination at the ballot box. However, African Americans still faced racism, disenfranchisement and poverty, particularly in the South, where states passed the segregationist Jim Crow laws. Booker T. Washington (1856–1915), born into slavery in Virginia, was the first principal of Tuskegee Institute in Alabama, founded in 1881 to train African-American teachers. In 1895, when lynchings were becoming more widespread, Washington made a speech at the Atlanta Exposition where he announced a compromise he had agreed with other leaders, black and white, in the South. He advocated a gradualist approach to equality where African Americans would not demand major reforms in return for peace and rights to basic education. Other African-American leaders later criticized Washington's conciliatory policies, and campaigned for change, although he continued to be influential until his death in 1915.

"To those of the white race who look to the incoming of those of foreign birth and strange tongue and habits for the prosperity of the South, were I permitted, I would repeat what I say to my own race, cast down your bucket where you are. Cast it down among the eight million Negroes whose habits you know, whose loyalty and love you have tested in days when to have proved treacherous meant the ruin of your firesides. Cast it down among those people who have, without strikes and labour wars, tilled your fields, cleared your forests, built your railroads and cities and brought forth treasures from the bowels of the earth and helped make possible this magnificent representation of the progress of the South. Casting down your bucket among my people, helping and encouraging as you are doing on these grounds, and with education of head, hand and heart, you will find that they will buy your surplus land, make blossom the waste places in your fields and run your factories. While doing this you can be sure in the future, as you have been in the past, that you and your families will be surrounded by the most patient, faithful, law-abiding and unresentful people that the world has seen.

As we have proved our loyalty to you in the past, in nursing your children, watching by the sickbeds of your mothers and fathers and often following them with tear-dimmed eyes to their graves, so in the future, in our humble way, we shall stand by you with a devotion that no foreigner can approach, ready to lay down our lives, if need be, in defense of yours, interlacing our industrial, commercial, civil and religious life with yours in a way that shall make the interests of both races one. In all things that are purely social we can be as separate as the fingers, yet one as the hand in all things essential to mutual progress."

Atlanta, Georgia, USA, 18th September 1895

Alfred Deakin

'THESE ARE TIMES THAT TRY MEN'S SOULS'

By the late 19th century, Australia existed as six separate British colonies: New South Wales, Queensland, South Australia, Tasmania, Victoria and Western Australia. A sense of national identity was emerging amongst the descendants of European settlers, and support for joining the colonies together began to build. Amongst those in favour of federalism was the Australian Natives' Association (ANA), a mutual society for white, Australian-born men. One of its members was Melbourne-born politician Alfred Deakin (1856–1919). After a proposed constitution was adopted in 1898, it had to be ratified by referenda, and Deakin campaigned in support of this. That March he spoke before ANA members. His passionate words in favour of federation were crucial in galvanizing media and public support, and by 1900 the constitution had been approved in all six colonies. The next year the Commonwealth of Australia officially came into being. From 1903–4 Deakin served as its second prime minister, holding the post twice more, from 1905–8 and 1909–10.

"I propose to speak to Australians simply as an Australian. …The number actually against us is probably greater than ever. The timorous and passive will be induced to fall away. The forces against us are arrayed under capable chiefs. But few as we may be, and weak by comparison, it will be the greater glory, whether we succeed or fail. These are the times that try men's souls. The classes may resist us, the masses may be inert, politicians may falter, our leaders may sound the retreat. But it is not a time to surrender. Let us nail our standard to the mast. Let us stand shoulder to shoulder in defence of the enlightened liberalism of the constitution. Let us recognize that we live in an unstable era, and that, if we fail in the hour of crisis, we may never be able to recall our lost national opportunities. …You must realize that upon you, and perhaps upon you alone, will rest the responsibility of organizing and carrying on this campaign. The greater the odds, the greater the honour. This cause dignifies every one of its servants and all efforts that are made on its behalf. The contest in which you are about to engage is one in which it is a privilege to be enrolled. It lifts your labours to the loftiest political levels, where they may be inspired with the purest patriotic passion for national life and being."

Bendigo, Victoria, Australia, 15th March 1898

Rosa Luxemburg

SPEECH TO THE STUTTGART CONGRESS

During the late 19th century, socialist parties, influenced by Karl Marx, sprang up across Europe, their members frequently subjected to suppression. In 1889, the threat of persecution forced Rosa Luxemburg (1871–1919) to flee southeastern Poland, then part of the Russian Empire, and move to Switzerland, where she became an important figure in the international socialist movement. In 1898, she emigrated to Berlin. That year she attended the Stuttgart Congress, where the Social Democratic Party of Germany was debating revising Marxist theory and adopting a gradual approach to building a socialist society by winning power democratically. In her address, Luxemburg opposed this, defending Marx's views and arguing that revolution was necessary. When World War I broke out, Luxemburg cofounded the Spartacus League, which sought to end the conflict through revolutionary action. As a result of her activities she was imprisoned from 1916–18. In January 1919, with Germany facing postwar political upheaval, she helped launch a communist uprising in Berlin. The insurgency was defeated and Luxemburg was arrested and executed.

"Perhaps there are some comrades who think speculations about final goals are academic questions. To them I would say that for us, as a revolutionary proletarian party, there exists no more practical question than that concerning ultimate goals.

…I think that arguments about whether, once we come to power, we will be able to make the production process serve society, whether things are ripe for that, that is an academic question. For us there can never be any question that we must struggle to seize political power. A socialist party must always have a response appropriate to the situation. It can never shrink back from its task. Therefore our views on what our final goals are must be fully clarified. And we will fulfil them, in spite of storm, wind and weather."

Stuttgart, Germany, 3rd October 1898

Theodore Roosevelt

'THE LIAR IS NO WHIT BETTER THAN THE THIEF'

Rising to fame after leading a volunteer cavalry regiment during the Spanish-American War, Theodore Roosevelt (1858–1919) was one of the United States's most charismatic leaders. He became running mate during William McKinley's successful 1900 presidential campaign, and when McKinley was assassinated the following year, Roosevelt became president. Re-elected in 1904, he pursued reforms aimed at delivering the American people a 'Square Deal', preserved vast swathes of the nation's landscape and won the Nobel Peace Prize for mediating an end to the Russo-Japanese War. In this speech from 1906, Roosevelt spoke of the need for journalists to uncover corruption, but also warned against 'muckrakers' who made exaggerated claims. He promised to continue reforming whilst reminding citizens of the need to maintain the highest personal standards. Roosevelt did not run for re-election in 1908, and was succeeded by his friend William Howard Taft. Disappointed with Taft's presidency, Roosevelt made a brief return to politics, founding his own Progressive Party, but was defeated in the 1912 presidential elections.

"There are, in the body politic, economic and social, many and grave evils, and there is urgent necessity for the sternest war upon them. There should be relentless exposure of, and attack upon, every evil man whether politician or business man, every evil practice, whether in politics, in business or in social life. I hail as a benefactor every writer or speaker, every man who, on the platform, or in book, magazine or newspaper, with merciless severity makes such attack, provided always that he in his turn remembers that the attack is of use only if it is absolutely truthful. The liar is no whit better than the thief, and if his mendacity takes the form of slander, he may be worse than most thieves. It puts a premium upon knavery untruthfully to attack an honest man, or even with hysterical exaggeration to assail a bad man with untruth. An epidemic of indiscriminate assault upon character does not good, but very great harm. The soul of every scoundrel is gladdened whenever an honest man is assailed, or even when a scoundrel is untruthfully assailed.

…Materially we must strive to secure a broader economic opportunity for all men, so that each shall have a better chance to show the stuff of which he is made. Spiritually and ethically we must strive to bring about clean living and right thinking. We appreciate that the things of the body are important, but we appreciate also that the things of the soul are immeasurably more important. The foundation stone of national life is, and ever must be, the high individual character of the average citizen."

Washington, DC, USA, 14th April 1906

Constance Markievicz

WOMEN, IDEALS AND THE NATION

The first woman to be elected to the UK's parliament, Constance Markievicz (1868–1927) was born into an aristocratic Anglo-Irish family. In 1893, she went to London to study art. Back in Ireland, Markievicz became involved in nationalist politics, joining Sinn Féin in 1908.

Famed for her fiery oratory in favour of Irish independence, in this speech from 1909 she urged women to join the armed struggle against the British she believed was inevitable. Taking part in the 1916 Easter Rising, she was arrested and only escaped execution because of her gender. In December 1918, Markievicz made history by being elected an MP, but like the rest of her Sinn Féin colleagues, refused to take her seat in Westminster. Instead, in 1919, the Sinn Féin MPs formed their own revolutionary parliament and government in Ireland, with Markievicz serving as minister for labour until 1922. For the rest of her life she continued to fight for the republican cause whilst also strongly opposing the division of Ireland.

"To sum up in a few words what I want the Young Ireland women to remember from me. Regard yourselves as Irish, believe in yourselves as Irish, as units of a nation distinct from England, your conquerer, and as determined to maintain your distinctiveness and gain your deliverance. Arm yourselves with weapons to fight your nation's cause. Arm your souls with noble and free ideas. Arm your minds with the histories and memories of your country and her martyrs, her language and a knowledge of her arts and her industries. And if in your day the call should come for your body to arm, do not shirk that either. May this aspiration towards life and freedom among the women of Ireland bring forth a Joan of Arc to free our nation!"

Dublin, Ireland, 1909

Emmeline Pankhurst

'FREEDOM OR DEATH'

Born in Manchester, England, Emmeline Pankhurst (1858–1928) attended her first women's suffrage meeting at the age of 14, and spent the rest of her life fighting to give females the vote. Frustrated at the restrained tactics and moderate demands of the suffragists, Pankhurst founded the Women's Social and Political Union in 1903. Using 'deeds, not words', the organization deployed mass rallies, vandalism and even arson. Its members were often arrested. Whilst imprisoned they were subjected to degrading treatment; many went on hunger strike and were brutally force-fed. When, on her 1913 speaking tour of the United States, Pankhurst made a speech stating she was willing to make the ultimate sacrifice to win the vote for women, no one could doubt her. On the outbreak of World War I, Pankhurst urged her followers to cease their militancy and support the conflict. In 1918, women won the right to vote, but only those over 30 who met certain qualifications. By this time Pankhurst was entering her last decade – she died in 1928, just weeks before legislation was passed that gave all adult women the vote.

"Since I am a woman, it is necessary to explain why women have adopted revolutionary methods in order to win the rights of citizenship. We women, in trying to make our case clear, always have to make as part of our argument, and urge upon men in our audience the fact – a very simple fact – that women are human beings… We were called militant, and we were quite willing to accept the name. We were determined to press this question of the enfranchisement of women to the point where we were no longer to be ignored by the politicians… We wear no mark, we belong to every class, we permeate every class of the community from the highest to the lowest. And so you see in the woman's civil war the dear men of my country are discovering it is absolutely impossible to deal with it. You cannot locate it, and you cannot stop it… Human life for us is sacred, but we say if any life is to be sacrificed it shall be ours. We won't do it ourselves, but we will put the enemy in the position where they will have to choose between giving us freedom or giving us death."

Hartford, Connecticut, USA, 13th November 1913

Keir Hardie

'THE SUNSHINE OF SOCIALISM'

In 1893, the Independent Labour Party (ILP) was founded in Bradford, England. Its was led by Keir Hardie (1856–1915), a Scottish former miner and socialist trade unionist who had been elected to Parliament the previous year. Giving a voice to the nation's working-class population, the party called for sweeping reforms to improve their lives. Their goals did not resonate with voters and all of the ILP's parliamentary candidates, including Hardie, lost in the 1895 general election. In 1900, Hardie helped form the Labour Representation Committee, an alliance of socialist groups (including the ILP) and trade unions. In 1906, this became the Labour Party, with Hardie, an MP once more, as its leader. Resigning from the post two years later, Hardie focused his energies on votes for women, self-rule for India and ending racial segregation in South Africa. By 1914, he was the elder statesman of British socialism, and delivered a speech detailing the benefits it would bring the people. When World War I broke out, Hardie, a pacifist, publicly opposed it, facing criticism and abuse for this stance and dying of pneumonia one year later.

"Think of the thousands of men and women who, during the past 21 years, have toiled unceasingly for the good of the race. The results are already being seen on every hand, alike in legislation and administration. And who shall estimate or put a limit to the forces and powers, which yet lie concealed in human nature? Frozen and hemmed in by a cold, callous greed, the warming influence of socialism is beginning to liberate them. We see it in the growing altruism of trade unionism. We see it, perhaps, most of all in the awakening of women… Woman, even more than the working class, is the great unknown quantity of the race. Already we see how their emergence into politics is affecting the prospects of men. Their agitation has produced a state of affairs in which even radicals are afraid to give more votes to men, since they cannot do so without also enfranchising women. Henceforward we must march forward as comrades in the great struggle for human freedom… The past 21 years have been years of continuous progress, but we are only at the beginning. The emancipation of the worker has still to be achieved and just as the ILP in the past has given a good, straight lead, so shall the ILP in the future, through good report and through ill, pursue the even tenor of its way, until the sunshine of socialism and human freedom break forth upon our land."

Bradford, England, 11th April 1914

Patrick Pearse

'IRELAND UNFREE SHALL NEVER BE AT PEACE'

In 1914, repeated protests and political campaigns against British rule in Ireland culminated in Parliament passing the Government of Ireland Act. This would have given Ireland devolved self-government within the United Kingdom but was postponed due to World War I. Many Irish nationalists, including Patrick Pearse (1879–1916), believed home rule did not go far enough, but wanted a wholly independent republic. A leader of the militant Irish Volunteers, Pearse sat on the supreme council of the Irish Republican Brotherhood, a secret revolutionary fraternity. On 1st August 1915, he spoke at the funeral of Jeremiah O'Donovan Rossa, a veteran Irish republican and revolutionary, promising resistance to British rule until Irish independence had been achieved. His words pre-empted the Easter Rising of 1916, when Pearse proclaimed an independent Irish republic. After six days of fighting the rebellion was put down; Pearse surrendered and was killed by firing squad, as were many other republican leaders. Despite this defeat, Irish independence was achieved in 1922, albeit with Northern Ireland remaining part of the United Kingdom.

"In a closer spiritual communion with him now than ever before or perhaps ever again, in spiritual communion with those of his day, living and dead, who suffered with him in English prisons, in communion of spirit too, with our own dear comrades who suffer in English prisons today, and speaking on their behalf as well as on our own. We pledge to Ireland our love, and we pledge to English rule in Ireland our hate… Our foes are strong and wise and wary but, strong and wise and wary as they are, they cannot undo the miracles of God who ripens in the hearts of young men the seeds sown by the young men of a former generation.

…Rulers and Defenders of Realms had need to be wary if they would guard against such processes. Life springs from death and from the graves of patriot men and women spring living nations. The defenders of this realm have worked well in secret and in the open. They think that they have pacified Ireland. They think that they have purchased half of us and intimidated the other half. They think that they have foreseen everything, think that they have provided against everything but the fools, the fools, the fools! They have left us our Fenian dead, and, while Ireland holds these graves, Ireland unfree shall never be at peace."

Dublin, Ireland, 1st August 1915

Dragutin Gavrilović

'LONG LIVE BELGRADE!'

On 28th June 1914, Archduke Franz Ferdinand, heir to the Austro-Hungarian throne, was killed in Sarajevo by a Bosnian student who wanted to create an independent Southern Slav state. This increased tensions between Austria-Hungary and Serbia, an important sponsor of Southern Slav rebels. Tensions escalated, drawing in Europe's great powers and culminating in the outbreak of World War I. On 7th October 1915, an Austro-Hungarian invasion threatened Belgrade, the Serb capital. Commanding one of the battalions defending the city was Dragutin Gavrilović (1882–1945), a veteran Serb officer. Under heavy artillery attack and outnumbered, he resisted the enemy onslaught. Launching a counterattack, he rallied his men, personally leading a charge and being seriously wounded. Belgrade fell and most of Serbia remained under enemy occupation until the country was liberated in September 1918. After the war, Serbia formed the nucleus for the Kingdom of Yugoslavia, whilst Gavrilović, who survived the conflict, was garlanded with decorations and honours.

"Soldiers, exactly at three o'clock, the enemy is to be crushed by your fierce charge, destroyed by your grenades and bayonets. The honour of Belgrade, our capital, must not be stained. Soldiers! Heroes! The supreme command has erased our regiment from its records. Our regiment has been sacrificed for the honour of Belgrade and the Fatherland. Therefore, you no longer need to worry about your lives: they no longer exist. So, forward to glory! For the King and the Fatherland! Long live the King, Long live Belgrade!"

Belgrade, modern-day Serbia, 7th October 1915

Roger Casement

SPEECH FROM THE DOCK

Born into a Protestant Anglo-Irish family, Roger Casement (1864–1916) had a distinguished career as a British consul in Africa and South America. As part of his work, he investigated treatment of local workers in rubber plantations in Congo and the Amazon, revealing systematic brutality and violence against them. Casement retired from the civil service in 1913, devoting himself to another movement: Irish independence. Fund-raising for the cause when World War I broke out in 1914, Casement travelled to Germany, where he tried unsuccessfully to gain formal military support for a revolt in Ireland. Returning to Ireland in a German U-boat in April 1916, he was captured by the British and imprisoned in London. Meanwhile the Easter Rising had been launched. The rebels declared independence, but after six days they were defeated by British forces. Casement was found guilty of high treason and sentenced to death. Speaking from the dock, he challenged the court's right to try him and defended his decision to rebel against British rule. He was executed by hanging at Pentonville Prison on 3rd August.

"If we are to be indicted as criminals, to be shot as murderers, to be imprisoned as convicts because our offence is that we love Ireland more than we value our lives, then I know not what virtue resides in any offer of self-government held out to brave men on such terms. Self-government is our right, a thing born in us at birth. It is a thing no more to be doled out to us or withheld from us by another people than the right to life itself, than the right to feel the sun or smell the flowers or to love our kind. It is only from the convict these things are withheld for crime committed and proven, and Ireland that has wronged no man, that has injured no land, that has sought no dominion, over others, Ireland is treated today among the nations of the world as if she were a convicted criminal. If it be treason to fight against such an unnatural fate as this, then I am proud to be a rebel, and shall cling to my rebellion with the last drop of my blood.

…Where all your rights become only an accumulated wrong. Where men must beg with bated breath for leave to subsist in their own land, to think their own thoughts, to sing their own songs, to garner the fruits of their own labours. And even while they beg, to see things inexorably withdrawn from them, then surely it is a braver, a saner and a truer thing, to be a rebel in act and deed against such circumstances as these than tamely to accept it as the natural lot of men."

London, England, 29th June 1916

Robert Laird Borden

'HEIRS OF THE PAST, TRUSTEES OF THE FUTURE'

When the United Kingdom declared war on Germany on 4th August 1914, it committed the British Empire to join the conflict. This applied to 'dominions' such as Canada, which had domestic self-government but no independent foreign policy. The Canadian prime minister was Robert Laird Borden (1854–1937), a former teacher and lawyer who had led the country since 1911. He pledged Canada would raise half a million soldiers. Tens of thousands of Canadians volunteered, but as the fighting dragged on and its brutality became known, their numbers dwindled. Furthermore, relatively few in the French-speaking population joined up. In his speech from 1916, Borden, reluctant to introduce conscription, publicly urged more Canadians to volunteer. The appeal did not have the desired effect and, in August 1917, conscription was controversially introduced, leading to violent rioting in Quebec at Easter 1918, with Borden sending in government troops to maintain order. In all, around one-fifth of the 600,000 Canadians who served in World War I were conscripts.

"In the history of every people there may come such a challenge to the spirit of its citizens as must be answered in service and devotion if the nation is to have an abiding place in the future. The events of this war bring that challenge today to the manhood of Canada.

…To men of military age I make appeal that they place themselves at the service of the State for military duty. To all others I make appeal that they place themselves freely at the disposition of their country for such service as they are deemed best fitted to perform.

And to the women of Canada, whose spirit has been so splendid and so inspiring in this hour of devotion and sacrifice, I bid God-speed in the manifold works of beneficence in which they are now engaged, and I pray them to aid still more in every field of national service for which they may feel themselves fitted.

Let us never forget the solemn truth that the nation is not constituted of the living alone. There are those as well who have passed away and those yet to be born. So this great responsibility comes to us as heirs of the past and trustees of the future. But with that responsibility there has come something greater still, the opportunity of proving ourselves worthy of it, and I pray that this may not be lost."

Ottawa, Canada, 23rd October 1916

Vladimir Lenin

THE APRIL THESES

In 1917, with war-weary Russia facing food shortages, its tsarist regime was overthrown and replaced by a republican provisional government. At this time, the Russian Bolshevik leader Vladimir Lenin (1870–1924) was in exile in Switzerland; he gained permission from German authorities to pass through their territory in a sealed train so he could return home. Lenin arrived in Petrograd on 16th April and the next day issued ten directives, his 'theses', criticizing the provisional government and calling for radical socialist policies and delivering more power to the soviets (workers' councils). The Bolsheviks steadily won popular support, particularly as the provisional government decided to continue to participate in World War I. In the October Revolution, Lenin led the Bolsheviks to power by launching an armed insurrection in Petrograd. Established as the leader of the new government, Lenin withdrew the nation from World War I and by 1922 had overseen victory in the Russian Civil War, after which the Soviet Union was established. By this point Lenin's health was in decline and he died in 1924.

"The specific feature of the present situation in Russia is that the country is passing from the first stage of the revolution, which – owing to the insufficient class-consciousness and organization of the proletariat – placed power in the hands of the bourgeoisie, to its second stage, which must place power in the hands of the proletariat and the poorest sections of the peasants. …The masses must be made to see that the Soviets of Workers' Deputies are the only possible form of revolutionary government, and that therefore our task is, as long as this government yields to the influence of the bourgeoisie, to present a patient, systematic, and persistent explanation of the errors of their tactics, an explanation especially adapted to the practical needs of the masses."

Petrograd, now St Petersburg, Russia, 17th April 1917

Jan Smuts

'A NEW AND RICHER NATIONAL TYPE'

In 1899, war broke out in South Africa between the Boer republics of Orange Free State and Transvaal and the British Empire. A British victory in 1902 saw a peace that allowed the Boers self-government as part of the Union of South Africa, which was declared in 1910. When World War I broke out, the leading political figure was Jan Smuts (1870–1950), who had led a Boer guerrilla unit during the earlier conflict. South Africa remained loyal to the British, although Smuts had to help suppress a Boer revolt before leading campaigns against German colonial forces in Africa. In 1917, Smuts travelled to London for an imperial conference, going on to play a major role in setting Allied strategy; whilst there he gave a speech on South African matters, presaging the legislation that would limit the rights of the non-white population. Smuts then served as prime minister of South Africa from 1919–24, resuming the position when World War II broke out in 1939 and serving in the Imperial War Cabinet. He was voted out of office in 1948, dying two years later.

"When we look at that wonderful history of South Africa we are all cheered and encouraged to move forward in the hope that as our task has not been too difficult for us in the past, it may not prove entirely beyond us in the future. …Instead of mixing up black and white in the old haphazard way, which instead of lifting up the black degraded the white, we are now trying to lay down a policy of keeping them apart as much as possible in our institutions. In land ownership, settlement and forms of government, we are trying to keep them apart, and in that way laying down in outline a general policy which it may take a hundred years to work out, but which in the end may be the solution of our native problem… We know we have tremendous problems to contend with. We know we have tremendous tasks before us, and in dealing with these problems and in trying to fulfil these tasks one generation of South Africans after another will brace its nerves and strengthen its intellect and broaden its mind and character. Although these difficulties may seem to us, and indeed are, grave perils to our future, I trust that in the long run these difficulties may prove a blessing in disguise and may prove to have afforded the training school for a large-minded, broad-minded, magnanimous race, capable not only of welding together different racial elements into a new and richer national type, but capable of dealing as no other white race in history has ever dealt with the question of the relations between black and white."

London, England, 22nd May 1917

David Lloyd George

'GERMANY EXPECTED TO FIND A LAMB'

The United Kingdom committed itself to defending Belgian neutrality under the 1839 Treaty of London. Despite this, Germany had invaded Belgium on 4th August 1914, believing the British would take no action; they were proved wrong, as the United Kingdom duly declared war. The prime minister at the time was the Liberal H. H. Asquith and the Welshman David Lloyd George (1863–1945) was chancellor of the exchequer. In 1915, after a public outcry over shortage of shells, Asquith went into coalition with the Conservatives and Lloyd George became minister of munitions. When the beleaguered Asquith was forced out of office in December 1916, Lloyd George replaced him. He was an energetic and decisive wartime leader, and his June 1917 speech to Parliament outlined Germany's responsibility for starting the conflict. Lloyd George remained prime minister after the war ended in 1918 but, despite his previous harsh words, resisted demanding overly punitive measures against Germany. Following a scandal about the sale of honours, Lloyd George resigned the prime ministership but remained an MP until 1945.

"There were six countries which entered the war at the beginning. Britain was last, and not the first. Before she entered the war Britain made every effort to avoid it, begged, supplicated and entreated that there should be no conflict… We begged Germany not to attack Belgium, and produced a treaty, signed by the King of Prussia, as well as the King of England, pledging himself to protect Belgium against an invader, and we said, If you invade Belgium we shall have no alternative but to defend it. The enemy invaded Belgium, and now they say, Why, forsooth, you, England, provoked this war. It is not quite the story of the wolf and the lamb. I will tell you why – because Germany expected to find a lamb and found a lion."

London, England, 21st June 1917

Emma Goldman

ADDRESS TO THE JURY

Anarchism, which believes traditional government structures ought to be swept away and that society needs to be wholly transformed, was globally influential from the late 19th century. Due to their radical beliefs and involvement in rioting, authorities regarded anarchists as a fundamental threat to public order. Anarchist Emma Goldman (1869–1940) was born into a Jewish family in Lithuania (then part of the Russian Empire), and emigrated to the United States in 1885. She became involved in radical politics, publishing, campaigning and lecturing, and earned the enmity of the government for her activities. Opposing America's entry into World War I, Goldman was arrested in July 1917 for agitating against conscription. At her trial, she argued that her activities were protected under the First Amendment, which guarantees the right to free speech. Nonetheless she was found guilty and sentenced to two years' imprisonment. Upon her release in 1919, Goldman was deported to the Soviet Union as a subversive alien. She left in 1921 and spent the rest of her life living and working in Europe and North America, dying in Canada in 1940.

"Gentlemen of the jury, we respect your patriotism. We would not, if we could, have you change its meaning for yourself. But may there not be different kinds of patriotism as there are different kinds of liberty? I for one cannot believe that love of one's country must needs consist in blindness to its social faults, to deafness to its social discords, of inarticulation to its social wrongs. Neither can I believe that the mere accident of birth in a certain country or the mere scrap of a citizen's paper constitutes the love of country.

I know many people – I am one of them – who were not born here, nor have they applied for citizenship, and who yet love America with deeper passion and greater intensity than many natives whose patriotism manifests itself by pulling, kicking and insulting those who do not rise when the national anthem is played.

...We say that if America has entered the war to make the world safe for democracy, she must first make democracy safe in America. How else is the world to take America seriously, when democracy at home is daily being outraged, free speech suppressed, peaceable assemblies broken up by overbearing and brutal gangsters in uniform, when free press is curtailed and every independent opinion gagged. Verily, poor as we are in democracy, how can we give of it to the world? We further say that a democracy conceived in the military servitude of the masses, in their economic enslavement, and nurtured in their tears and blood, is not democracy at all. It is despotism, the cumulative result of a chain of abuses which, according to that dangerous document, the Declaration of Independence, the people have the right to overthrow."

New York City, NY, USA, 9th July 1917

Woodrow Wilson

14 POINTS FOR PEACE

The United States entered World War I in April 1917. Woodrow Wilson (1856–1924), president since 1913, had declared war on Germany as a response to its unrestricted targeting of shipping in the Atlantic and attempts to ally with Mexico. American involvement ultimately helped deliver Allied victory. Whilst the fighting was ongoing, Wilson looked towards the postwar settlement, and in January 1918 delivered a speech to Congress detailing his diplomatic principles. These '14 points' proposed goals such as free trade, reduction of armaments, open negotiation, the right of nations to democracy and self-determination and the establishment of the League of Nations as an international organization to promote peace. Attending the Paris Peace Conference, Wilson was unable to persuade other Allied leaders to share in his idealism, and the Treaty of Versailles failed to meet many of his aims although his proposed League of Nations was founded. Wilson returned home, but was unable to persuade the Senate to ratify entry into the body, which the United States would never join.

"What we demand in this war, is nothing peculiar to ourselves. It is that the world be made fit and safe to live in, and particularly that it be made safe for every peace-loving nation which, like our own, wishes to live its own life, determine its own institutions, be assured of justice and fair dealing by the other peoples of the world as against force and selfish aggression. All the peoples of the world are in effect partners in this interest, and for our own part we see very clearly that unless justice be done to others it will not be done to us.

...For such arrangements and covenants we are willing to fight and to continue to fight until they are achieved, but only because we wish the right to prevail and desire a just and stable peace such as can be secured only by removing the chief provocations to war, which this programme does remove.

We have no jealousy of German greatness, and there is nothing in this programme that impairs it. We grudge her no achievement or distinction of learning or of pacific enterprise such as have made her record very bright and very enviable. We do not wish to injure her or to block in any way her legitimate influence or power. We do not wish to fight her either with arms or with hostile arrangements of trade if she is willing to associate herself with us and the other peace-loving nations of the world in covenants of justice and law and fair dealing. We wish her only to accept a place of equality among the peoples of the world – the new world in which we now live – instead of a place of mastery."

Washington, DC, USA, 8th January 1918

Leon Trotsky

RALLYING THE RED ARMY

A central figure in the Bolshevik seizure of power in the 1917 October Revolution was Leon Trotsky (1879–1940), a Ukrainian-Jewish politician and Lenin's top lieutenant. As foreign commissar, Trotsky had the task of negotiating peace with Russia's enemies. The resulting Treaty of Brest-Litovsk, signed March 1918, ended Russian involvement in World War I. The Bolsheviks then had to contend with the ongoing Russian Civil War, fought against the White Army, an anti-communist alliance supported by foreign powers. Trotsky was named war commissar, and oversaw the growth of the Red Army into an effective fighting force. Constantly on the move, he frequently gave speeches to remind troops of the importance of their struggle, and was instrumental to the communist victory in 1922. After Lenin died in 1924, Trotsky was outmanoeuvred by Joseph Stalin, who became the paramount figure in the Soviet Union. Trotsky led the opposition to the Stalinist regime, and was expelled from the country in 1929. He settled in Mexico in 1936, where he was assassinated in 1940.

"Less than six months have passed since the decisive victory of the Allies over the central empires. Six months ago it seemed that the power of the Anglo-French and American imperialism was without limits.

At that time all the Russian counter-revolutionists had no doubt that the days of the Soviet Republic were numbered, but events now move steadfastly along the Soviet road. The working masses of the whole world are joining the flag of the Soviet authority, and the world robbers of imperialism are being betrayed even by the Crimean donkeys. At the present moment one awaits from day to day the victory of the Soviet Republic in Austria and in Germany. It is not impossible that the proletariat of Italy, Poland or France will violate the logical order and outstrip the working class in other countries.

These spring months become the decisive months in the history of Europe. At the same time this spring will decide definitely the fate of the bourgeois and rich peasant, anti-Soviet Russia.

…Only stubbornness, steadfastness, watchfulness and courage in the military struggle have guaranteed til now to the Russian Soviet Republic its international success. The victorious struggle of the Red Army on all fronts aroused the spirit of the European working class."

Russia, April 1919

Marcus Garvey

'IF YOU BELIEVE THE NEGRO HAS A SOUL'

One of the United States's most charismatic black nationalists was the Jamaican-born Marcus Garvey (1887–1940), who migrated to the country in 1916. Founder of the Universal Negro Improvement Association, an organization that aimed to promote black self-pride and unity, Garvey spread his message of empowerment through lecture tours and writing, winning hundreds of thousands of followers. He advocated progress through self-sufficiency and self-determination, and proposed the creation of an autonomous state for black Americans in Africa. To this end Garvey founded the Black Star Line to empower the African diaspora to trade goods and also to facilitate migration to Africa. It attracted financial investment from thousands of African Americans but operational problems forced it to fold in 1921. Garvey was eventually found guilty of mail fraud related to sale of Black Star Line stock and was imprisoned. Upon his release in 1927, he was deported to Jamaica, before moving to London in 1935. Garvey continued to be politically active up until his death in 1940, and continues to be hailed as a champion of Pan-Africanism.

"If you believe that the Negro has a soul, if you believe that the Negro is a man, if you believe the Negro was endowed with the senses commonly given to other men by the Creator, then you must acknowledge that what other men have done, Negroes can do. We want to build up cities, nations, governments, industries of our own in Africa, so that we will be able to have a chance to rise from the lowest to the highest position in the African Commonwealth."

New York City, NY, USA, July 1921

Margaret Sanger

A MORAL NECESSITY FOR BIRTH CONTROL

During the early 20th century, people who promoted access to birth control and spread information about family planning were subject to legal prosecution in many countries. Margaret Sanger (1879–1966), an obstetrical nurse in New York City, witnessed first-hand how a lack of information about methods of birth control could lead to increased maternal and infant mortality, particularly in poorer communities. She gave up nursing in 1912, devoting herself to helping women avoid unwanted pregnancies. Besides lecturing, importing contraceptive devices and publishing pamphlets, she opened a family planning clinic in Brooklyn. She faced legal harassment and imprisonment for her activities, but carried on regardless. In 1921 Sanger founded the American Birth Control League, a nationwide organization aimed at appealing to a broader base of society. That same year she delivered a speech that emphasized the social benefits of legalizing contraception. By the 1930s and 1940s, thanks in large part to Sanger's efforts, birth control was widely used and accepted in the United States, and laws against using and promoting it were no longer enforced.

"We stand on the principle that birth control should be available to every adult man and woman. We believe that every adult man and woman should be taught the responsibility and the right use of knowledge. We claim that woman should have the right over her own body and to say if she shall or if she shall not be a mother, as she sees fit. We further claim that the first right of a child is to be desired. While the second right is that it should be conceived in love and the third, that it should have a heritage of sound health. ...We desire to stop at its source the disease, poverty and feeble-mindedness and insanity which exist today, for these lower the standards of civilization and make for race deterioration. We know that the masses of people are growing wiser and are using their own minds to decide their individual conduct. The more people of this kind we have, the less immorality shall exist. For the more responsible people grow, the higher do they and shall they attain real morality."

New York City, NY, USA,
18th November 1921

Joseph Stalin

ON THE DEATH OF LENIN

On 21st January 1924, Vladimir Lenin, founder and first leader of the Soviet Union, died after a series of strokes. The leading figures of the state gathered in Moscow to pay their respects. They included Joseph Stalin (1878–1953) a Georgian-born revolutionary who had risen to the powerful position of General Secretary of the Communist Party of the Soviet Union. Although Stalin had often clashed with Lenin, who had grown concerned about his rising influence, he played a prominent role in the ceremonies to mark his death. On 26th January, he made a speech extolling Lenin's virtues and his contribution to communism. The funeral took place the next day. Lenin's corpse was carried through Red Square to a mausoleum where his embalmed body remains on public display to this day. The Soviet Union was briefly ruled by a *troika* (triumvirate) made up of Stalin and two other politicians, Lev Kamenev and Grigory Zinoviev. However, using a mixture of ruthlessness and political skill, Stalin outmanoeuvred both men, as well as marginalizing his rival, Leon Trotsky, to establish himself as sole leader, ruling until his death in 1953.

"Like a huge rock, our country stands out amid an ocean of bourgeois states. Wave after wave dashes against it, threatening to submerge it and wash it away. But the rock stands unshakable. Wherein lies its strength? Not only in the fact that our country rests on an alliance of the workers and peasants, that it embodies a union of free nationalities, that it is protected by the mighty arm of the Red Army and the Red Navy. The strength, the firmness, the solidity of our country is due to the profound sympathy and unfailing support it finds in the hearts of the workers and peasants of the whole world. The workers and peasants of the whole world want to preserve the Republic of Soviets as an arrow shot by the sure hand of Comrade Lenin into the camp of the enemy, as the pillar of their hopes of deliverance from oppression and exploitation, as a reliable beacon pointing the path to their emancipation. They want to preserve it, and they will not allow the landlords and capitalists to destroy it. Therein lies our strength. Therein lies the strength of the working people of all countries. And therein lies the weakness of the bourgeoisie all over the world!"

Moscow, former USSR, 26th January 1924

Mahatma Gandhi

ON THE EVE OF THE SALT MARCH

Having dominated the Indian subcontinent since the mid-18th century, Britain assumed direct rule in 1858. Reforms introducing elements of self-government were limited and demands for independence emerged, led by the Indian National Congress. The movement's most influential figure was Mohandas Gandhi (1869–1948), who had studied law in London. Living in South Africa from 1893–1914, Gandhi campaigned against racial discrimination and it was here that he was given the honorific *Mahatma*, meaning 'great soul'. Returning to India in 1915, Gandhi joined Congress, where he advocated protest against British rule using *satyagraha* (nonviolent civil resistance). In March 1930, Gandhi announced a march against the salt tax. The day before the march, he explained the importance of nonviolence. Growing to 2,500 people, the 26-day march progressed peacefully over 240 miles from Ahmedabad to the coastal village of Dandi, where Gandhi gathered sea salt without paying tax. The march inspired many to join the independence movement but did not lead to any major changes in British policy; Gandhi's great work was yet to be completed.

"But let there be not a semblance of breach of peace even after all of us have been arrested. We have resolved to utilize all our resources in the pursuit of an exclusively nonviolent struggle. Let no one commit a wrong in anger. This is my hope and prayer. I wish these words of mine reached every nook and corner of the land. My task shall be done if I perish and so do my comrades.

…I believe there are men in India to complete the work begun by me. I have faith in the righteousness of our cause and the purity of our weapons. And where the means are clean, there God is undoubtedly present with His blessings."

Ahmedabad, India, 11th March 1930

Albert Einstein

'THE WONDERS OF SCIENCE'

Born into a German-Jewish family, in 1905 Albert Einstein (1879–1955) was a technical assistant in the Swiss Patent Office, having failed to secure an academic position. That year, he published four groundbreaking articles that would transform the perception of the universe. They made his reputation, winning him international recognition and university lectureships. In 1913, Einstein was appointed director of the Kaiser Wilhelm Institute for Physics at the University of Berlin, where he continued his research, winning the Nobel Prize in 1921. He became a globally known figure, and this speech from 1930 encapsulates his optimistic faith in the benefits of science for humanity. In 1933, the rise of the Nazis led to growing anti-semitic sentiment that forced Einstein to emigrate to the United States. Despite his pacifist beliefs, in 1939 Einstein recommended that the United States should develop an atomic bomb, but from 1945 campaigned against the perils of atomic warfare. Einstein's last decade was devoted to finding a unified field theory to bring together all the laws of physics, but he died in 1955 before he could complete it.

" And everybody should be ashamed who uses the wonders of science and engineering without thinking and having mentally realized not more of it than a cow realizes of the botany of the plants that it eats with pleasure.

Think also about the fact that it is the engineers who make true democracy possible. They facilitate not only the daily work of the people, but also make the works of the finest thinkers and artists accessible to the public. The pleasure of these works had recently still been a privilege of the preferred classes. Thus the engineers wake the peoples from their sleepy bluntness. "

Berlin, Germany, 22nd August 1930

Stanley Baldwin

A FEAR FOR THE FUTURE

During the 1920s and 1930s, with the power of aircraft and explosives increasing, military theorists in the UK argued that strategic bombing of enemy cities would be a virtually unstoppable method of achieving victory in a future war. These ideas were widely believed by military and civilian leaders, including the Conservative statesman Stanley Baldwin (1867–1947).

In 1932, having already served twice as prime minister himself, Conservative leader Baldwin held a senior role in Prime Minister Ramsay MacDonald's coalition government. He made a speech in parliament advocating international disarmament. He stated that the abolition of aerial weaponry was vital because its potential for destruction was so great and unstoppable it would always create fear and tension between nations. Ultimately, the bellicosity of Nazi Germany led Baldwin to switch to favouring rearmament, which he continued to promote after he became prime minister for the third time in 1935. Baldwin resigned from politics in 1937, and died in his sleep a decade later.

"What the world suffers from is a sense of fear, a want of confidence. And it is a fear held instinctively and without knowledge very often. But my own view – and I have slowly and deliberately come to this conclusion – is that there is no one thing that is more responsible for that fear... than the fear of the air.

...That is, the appalling speed which the air has brought into modern warfare, the speed of the attack. The speed of the attack, compared with the attack of an army, is as the speed of a motorcar to that of a four-in-hand. In the next war you will find that any town within reach of an aerodrome can be bombed within the first five minutes of war to an extent inconceivable in the last war... I think it is well also for the man in the street to realize that there is no power on Earth that can protect him from being bombed, whatever people may tell him. The bomber will always get through."

London, England, 10th November 1932

Franklin D. Roosevelt

FIRST INAUGURAL ADDRESS

After the Wall Street Crash of 1929, the United States – and the world – went into the Great Depression, a decade-long economic slump that left millions unemployed. The incumbent president, the Republican Herbert Hoover, was widely blamed for the unfolding crisis, and suffered a landslide defeat in the 1932 elections. The victor was Franklin D. Roosevelt (1882–1945), the Democrat governor of New York, who had overcome an attack of polio that left him unable to walk unaided. The heart of his campaign was the 'New Deal' – a programme of reforms that aimed to regulate the financial system, provide relief for the poor and unemployed and return the economy to its pre-crisis state. Roosevelt was inaugurated in March 1933; in his address he promised the American people he would take bold action. He urged them not to succumb to fear, but to have confidence in the future. Roosevelt's New Deal was unprecedented in its ambition and scale, and succeeded in reducing unemployment and beginning to rebuild the economy. Roosevelt was re-elected in 1936, and continued to lead the United States towards economic recovery.

"This is preeminently the time to speak the truth, the whole truth, frankly and boldly. Nor need we shrink from honestly facing conditions in our country today. This great nation will endure as it has endured, will revive and will prosper. So, first of all, let me assert my firm belief that the only thing we have to fear is fear itself – nameless, unreasoning, unjustified terror which paralyses needed efforts to convert retreat into advance. In every dark hour of our national life, a leadership of frankness and vigour has met with that understanding and support of the people themselves which is essential to victory."

Washington, DC, USA, 4th March 1933

...al Atatürk

...es dismantled the defeated
...ng it of most of its non-Turkish
...anbul. As a protest to this harsh
...(1881–1938), an army officer
who had ... at Gallipoli, launched a Turkish
nationalist uprising in 1919. He rapidly gathered support and,
by 1923, had won victory over the Allies in the Turkish War of
Independence. The sultanate was overthrown and the Republic
of Turkey was declared in its place, with Kemal as president. He
launched a swathe of reforms to modernize and secularize the
nation, including giving women equal civil and political rights and
making primary education free and compulsory. A decade after
the foundation of the republic, Kemal made a speech detailing
the progress that had been made whilst pledging to continue
his work. In 1934, four years before his death, he announced
that all Turkish citizens should have hereditary surnames.
Parliament granted him the name Atatürk, 'Father of the Turks',
befitting the great esteem that his nation held him in.

"We shall raise our country to the level of the most prosperous and civilized nations of the world. We shall endow our nation with the broadest means and sources of welfare. We shall raise our national culture above the contemporary level of civilization. ...Compared to the past, we shall work harder. We shall perform greater tasks in a shorter time. I have no doubt that we shall succeed in this, because the Turkish nation is of excellent character. The Turkish nation is intelligent, because the Turkish nation is capable of overcoming difficulties of national unity, and because it holds the torch of positive sciences.

...Today, I repeat with the same faith and determination that it will soon be acknowledged once again by the entire civilized world that the Turkish nation, who has been progressing towards the national ideal in exact unison, is a great nation. Never have doubted that the great, but forgotten, civilized characteristic and the great civilized talents of the Turkish nation will, in its progress henceforth, rise like a new sun from the high horizon of civilization for the future."

Ankara, Turkey, 29th October 1933

Haile Selassie I

APPEAL TO THE LEAGUE OF NATIONS

The Scramble for Africa left most of the continent divided between European powers. Standing independent was the Ethiopian Empire, which had fought off an Italian invasion in 1895–96. In 1930, Tafari Makonnen (1892–1975), better known by his regnal name Haile Selassie, inherited the throne. He was a modernizer – while heir, he had been central to Ethiopia joining the League of Nations in 1923. As emperor he centralized power and, in 1931, promulgated the country's first written constitution. Ethiopian independence was again threatened by Italy, which invaded in October 1935. Haile Selassie helped lead the resistance, but by May 1936 the Italians were on the verge of victory. With his capital of Addis Ababa under threat, Haile Selassie left for Geneva to appeal to the League of Nations. They did nothing to help preserve the independence of one of their member states, and Ethiopia fell under foreign occupation. Haile Selassie lived in exile in England and was restored after the Allied liberation of Ethiopia in 1941. He ruled until 1974, when he was deposed by a military coup, dying a year later while under house arrest.

" It is to defend a people struggling for its age-old independence that the head of the Ethiopian Empire has come to Geneva. …I pray to Almighty God that He may spare nations the terrible sufferings that have just been inflicted on my people, and of which the chiefs who accompany me here have been the horrified witnesses. It is my duty to inform the governments assembled in Geneva, responsible as they are for the lives of millions of men, women and children, of the deadly peril that threatens them, by describing to them the fate that has been suffered by Ethiopia. It is not only upon warriors that the Italian government has made war. It has above all attacked populations far removed from hostilities, in order to terrorize and exterminate them. …Apart from the Kingdom of the Lord there is not on this earth any nation that is superior to any other. Should it happen that a strong government finds it may with impunity destroy a weak people, then the hour strikes for that weak people to appeal to the League of Nations to give its judgment in all freedom. God and history will remember your judgment. "

Geneva, Switzerland, 30th June 1936

Dolores Ibárruri

'THEY SHALL NOT PASS!'

The Spanish Civil War started in July 1936, after a group of right-wing army officers tried to seize power from the Popular Front, a left-wing coalition elected the previous February. The coup left the Nationalists controlling just part of Spain, and they had failed to seize Madrid. Many in the capital had been inspired by the words of Dolores Ibárruri (1895–1989), a Communist politician and orator known as *La Pasionaria* (The Passionflower), who in a radio broadcast had urged the people to resist the coup with her declaration of *¡No Pasarán!* (They Shall Not Pass!). The phrase became a rallying cry for the Republicans. As the war went on, the Nationalists, led by Francisco Franco made steady gains. In March 1939, just before Franco captured Madrid and declared victory, Ibárruri fled overseas. She lived in the Soviet Union until 1977, returning home 18 months after Franco's death. That year marked Spain's first elections since 1936, and Ibárruri was elected as a deputy to the legislature. Although poor health prevented her from running for re-election in 1979, she remained politically active until her death in 1989.

"The whole country cringes in indignation at these heartless barbarians that would hurl our democratic Spain back down into an abyss of terror and death. However, they shall not pass! …All workers, all antifascists must now look upon each other as brothers in arms. Peoples of Catalonia, Basque Country and Galicia! All Spaniards! Defend our democratic Republic. …The Communist Party calls you to arms. We especially call upon you, workers, farmers, intellectuals to assume your positions in the fight to finally smash the enemies of the Republic and of the popular liberties. Long live the Popular Front! Long live the union of all antifascists! Long live the Republic of the people! The Fascists shall not pass!"

Madrid, Spain, 19th July 1936

Neville Chamberlain

'PEACE FOR OUR TIME'

The bloodshed of the Great War left many leaders determined to avoid another conflict. They included Neville Chamberlain (1869–1940), who became prime minister of the United Kingdom in 1937 and adopted a policy of appeasement towards fascist Italy and Germany, even when they behaved aggressively. Adolf Hitler was particularly provocative, breaking many terms of the Treaty of Versailles, including annexing Austria in March 1938. In September, Chamberlain travelled to Munich for talks with Hitler, also joined by the French and Italian leaders. Together, they signed an agreement allowing Germany to annexe the Sudetenland. When Chamberlain returned to London he was hailed as hero and gave a speech to cheering crowds, declaring he had preserved peace. But his triumphalism proved hollow. In March, Germany occupied the remaining Czech territory and in September Europe was plunged into war following the invasion of Poland. Losing the support of many MPs, Chamberlain stepped down as leader in May 1940. He then served in Winston Churchill's coalition government until ill health forced him to retire in September – he died the next month.

"We, the German Führer and Chancellor, and the British Prime Minister, have had a further meeting today and are agreed in recognizing that the question of Anglo-German relations is of the first importance for our two countries and for Europe.
We regard the agreement signed last night and the Anglo-German Naval Agreement as symbolic of the desire of our two peoples never to go to war with one another again.
We are resolved that the method of consultation shall be the method adopted to deal with any other questions that may concern our two countries, and we are determined to continue our efforts to remove possible sources of difference, and thus to contribute to assure the peace of Europe.
My good friends, for the second time in our history, a British Prime Minister has returned from Germany bringing peace with honour. I believe it is peace for our time.
Go home and get a nice quiet sleep."

London, England, 30th September 1938

Adolf Hitler

'OUR GERMAN MIGHT SHALL PREVAIL'

After the Nazis won power in 1933, Adolf Hitler (1889–1945) transformed Germany into an authoritarian dictatorship. From 1938, his ambition to unite all German-speaking peoples saw him annex Austria and occupy territory in the former Czechoslovakia. He then turned to Poland, seeking its territory as *Lebensraum* ('living space') for the German people. France and the United Kingdom, having previously appeased Germany, allied with Poland and guaranteed its independence, but Hitler carried on his invasion plans. On 23rd August, Germany and the Soviet Union signed a non-aggression pact including secret protocols dividing Polish territory. Eight days later, to create a pretext for war, German soldiers disguised as Poles staged false attacks on their own territory to give the appearance of Polish aggression. The next day, Poland was invaded and Hitler spoke before the Reichstag falsely claiming Germany had been provoked and pledging to lead them to victory. Although the British and French declared war on Germany two days later, they could not help Poland, particularly after the Soviet Union invaded from the east.

> "As a National Socialist and a German soldier I enter upon this struggle with a stout heart. My whole life has been nothing but one long struggle for my people, for its restoration, and for Germany. There was only one watchword for that struggle: faith in this people. One word I have never learned is surrender. …We have nothing to do with traitors. We are all faithful to our old principle. It is quite unimportant whether we ourselves live, but it is essential that our people shall live, that Germany shall live. The sacrifice that is demanded of us is not greater than the sacrifice that many generations have made. If we form a community closely bound together by vows, ready for anything, resolved never to surrender, then our will will master every hardship and difficulty. And I would like to close with the declaration that I once made when I began the struggle for power in the Reich. I then said: If our will is so strong that no hardship and suffering can subdue it, then our will and our German might shall prevail."

Berlin, Germany, 1st September 1939

Michael Joseph Savage

'WHERE SHE GOES, WE GO'

The Commonwealth nations played a vital role in World War II. They included New Zealand, which at the start of the conflict was led by Michael Joseph Savage (1872–1940). He had been born in Australia but emigrated to New Zealand in 1907, where he became involved in socialist politics and trade unionism and in 1935 became the country's first Labour prime minister. As leader, he helped New Zealand recover from the Great Depression, established the nation's welfare state and opposed the appeasement of fascism. By 1939, he was suffering from colon cancer and was terminally ill. When the United Kingdom declared war on Germany on 3rd September, Savage was recovering from surgery but gave his support for New Zealand to formally enter the conflict. Two days later Savage spoke to the country, setting forth the evils of the Nazi regime and pledging to support the British. The New Zealand people lived up to his promise – 140,000 of them served overseas during the war, representing just under one-tenth of the population. Savage remained in office until his death on 27th March, and is remembered as New Zealand's greatest prime minister.

"Nazism is militant and insatiable paganism. In short but terrible history it has caused incalculable suffering. If permitted to continue, it will spread misery and desolation throughout the world. It cannot be appeased or conciliated. Either it or civilization must disappear. To destroy it, but not the great nation it has so cruelly treated, is the task of those who have taken up arms against Nazism. May God prosper those arms. I am satisfied that nowhere will the issue be more clearly understood than in New Zealand, where for almost a century, behind the sure shield of Britain, we have enjoyed and cherished freedom and self-government. Both with gratitude for the past and with confidence in the future, we range ourselves without fear beside Britain. Where she goes, we go. Where she stands, we stand. We are only a small and young nation, but we are one and all a band of brothers and we march forward with union of hearts and wills to a common destiny."

Wellington, New Zealand, 5th September 1939

Winston Churchill

'WE SHALL FIGHT ON THE BEACHES'

The United Kingdom's situation at the end of May 1940 was bleak. Nazi Germany had invaded and occupied Poland, Denmark, Norway and the Low Countries and was advancing into France. The Allied forces were overwhelmed and a large, mostly British, contingent had been cut off and surrounded around Dunkirk. Winston Churchill (1874–1965), who had been prime minister for just a few weeks, faced pressure to make peace with Germany, but he refused to consider surrender. He was helped by the fact that German forces delayed in pushing on to attack the isolated and vulnerable army marooned at Dunkirk, giving the Allies time to cobble together a rescue fleet to ferry their men to safety; 338,226 soldiers were saved from 26th May–4th June. On the final day of the Dunkirk Evacuation, Churchill addressed the House of Commons, telling them that though France may soon fall, the United Kingdom would carry on, and fight until the bitter end. The speech was a resounding success, and helped to galvanize both the political establishment and the nation behind Churchill's leadership.

" I have, myself, full confidence that if all do their duty, if nothing is neglected, and if the best arrangements are made, as they are being made, we shall prove ourselves once again able to defend our island home, to ride out the storm of war, and to outlive the menace of tyranny, if necessary for years, if necessary alone. ...Even though large tracts of Europe and many old and famous states have fallen or may fall into the grip of the Gestapo and all the odious apparatus of Nazi rule, we shall not flag or fail. We shall go on to the end. We shall fight in France, we shall fight on the seas and oceans, we shall fight with growing confidence and growing strength in the air, we shall defend our island, whatever the cost may be. We shall fight on the beaches, we shall fight on the landing grounds, we shall fight in the fields and in the streets, we shall fight in the hills. We shall never surrender. "

London, England, 4th June 1940

Benito Mussolini

DECLARATION OF WAR

In 1922, Benito Mussolini (1883–1945) marched his fascist Blackshirts on Rome and was appointed prime minister. By 1925, Mussolini had made himself dictator, calling himself *Il Duce* (The Leader). Seeking to grow Italy's empire, he invaded and occupied Ethiopia from 1935–36. He also pursued close links with Adolf Hitler; in May 1939 their two countries allied through the Pact of Steel. Mussolini did not enter World War II when Germany invaded Poland, as he believed Italy was not yet militarily prepared to join the conflict. By June 1940, however, Germany's military triumphs convinced Mussolini the fighting would soon be over. Hoping to use the conflict to win more territory for Italy, he declared war on the Allies. Italy temporarily gained land in Greece, the Balkans and Africa, but the war was ultimately disastrous for Mussolini. In July 1943, the Allies invaded Sicily, leading to Mussolini's removal from power; that September Italy made peace with the Allies. Mussolini continued as leader of the Italian Social Republic, a Nazi puppet state in the north of the country, until 1945 – when he was captured and summarily executed by communist partisans.

"An hour appointed by destiny has struck in the heavens of our fatherland. The declaration of war has already been delivered to the ambassadors of Great Britain and France. We go to battle against the plutocratic and reactionary democracies of the West who, at every moment, have hindered the advance and have often endangered the very existence of the Italian people.

…If now today we have decided to face the risks and the sacrifices of a war, it is because the honour, the interests, the future impose an iron necessity, since a great people is truly such if it considers sacred its own duties and does not evade the supreme trials that detemine the course of history.

…This gigantic struggle is nothing other than a phase in the logical development of our revolution. It is the struggle of peoples who are poor but rich in workers against the exploiters who hold on ferociously to the monopoly of all the riches and all the gold of the earth. It is the struggle of the fertile and young people against the sterile people moving to the sunset. It is the struggle between two centuries and two ideas."

Rome, Italy, 10th June 1940

Winston Churchill

'THEIR FINEST HOUR'

On the afternoon of 18th June 1940, just over one month after he had become British prime minister as the leader of a coalition government, Winston Churchill addressed the House of Commons on the state of the war. The country was in a perilous position; France, its main ally, had collapsed and was about to commence peace talks with Nazi Germany. In his speech, Churchill reminded Parliament of the successful evacuation of the majority of British forces from France, the power of the military personnel still available to them and the support of the Commonwealth nations. As his address came to an end, Churchill spoke of the impending German invasion of Britain. He portrayed this as a final struggle between good and evil, where defeat would have dire repercussions for the whole world. Later that day, Churchill repeated the speech on a national radio broadcast, seeking to rally the nation to do their utmost to prevent Nazi victory. Four days after this speech, France and Germany signed an armistice; as Churchill had predicted, the Battle of Britain was about to begin.

"Of this I am quite sure, that if we open a quarrel between the past and the present, we shall find that we have lost the future.

...I expect that the battle of Britain is about to begin. Upon this battle depends the survival of Christian civilization. Upon it depends our own British life and the long continuity of our institutions and our empire. The whole fury and might of the enemy must very soon be turned on us. Hitler knows that he will have to break us in this island or lose the war. If we can stand up to him, all Europe may be free, and the life of the world may move forward into broad, sunlit uplands. But if we fail then the whole world, including the United States, and all that we have known and cared for, will sink into the abyss of a new dark age made more sinister, and perhaps more prolonged, by the lights of a perverted science. Let us therefore brace ourselves to our duty and so bear ourselves that if the British Commonwealth and Empire lasts for a thousand years men will still say, This was their finest hour."

London, England, 18th June 1940

Charles de Gaulle

'FLAME OF FRENCH RESISTANCE'

During the Battle of France, Charles de Gaulle (1890–1970), a veteran of World War I and expert in tank warfare, had led an armoured division and been one of the few Allied commanders able to resist the German onslaught. His successes led to him being appointed to the French cabinet as undersecretary of state for defence and war. Unlike some French politicians, de Gaulle was determined to fight on and when he heard that an armistice with Germany was imminent, he flew to London. The next day de Gaulle delivered a speech, broadcast by the BBC, urging the French people to continue fighting the Germans and to rally under his leadership.

Although his appeal is now regarded as the clarion-call of French resistance, it was not widely heard at the time. Furthermore, de Gaulle was only a relatively junior government minister without a particularly high profile. Despite this, the force of his personality led him to become leader of Free France, heading the government-in-exile that carried on the military struggle against the Axis.

"France does not stand alone. She is not isolated. Behind her is a vast empire, and she can make common cause with the British Empire, which commands the seas and is continuing the struggle. Like England, she can draw unreservedly on the immense industrial resources of the United States.

This war is not limited to our unfortunate country. The outcome of the struggle has not been decided by the battle of France. This is a world war. Mistakes have been made, there have been delays and untold suffering, but the fact remains that there still exists in the world everything we need to crush our enemies some day.

Today we are crushed by the sheer weight of mechanized force hurled against us, but we can still look to a future in which even greater mechanized force will bring us victory.

The destiny of the world is at stake.

I, General de Gaulle, now in London, call on all French officers and men who are at present on British soil, or may be in the future, with or without their arms. I call on all engineers and skilled workmen from the armaments factories who are at present on British soil, or may be in the future, to get in touch with me. Whatever happens, the flame of French resistance must not and shall not die."

London, England, 18th June 1940

Winston Churchill

THE FEW

After the Fall of France in June 1940, Germany turned its attention across the channel. The next month German forces began a blockade of the United Kingdom to force its surrender, beginning the Battle of Britain. On 16th July, with Prime Minister Winston Churchill refusing to submit, Adolf Hitler ordered preparations for an invasion. For this to have any chance of success, Germany needed aerial superiority. The Luftwaffe launched raids against British shipping, ports and air bases, before moving on to bomb factories and civilian targets.

They were staunchly resisted by the outnumbered Royal Air Force, which included pilots from the British Commonwealth and Empire and occupied Europe. Also vital was the British radar system, which provided strategic information about the positions of German aircraft. Churchill was moved by the valour and self-sacrifice of the pilots and aircrews, and on 20th August hailed them in a speech in the House of Commons as vital to the survival of the nation and the Allied cause.

"The gratitude of every home in our island, in our empire, and indeed throughout the world, except in the abodes of the guilty, goes out to the British airmen who, undaunted by odds, unwearied in their constant challenge and mortal danger, are turning the tide of the World War by their prowess and by their devotion. Never in the field of human conflict was so much owed by so many to so few. All hearts go out to the fighter pilots, whose brilliant actions we see with our own eyes day after day. But we must never forget that all the time, night after night, month after month, our bomber squadrons travel far into Germany, find their targets in the darkness by the highest navigational skill, aim their attacks, often under the heaviest fire, often with serious loss, with deliberate careful discrimination, and inflict shattering blows upon the whole of the technical and war-making structure of the Nazi power. On no part of the Royal Air Force does the weight of the war fall more heavily than on the daylight bombers, who will play an invaluable part in the case of invasion and whose unflinching zeal it has been necessary in the meanwhile on numerous occasions to restrain."

London, England, 20th August 1940

Joseph Stalin

'EVERY INCH OF SOVIET SOIL'

During the 1930s, Joseph Stalin (1878–1953) had solidified his position as paramount leader of the Soviet Union, brutally crushing domestic opposition and purging political rivals. To secure his western border, in August 1939 he concluded a non-aggression pact with Germany. This agreement ignored the Nazi regime's fundamental and implacable opposition to communism, as well as Adolf Hitler's desire to win 'living space' for the German people. Accordingly, Germany made plans to invade the Soviet Union, with Stalin stubbornly refusing to believe an attack was forthcoming. On 22nd June 1941, Operation Barbarossa was launched; an Axis army of 3.6 million advanced into Soviet territory. The unprepared Soviet forces were caught by surprise, and the Axis made rapid gains. To slow the invasion, Stalin made a radio address on 3rd July proclaiming a scorched-earth policy, where anything of value to the enemy would be destroyed, and demanded steadfast and determined resistance. The Eastern Front would see the most bitter and savage fighting of World War II, and ended with the Red Army forcing the invaders back and capturing Berlin in 1945.

"The Red Army, Red Navy and all citizens of the Soviet Union must defend every inch of Soviet soil, must fight to the last drop of blood for our towns and villages, must display the daring, initiative and mental alertness that are inherent in our people.

…In case of a forced retreat of Red Army units, all rolling stock must be evacuated, the enemy must not be left a single engine, a single railway car, not a single pound of grain or gallon of fuel. The collective farmers must drive off all their cattle and turn over their grain to the safe keeping of the state authorities for transportation to the rear. All valuable property, including nonferrous metals, grain and fuel that cannot be withdrawn must be destroyed without fail. In areas occupied by the enemy, guerilla units, mounted and on foot, must be formed. Sabotage groups must be organized to combat enemy units, to foment guerilla warfare everywhere, blow up bridges and roads, damage telephone and telegraph lines, set fire to forests, stores and transports. In occupied regions conditions must be made unbearable for the enemy and all his accomplices. They must be hounded and annihilated at every step, and all their measures frustrated."

Former USSR, 3rd July 1941

Franklin D. Roosevelt

'A DATE WHICH WILL LIVE IN INFAMY'

With World War II raging, Franklin D. Roosevelt won a third term as president in 1940. The United States was still not involved in the conflict, but in March 1941, Roosevelt instituted the Lend-Lease programme, which saw the US government supply Allied nations with goods and weaponry in their fight against fascism. On 7th December, Japanese aircraft bombed the US base at Pearl Harbor in Hawaii, drawing the United States into the war. Although the raid was a surprise, American attempts to block Japanese expansionism in Asia had strained relations between the countries. The day after the Pearl Harbor attack, Roosevelt spoke before Congress, condemning Japanese aggression and asking for permission to declare war. It was duly granted. Three days later, Japan's fellow Axis powers, Germany and Italy, formally commenced hostilities with the United States. Roosevelt deployed the full might of the American nation against the Axis and won a fourth term in November 1944. Five months later he died after a massive stroke – too soon to see the confirmation of the Allied victory he had played such a vital role in securing.

"Yesterday, December 7, 1941, a date which will live in infamy, the United States of America was suddenly and deliberately attacked by naval and air forces of the Empire of Japan. ...As Commander in Chief of the Army and Navy, I have directed that all measures be taken for our defence. But always will our whole nation remember the character of the onslaught against us. No matter how long it may take us to overcome this premeditated invasion, the American people in their righteous might will win through to absolute victory. I believe that I interpret the will of the Congress and of the people when I assert that we will not only defend ourselves to the uttermost, but will make it very certain that this form of treachery shall never again endanger us. Hostilities exist. There is no blinking at the fact that our people, our territory, and our interests are in grave danger. With confidence in our armed forces, with the unbounding determination of our people, we will gain the inevitable triumph, so help us God. I ask that the Congress declare that since the unprovoked and dastardly attack by Japan on Sunday, December 7, 1941, a state of war has existed between the United States and the Japanese Empire."

Washington, DC, 8th December 1941

Mahatma Gandhi

ON THE QUIT INDIA MOVEMENT

In 1934, Mahatma Gandhi resigned from the Indian National Congress, believing they were not fully committed to nonviolent protest. Instead, he devoted himself to promoting social reforms, such as a new education system designed for rural Indians, encouraging economic self-sufficiency and fighting against prejudice towards 'untouchables'. When World War II started, Gandhi returned to politics, urging Indians not to support the conflict. He opposed fascism, but believed it was hypocritical to support a war supposedly being fought to preserve freedom and democracy whilst India was denied self-determination. In March 1942, Congress rejected a British offer of future democratic self-government in return for backing the war. That August, Gandhi and Congress launched the 'Quit India' movement, demanding the British withdraw immediately. Colonial authorities moved to suppress the movement, and arrested Gandhi and the Congress leadership. They were released by the end of the war, although by then the British government was moving towards supporting Indian independence.

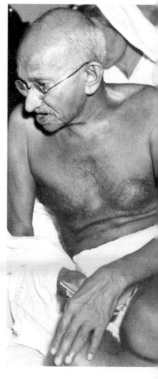

"Ours is not a drive for power, but purely a nonviolent fight for India's independence. In a violent struggle, a successful general has often been known to effect a military coup and to set up a dictatorship. But under the Congress scheme of things, essentially nonviolent as it is, there can be no room for dictatorship. A nonviolent soldier of freedom will covet nothing for himself, he fights only for the freedom of his country. The Congress is unconcerned as to who will rule, when freedom is attained. The power, when it comes, will belong to the people of India, and it will be for them to decide to whom they entrust it."

Mumbai, India, 8th August 1942

Josip Broz Tito

'THE DEFEAT OF THE FASCIST BEASTS'

In April 1941, Germany invaded the former Kingdom of Yugoslavia, dividing its territory between itself and its fellow Axis powers. There was a widespread domestic insurgency against the Axis occupation, broadly divided into two factions: the nationalist royalist Chetniks and the communist Partisans, both of whom received support from the Allies. The leader of the Partisans was Josip Broz Tito (1892–1980), general secretary of the Communist Party of Yugoslavia. Under Tito, the Partisans became the leading force in the Yugoslav resistance, even recapturing territory from the Axis. In late November 1942, Tito convened the Anti-Fascist Council of National Liberation of Yugoslavia, a meeting of representatives from several resistance groups, to discuss campaign plans and the postwar political structure of the country. Tito told the council that the defeat of the fascist occupiers was certain, and although it took until 1945 to fully dislodge the Axis from Yugoslav territory, his words were ultimately proved true. After the war ended, Yugoslavia was declared a federal communist republic, which Tito led until his death in 1980.

"The Hitlerite fascists hurl themselves in every direction, like wild beasts in a cage, but there is no hope for them. In their death throes they will perhaps try to wreak their rage upon the weaker, occupied countries, upon the occupied nations, but we can tell them that in Yugoslavia they will have a really tough time. Today we have an army. Today we have arms, everything from rifles to field guns. We can measure up to them all right. You may rest assured that their power in our country is not sufficient to realize and put into practice their diabolical intentions – that is, to destroy us. We have never lost faith, and today least of all do we doubt that victory is ours. Consequently, at this moment, when the hearts of all subjugated peoples are beating with joy as they see the inevitable defeat of the fascist beasts, we go forward, boldly and full of hope and faith, to meet all the difficulties awaiting us, convinced that by working together and fighting together we shall carry our long struggle and our sufferings to a triumphant close."

Bihać, modern-day Bosnia and Herzegovina, 26th November 1942

Joseph Goebbels

'RISE UP AND LET THE STORM BREAK LOOSE'

Central to the rise of the Nazis was their propaganda machine, which was organized by Joseph Goebbels (1897–1945). The journalist had joined the party in 1924 and had risen to become a member of Adolf Hitler's inner circle. As World War II dragged on, he played an increasingly prominent public role, frequently making speeches and broadcasts. By 1943, Germany was experiencing serious difficulties; its people were subjected to bombing and food shortages whilst progress on the Eastern Front had halted. On 18th February, 16 days after the last German forces at Stalingrad had surrendered, Goebbels spoke at a rally in Berlin. There, he demanded support for 'total war' and the complete commitment of the German people. In 1944, Hitler appointed Goebbels Reich Plenipotentiary for Total War. Tens of thousands of men previously deemed too young or old were recruited into military units, where they were given inadequate training and weaponry. As the regime crumbled, Goebbels and his family joined Hitler in his Berlin bunker. The day after Hitler committed suicide, Goebbels and his wife poisoned their six children before committing suicide themselves.

" The German people, raised, educated and disciplined by National Socialism, can bear the whole truth. It knows the gravity of the situation, and its leadership can therefore demand the necessary hard measures, yes even the hardest measures. We Germans are armed against weakness and uncertainty. The blows and misfortunes of the war only give us additional strength, firm resolve and a spiritual and fighting will to overcome all difficulties and obstacles with revolutionary elan.

…Total war is the demand of the hour… No one has any excuse for ignoring its demands. A storm of applause greeted my call on 30th January for total war. I can therefore assure you that the leadership's measures are in full agreement with the desires of the German people at home and at the front. The people are willing to bear any burden, even the heaviest, to make any sacrifice, if it leads to the great goal of victory.

…The nation is ready for anything. The Führer has commanded, and we shall follow him. In this hour of national reflection and contemplation, we believe firmly and unshakably in victory. We see it before us, we need only reach for it. We must resolve to subordinate everything to it. That is the duty of the hour. Let the slogan be: Now, people rise up and let the storm break loose! "

Berlin, Germany, 18th February 1943

Subhas Chandra Bose

'GIVE ME BLOOD AND I PROMISE YOU FREEDOM'

A broad range of views existed in the Indian independence movement on how to achieve its aims. Subhas Chandra Bose (1897–1945), who came from a wealthy Bengali family, had risen to prominence in the Indian National Congress, but clashed with other leaders over his support for socialism and militant action. Elected president of Congress in 1938, he resigned the next year because he lacked support from senior party officials, particularly Mahatma Gandhi. Bose then formed the All India Forward Bloc, a left-wing group that promoted armed struggle against the British. Bose was arrested, but escaped India in January 1941, travelling to Germany. He campaigned for independence, living in Berlin until 1943, before moving on to Japan. He then traveled across Japanese-occupied Southeast Asia recruiting Indians to fight against the British, giving frequent speeches to rally support, and declaring himself leader of the Provisional Government of Free India. When Japan announced its surrender on 15th August 1945, it dealt a terminal blow to Bose's efforts. Three days later Bose's life ended prematurely in a plane crash.

"Gird up your loins for the task that now lies ahead. I had asked you for men, money and materials. I have got them in generous measure. Now I demand more of you. Men, money and materials have the motive power that will inspire us to brave deeds and heroic exploits.

It will be a fatal mistake for you to wish to live and see India free, simply because victory is now within reach. No one here should have the desire to live to enjoy freedom. A long fight is still in front of us. We should have but one desire today, the desire to die so that India may live, the desire to face a martyr's death, so that the path to freedom may be paved with the martyr's blood.

Friends! My comrades in the War of Liberation! Today I demand of you one thing, above all. I demand of you blood. It is blood alone that can avenge the blood that the enemy has spilt. It is blood alone that can pay the price of freedom. Give me blood and I promise you freedom!"

Rangoon, now Yangon, Myanmar, 4th July 1944

Charles de Gaulle

'PARIS LIBERATED'

On 6th June 1944 the Allies invaded Normandy, beginning the liberation of France. Charles de Gaulle, leader of Free France, had frequently clashed with his allies and been excluded from the planning for D-Day, only arriving in England from his headquarters in Algiers two days before the landings. The Allied invasion was successful, and de Gaulle was able to visit France on 14th June. Paris remained in Nazi hands – reluctant to fight a potentially costly battle there, Allied commanders planned to bypass the city as they pushed east. De Gaulle successfully lobbied for its capture to be prioritized, and late on 24th August Free French forces entered Paris, followed the next morning by American troops. That day, the German military governor surrendered, allowing de Gaulle to proclaim Paris had been liberated. De Gaulle was then recognized as the chair of the French provisional government, remaining in the position until 1946. With France in chaos over the future of their colony in Algeria, de Gaulle returned to power in 1958, restoring order and overseeing a new constitution that saw him elected president, serving in the post until 1969.

"Why should we hide the emotion that seizes us all, men and women, who are here, at home, in Paris that stood up to liberate itself and that succeeded in doing this with its own hands?

No! We will not hide this deep and sacred emotion. These are minutes that go beyond each of our poor lives. Paris! Paris outraged! Paris broken! Paris martyred! But Paris liberated! Liberated by itself, liberated by its people with the help of the French armies, with the support and the help of all France, of the France that fights, of the only France, of the real France, of the eternal France!"

Paris, France, 25th August 1944

Adolf Hitler

FINAL SPEECH

By early 1945, the Third Reich was on the brink of destruction. Its cities were subjected to near-constant bombing raids that left them in ruins, whilst the military situation was dire. On the Eastern Front, the Soviet Red Army had pushed into Poland and the Baltic, whilst the Western Allies had just won the Battle of the Bulge, Hitler's last desperate attempt to push back their advance towards Germany. As defeat loomed, Adolf Hitler, who had survived a July 1944 attempt to assassinate and overthrow him, moved into the Führerbunker, an underground complex in Berlin. On 30th January 1945, he made his final broadcast to the German people, urging every able-bodied citizen to continue fighting with all their efforts. Tens of thousands heeded his words, continuing to fight the Allies even when defeat was inevitable. On 20th April, his 56th birthday, Hitler made a final public appearance to award medals to boy soldiers who had been fighting the Soviets outside Berlin. Hitler then permanently retreated to his bunker, committing suicide there on 30th April to escape being captured alive.

" The horrid fate that is now taking shape in the east and that exterminates hundreds of thousands in the villages and marketplaces, in the country and in the cities will be warded off in the end and mastered by us, with the utmost exertion and despite all setbacks and hard trials.

…I expect every German to do his duty to the last and that he be willing to take upon himself every sacrifice that is asked of him. I expect every able-bodied German to fight with the complete disregard for his personal safety. I expect the sick and the weak or those otherwise unavailable for military duty to work with their last strength. I expect city dwellers to forge the weapons for this struggle and I expect the farmer to supply the bread for the soldiers and workers of this struggle by imposing restrictions upon himself. I expect all women and girls to continue supporting this struggle with utmost fanaticism.

…However grave the crisis may be at the moment, it will, despite everything, finally be mastered by our unalterable will, by our readiness for sacrifice and by our abilities. We shall overcome this calamity, too, and this fight, too, will not be won by central Asia but by Europe, and at its head will be the nation that has represented Europe against the east for 1,500 years and shall represent it for all times: our Greater German Reich, the German nation. "

Berlin, Germany, 30th January 1945

Emperor Hirohito

JEWEL VOICE BROADCAST

In December 1941, having annexed Taiwan, Korea and parts of China, the Japanese Empire entered World War II. This followed invasions of Thailand, the Philippines, Hong Kong, Malaya and Singapore, as well as attacks on American bases in the Pacific. The emperor of Japan since 1926 was Hirohito (1901–89), although his ministers and generals determined much of Japan's policy. At first, the Pacific War went well for Japan – after their early conquests, they advanced into the Dutch East Indies (now Indonesia), New Guinea, the Solomon Islands and Burma. These gains left Japan overstretched, and from 1943–45, the Allies clawed back territory. The bitter nature of the struggle convinced Allied generals that an invasion of Japan itself would be incredibly costly. With Japan, which had been subjected to heavy bombing, refusing to surrender, the Allies dropped atomic bombs on Hiroshima on 6th August and on Nagasaki on 9th August. The devastating damage they caused convinced Hirohito to announce Japan's surrender, which was formally concluded on 2nd September, ending World War II. Hirohito remained emperor until his death in 1989.

"But now the war has lasted for nearly four years. Despite the best that has been done by everyone – the gallant fighting of our military and naval forces, the diligence and assiduity of our servants of the state and the devoted service of our 100,000,000 people – the war situation has developed not necessarily to Japan's advantage, while the general trends of the world have all turned against her interest. Moreover, the enemy has begun to employ a new and most cruel bomb, the power of which to do damage is, indeed, incalculable, taking the toll of many innocent lives. Should we continue to fight, it would not only result in an ultimate collapse and obliteration of the Japanese nation, but also it would lead to the total extinction of human civilization.

…We are keenly aware of the inmost feelings of all of you, our subjects. However, it is according to the dictates of time and fate that we have resolved to pave the way for a grand peace for all the generations to come by enduring the unavoidable and suffering what is unsufferable. Having been able to save and maintain the structure of the Imperial State, we are always with you, our good and loyal subjects, relying upon your sincerity and integrity."

Tokyo, Japan, 15th August 1945

Ho Chi Minh

DECLARATION OF VIETNAMESE INDEPENDENCE

The founding father of modern Vietnam was Nguyễn Sinh Cung (1890–1969), better known as Ho Chi Minh (He Who Enlightens). In May 1941, Ho founded the Vietminh, a coalition of groups united by a desire to gain independence from France, which had ruled the country since the late 19th century. By this time much of Vietnam had been occupied by Japan, and the Vietminh fought against them and the French colonial authorities. By August 1945, the Vietminh had won control and, on 2nd September, Ho declared Vietnamese independence in Hanoi. France attempted to regain its former colony, leading to a war that the French lost in 1954, but that split Vietnam in two. Ho led a communist state in the north, while an American-backed regime emerged in the south. War broke out once more – this time between north and south – with the United States sending in ground troops in 1965. With Ho refusing to give up his dream of a united, independent Vietnam, the North Vietnamese forces ultimately triumphed in 1975. Ho did not live to see it, having died of a heart attack in 1969.

"For more than 80 years, the French imperialists, abusing the standard of liberty, equality and fraternity, have violated our Fatherland and oppressed our fellow citizens. They have acted contrary to the ideals of humanity and justice.

…A people who have courageously opposed French domination for more than 80 years, a people who have fought side by side with the Allies against the Fascists during these last years, such a people must be free and independent. For these reasons, we, members of the Provisional Government of the Democratic Republic of Vietnam, solemnly declare to the world that Vietnam has the right to be a free and independent country, and in fact is so already. The entire Vietnamese people are determined to mobilize all their physical and mental strength, to sacrifice their lives and property in order to safeguard their independence and liberty."

Hanoi, Vietnam, 2nd December 1945

J. Robert Oppenheimer

'WE HAVE MADE A MOST TERRIBLE WEAPON'

In 1943, the Los Alamos Laboratory, located in New Mexico, was established to design and build the atomic bomb. Its director was J. Robert Oppenheimer (1904–67), a brilliant American theoretical physicist. A nuclear weapon was detonated in a test carried out on 16th July 1945 – the next month two atomic bombs were dropped on Japan. Seeing the destruction the weapons had caused, Oppenheimer came to believe they were so powerful that they should be placed in the hands of an international organization. That October, he resigned from Los Alamos and the following month he addressed the American Philosophical Society, arguing for the importance of scientific research, but also warning of its potential harm. In 1947, he was appointed chair of the advisory committee of the US Atomic Energy Commission, where he lobbied for the control of nuclear weapons. In 1954, he was removed from this, and his other political posts, because a past association with communists meant he was deemed a security risk. Oppenheimer continued his work, whilst also lecturing around the world, until his death from throat cancer in 1967.

> **"** We have made a thing, a most terrible weapon, that has altered abruptly and profoundly the nature of the world. We have made a thing that, by all standards of the world we grew up in, is an evil thing. By so doing, by our participation in making it possible to make these things, we have raised again the question of whether science is good for man, of whether it is good to learn about the world, to try to understand it, to try to control it, to help gift to the world of men increased insight, increased power.
>
> Because we are scientists, we must say an unalterable 'yes' to these questions. It is our faith and our commitment, seldom made explicit, even more seldom challenged, that knowledge is a good in itself. Knowledge and such power as must come with it. **"**

Philadelphia, Pennsylvania, USA, 16th November 1945

Winston Churchill

'AN IRON CURTAIN'

On 17th July 1945, nine weeks after VE Day, the Allied leaders convened for the Potsdam Conference to discuss the shape of postwar Europe. There were significant tensions and disagreements, mostly due to the ambitions of the Soviet leader Joseph Stalin in Central and Eastern Europe. Winston Churchill began the meetings as prime minister of the United Kingdom, but one week into the talks was voted out of office following a general election, and replaced by Labour's Clement Attlee. Churchill continued as the Conservative leader and remained an influential figure, writing and travelling around the world. On 5th March 1946, he made an address at Westminster College in Fulton, Missouri, in the United States, with President Harry S. Truman in attendance. In it, he criticized the Soviet Union and proclaimed that an 'iron curtain' had fallen across Europe, with nondemocratic communist regimes dominating much of the continent. Churchill was re-elected prime minister in 1951, serving until his resignation in 1955. The iron curtain he had identified remained in place until 1991.

"From Stettin in the Baltic to Trieste in the Adriatic, an iron curtain has descended across the Continent. Behind that line lie all the capitals of the ancient states of Central and Eastern Europe. Warsaw, Berlin, Prague, Vienna, Budapest, Belgrade, Bucharest and Sofia, all these famous cities and the populations around them lie in what I must call the Soviet sphere, and all are subject in one form or another not only to Soviet influence, but to a very high and, in many cases, increasing measure of control from Moscow.

…If we adhere faithfully to the Charter of the United Nations and walk forward in sedate and sober strength seeking no one's land or treasure, seeking to lay no arbitrary control upon the thoughts of men. If all British moral and material forces and convictions are joined with your own in fraternal association, the high-roads of the future will be clear not only for us, but for all, not only for our time, but for a century to come."

Fulton, Missouri, USA, 5th March 1946

Harry S. Truman

THE TRUMAN DOCTRINE

After President Franklin D. Roosevelt died on 12th April 1945, he was replaced by Vice President Harry Truman (1884–1972), a former senator for Missouri. Truman led the United States through the final months of World War II, approving the use of atomic bombs against Japan and helping to establish the United Nations. On 12th March 1947, after the near-bankrupt British government had withdrawn aid from Greece and Turkey, Truman addressed Congress asking it to approve funding to allow the United States to step in. He argued that this, and future involvement abroad, was essential to prevent the growth of communism. This 'Truman Doctrine' became a central component of US foreign policy during the Cold War, paving the way for the Marshall Plan, an initiative that saw the US provide European states with over $12 billion in financial assistance. Elected for a second term in 1948, Truman focused on domestic reforms, whilst continuing to pursue an active foreign policy. He helped found NATO in 1949 and led the United States into the Korean War in 1950.

"To ensure the peaceful development of nations, free from coercion, the United States has taken a leading part in establishing the United Nations. The United Nations is designed to make possible lasting freedom and independence for all its members. We shall not realize our objectives, however, unless we are willing to help free peoples to maintain their free institutions and their national integrity against aggressive movements that seek to impose upon them totalitarian regimes. This is no more than a frank recognition that totalitarian regimes imposed on free peoples, by direct or indirect aggression, undermine the foundations of international peace and hence the security of the United States.

...I believe that it must be the policy of the United States to support free peoples who are resisting attempted subjugation by armed minorities or by outside pressures. I believe that we must assist free peoples to work out their own destinies in their own way. I believe that our help should be primarily through economic and financial aid, which is essential to economic stability and orderly political processes."

Washington, DC, USA, 12th March 1947

Muhammad Ali Jinnah

'A UNITED INDIA COULD NEVER HAVE WORKED'

In 1906, the All-India Muslim League was founded to protect the interests of the Islamic population of the Indian subcontinent. Muhammad Ali Jinnah (1876–1948), born in Karachi and trained as a lawyer in London, joined the organization in 1913, quickly becoming its most influential figure. He was a supporter of Indian home rule and initially sought to secure a constitution that would guarantee Muslim rights within a self-governing India. Over time, he became convinced that a Muslim homeland was needed, and in 1940 the league officially called for the establishment of a separate state in Muslim-majority areas to be called Pakistan (Land of the Pure). Thanks to Jinnah's leadership both the British authorities and the Indian National Congress acceded to this demand. On 11th August 1947 Jinnah addressed the Constituent Assembly of Pakistan, the body elected to write a constitution in advance of independence. He urged the representatives to work together to create a fair and prosperous nation. Three days later Pakistan officially became independent, with Jinnah its first head of state. He is revered as the father of the nation to this day.

"This mighty subcontinent with all kinds of inhabitants has been brought under a plan that is titanic, unknown, unparalleled. And what is very important with regard to it is that we have achieved it peacefully and by means of an evolution of the greatest possible character.

…Any idea of a united India could never have worked, and in my judgment it would have led us to terrific disaster. Maybe that view is correct, maybe it is not. That remains to be seen. All the same, in this division, it was impossible to avoid the question of minorities being in one dominion or the other. Now that was unavoidable. There is no other solution. Now what shall we do? Now, if we want to make this great state of Pakistan happy and prosperous, we should wholly and solely concentrate on the wellbeing of the people, and especially of the masses and the poor. If you will work in cooperation, forgetting the past, burying the hatchet, you are bound to succeed. If you change your past and work together in a spirit that every one of you, no matter to what community he belongs, no matter what relations he had with you in the past, no matter what is his colour, caste or creed, is first, second and last a citizen of this state with equal rights, privileges, and obligations, there will be no end to the progress you will make."

Karachi, Pakistan, 11th August 1947

Jawaharlal Nehru

'TRYST WITH DESTINY'

Born in Allahabad, Jawaharlal Nehru (1889–1964) was the son of a wealthy lawyer and leading figure in the Indian independence movement. He followed in his father's footsteps, practising as a barrister and joining the Indian National Congress, where he met Mahatma Gandhi, who was an important mentor. Nehru became president of Congress in 1929, the year the party proclaimed that total independence from the United Kingdom was its aim. Arrested and imprisoned several times by the British authorities for civil disobedience, Nehru's last detention was from 1942–45, for his involvement in the Quit India Movement. After his release, India moved towards independence and he played a major role in the negotiations over its future, but was unable to prevent the division of the country on religious lines. On 14th August 1947, the day before India at last became an independent state, Nehru made a speech welcoming its imminent freedom whilst also reminding the country of the hard work that lay ahead. The next morning he was sworn in as the first prime minister of India.

" Long years ago, we made a tryst with destiny, and now the time comes when we shall redeem our pledge, not wholly or in full measure, but very substantially. At the stroke of the midnight hour, when the world sleeps, India will awake to life and freedom. A moment comes, which comes but rarely in history, when we step out from the old to the new, when an age ends, and when the soul of a nation, long suppressed, finds utterance. It is fitting that at this solemn moment we take the pledge of dedication to the service of India and her people and to the still larger cause of humanity. …We have hard work ahead. There is no resting for any one of us until we redeem our pledge in full, until we make all the people of India what destiny intended them to be. We are citizens of a great country, on the verge of bold advance, and we have to live up to that high standard. All of us, to whatever religion we belong, are equally the children of India with equal rights, privileges and obligations. We cannot encourage communalism or narrow-mindedness, for no nation can be great whose people are narrow in thought or in action. To the nations and peoples of the world we send greetings and pledge ourselves to cooperate with them in furthering peace, freedom and democracy. And to India, our much-loved motherland, the ancient, the eternal and the ever new, we pay our reverent homage and we bind ourselves afresh to her service. Victory to India. "

New Delhi, India, 14th August 1947

Mahatma Gandhi

ON THE EVE OF THE LAST FAST

After World War II ended, the British government announced that it was going to grant Indian independence. Mahatma Gandhi was involved in the subsequent negotiations over how the country would be structured but, by this point, Muhammad Ali Jinnah's demand for a separate homeland for Muslims was gaining popularity. Gandhi did not support this, but his appeals for unity increasingly fell on deaf ears as tensions grew between Hindus and Muslims. Although Gandhi's dream of Indian independence was achieved on 14th August 1947, it was as two separate states, India and Pakistan. Partition led to dislocation of millions of people, which was accompanied by widespread rioting and killings. Gandhi toured the country, appealing for calm and toleration, and fasting in protest against the violence. On 12th January 1948, he announced another fast, which lasted for six days and only ended when religious leaders in Delhi agreed to make peace in the city. Shortly after this last triumph of nonviolent protest Gandhi was assassinated, sending his country into mass mourning.

"I have no answer to return to the Muslim friends who see me from day to day as to what they should do. My impotence has been gnawing at me of late. It will go immediately the fast is undertaken. I have been brooding over it for the last three days. The final conclusion has flashed upon me and it makes me happy. No man, if he is pure, has anything more precious to give than his life. I hope and pray that I have that purity in me to justify the step.

…A pure fast, like duty, is its own reward. I do not embark upon it for the sake of the result it may bring. I do so because I must. Hence, I urge everybody dispassionately to examine the purpose and let me die, if I must, in peace, which I hope is assured. Death for me would be a glorious deliverance rather than that I should be a helpless witness of the destruction of India, Hinduism, Sikhism and Islam."

Delhi, India, 12th January 1948

Golda Meir

'IF WE HAVE ARMS TO FIGHT WITH'

Born in Kiev, in 1906 Golda Meir (1898–1978) and her family immigrated to the United States, where she joined the Zionist movement, and moved to Palestine in 1921. At the time, the region was administered by the United Kingdom, and there were frequent violent clashes between their forces, Palestinian Arabs and Jewish settlers. In 1947, the UN announced a plan that would end the British presence in Palestine, and partition it into Jewish and Arab states. Dissatisfaction with this proposal led to civil war between Jewish and Arab forces in November 1947. The next January, Meir returned to the United States to appeal for donations to buy weaponry. She made a series of rousing speeches, including this one in Chicago, and raised over $50,000,000. Returning to Palestine, Meir was one of the signatories of Israel's Declaration of Independence, made on 14th May. She was then elected to Israel's parliament, serving as minister of labour from 1949–56 and foreign minister from 1956–66. Meir became prime minister in 1969, leading Israel through the Yom Kippur War, before retiring from the post in 1974.

"We have to fight for our lives, for our safety and for what we have accomplished in Palestine, and perhaps above all, we must fight for Jewish honour and Jewish independence. Without exaggeration, I can tell you that the Jewish community in Palestine is doing this well. Many of you have visited Palestine. All of you have read about our young people and have a notion as to what our youth is like.

I have known this generation for the last 27 years.

I thought I knew them. I realize now that even I did not.

These young boys and girls, many in their teens, are bearing the burden of what is happening in the country with a spirit that no words can describe. You see these youngsters in open cars, not armoured cars, in convoys going from Tel Aviv to Jerusalem, knowing that every time they start out from Tel Aviv or from Jerusalem there are probably Arabs behind the orange groves or the hills, waiting to ambush the convoy.

These boys and girls have accepted the task of bringing Jews over these roads in safety as naturally as though they were going out to their daily work or to their classes in the university. We must ask the Jews the world over to see us as the front line. All we ask of Jews the world over, and mainly of the Jews in the United States, is to give us the possibility of going on with the struggle.

...I want to say to you, friends, that the Jewish community in Palestine is going to fight to the very end. If we have arms to fight with, we will fight with those, and if not, we will fight with stones in our hands."

Chicago, Illinois, USA, 21st January 1948

Jawaharlal Nehru

'THE LIGHT HAS GONE OUT OF OUR LIVES'

On 30th January 1948, Mahatma Gandhi was murdered by Nathuram Godse, a Hindu fundamentalist who opposed his calls for religious toleration. That evening, Jawaharlal Nehru, prime minister of India, spoke to the nation in a radio broadcast to inform them of the tragedy. Nehru, who had first met Gandhi in 1916, delivered an extempore speech sharing his sorrow with India and urging them to honour the great man's legacy by working towards peace and unity. After the assassination, Nehru continued an ongoing war with Pakistan over Kashmir, which ended with the region being divided between the two countries in 1949. Committed to secularism and socialism, whilst also seeking to modernize and reform India's society and economy, he remained popular, winning electoral victories in 1951, 1957 and 1962. In foreign policy he was supportive of pacifism and instrumental in the founding of the Non-Aligned Movement, a group of nations that sought to be neutral in the Cold War. In 1962, Nehru led India into a brief war with China – by then his health was deteriorating and he died in 1964 after a series of strokes.

"The light has gone out of our lives and there is darkness everywhere. I do not know what to tell you and how to say it. Our beloved leader, Bapu as we called him, the Father of the Nation, is no more. …The light has gone out, I said, and yet I was wrong. For the light that shone in this country was no ordinary light. The light that has illumined this country for these many years will illumine this country for many more years, and a thousand years later, that light will be seen in this country and the world will see it and it will give solace to innumerable hearts. For that light represented something more than the immediate past, it represented the living, the eternal truths, reminding us of the right path, drawing us from error, taking this ancient country to freedom."

Dehli, India, 30th January 1948

Aneurin Bevan

ON THE NATIONAL HEALTH SERVICE

I n the United Kingdom, the foundation of Labour's landslide
victory in the 1945 general election was its pledge to
deliver wholesale reforms, the centrepiece of which was the
National Health Service. Leading this effort was the minister
of health, Aneurin Bevan (1897–1960), a former miner and
trade unionist. The National Health Service Act was passed in
November 1946 and would come into effect on 5th July 1948.
With a few exceptions, the care provided would be free and
funded by taxation. Many doctors opposed the legislation,
and the British Medical Association, the country's largest
association of doctors, threatened to boycott it. In this speech
to Parliament, Bevan addressed their concerns, whilst urging
them to reconsider their intransigence. He ultimately secured
their agreement by that July, through making concessions on
pay, ensuring successful implementation of the National Health
Service. Bevan resigned from government in 1951, in protest
against the high costs of its rearmament programme, and died
prematurely of cancer in 1960.

"That this House takes note that the appointed day for the National Health Service has been fixed for July 5th, welcomes the coming into force on that date of this measure which offers to all sections of the community comprehensive medical care and treatment and lays for the first time a sound foundation for the health of the people, and is satisfied that the conditions under which all the professions concerned are invited to participate are generous and fully in accord with their traditional freedom and dignity.

…May I say this in conclusion? I think it is a sad reflection that this great act, to which every party has made its contribution, in which every section of the community is vitally interested, should have so stormy a birth. I should have thought, and we all hoped, that the possibilities contained in this act would have excited the medical profession, that they would have realized that we are setting their feet on a new path entirely, that we ought to take pride in the fact that, despite our financial and economic anxieties, we are still able to do the most civilized thing in the world: put the welfare of the sick in front of every other consideration."

London, England, 9th February 1948

David Ben-Gurion

DECLARATION OF THE STATE OF ISRAEL

In 1906, David Gruen (1886–1973), born in the Polish town of Płońsk, then part of the Russian Empire, immigrated to Palestine, where he worked as a farmer, becoming politically active and adopting the Hebrew surname Ben-Gurion.

By 1935, he had become chair of the Jewish Agency, the organization that led the Zionist movement. Palestine had been placed under a British mandate since 1920. In November 1947, when the UN adopted a plan to partition Palestine, war broke out between Arabs and Jews there, with the British unable to prevent the violence. On 14th May 1948, with the British mandate due to end at midnight, Ben-Gurion declared the creation of the State of Israel. As prime minister and minister of defence, he oversaw Israel's victory in its war for independence against a coalition of Arab states, remaining in both posts until resigning in 1954. He returned to power after winning elections the next year, leading Israel through the 1956 Suez Crisis, before stepping down as prime minister in 1963.

Eretz-Israel was the birthplace of the Jewish people. Here their spiritual, religious and political identity was shaped… After being forcibly exiled from their land, the people kept faith with it throughout their dispersion and never ceased to pray and hope for their return to it and for the restoration in it of their political freedom. Impelled by this historic and traditional attachment, Jews strove in every successive generation to reestablish themselves in their ancient homeland. In recent decades they returned in their masses… they made deserts bloom, revived the Hebrew language, built villages and towns and created a thriving community controlling its own economy and culture, loving peace but knowing how to defend itself, bringing the blessings of progress to all the country's inhabitants, and aspiring towards independent nationhood.**"**

Tel Aviv, Israel, 14th May 1948

Yusuf Mohamed Dadoo

'THAT IS APARTHEID'

Racial discrimination and segregation had been practised in South Africa since the country's formation in 1910, but it was formalized after the victory of the Reunited National Party in the general election of May 1948. It promised to legally implement strict social segregation based on race in a system known as apartheid ('apartness' in Afrikaans) that would ensure dominance for the white minority. One of the early leaders in the struggle against apartheid was Yusuf Dadoo (1909–83), a communist and medical doctor who was active in fighting for the rights of South Africa's Indian community. In late July 1948, he made a speech in Cape Town appealing to 'non-Europeans' to work together against apartheid. Dadoo was elected president of the South African Indian Congress in 1950, and worked with the leaders of the African National Congress to mobilize mass protests against apartheid. In response, the South African government banned Dadoo from any political activity, and he was forced to go into exile in 1960. He continued to play a leading role in the anti-apartheid struggle while living overseas, dying in London in 1983.

"They want to tell us, the non-Europeans, that they are going to put us into separate compartments in our own interests. The application of the policy of apartheid can only mean further repression and oppression for the non-European people of this country. Policy of apartheid means creating by brute force a permanent force of cheap migratory labour for the mines and on the farms. That is apartheid. …The hour has struck for serious and hard work. The time has come when on this policy we must go forward. This is the only policy that, at the present moment, can meet the dangers that face us in this country. We have vast and progressive forces throughout the world. If we can unite the progressive forces in South Africa we can beat back the reactionary forces in this country. Let us not panic. We have the strength and power in our hands if we act rightly. It may entail suffering and sacrifice and plenty of hard work, but we must realize that these reactionary forces can be defeated and must be defeated in South Africa. On those lines, we must go forward. My warning to the people, both Europeans and non-Europeans, is this: in the present circumstances, either we hang together or we hang separately. That is the question before South Africa. That is the lesson that every democrat in South Africa must learn at the present moment."

Cape Town, South Africa, July 1948

Eleanor Roosevelt

THE STRUGGLE FOR HUMAN RIGHTS

The longest-serving first lady in US history, Eleanor Roosevelt (1884–1962) married Franklin in 1905. She became involved in politics during the 1920s, often making campaign appearances on the behalf of her husband on his rise to the presidency in 1932. Roosevelt transformed the role of the first lady by playing a major public role. She held press conferences, wrote a daily newspaper column and advocated for a wide range of social causes including greater civil rights for women and African Americans. Still active after Franklin's death, in 1945 she was appointed a delegate to the UN, where she served as the first chair of the Commission on Human Rights from 1946–51. In 1948, she oversaw the drafting of the Universal Declaration of Human Rights, and in a speech given in Paris that September, argued for its importance, paving the way for its ratification on 10th December. During the 1950s, Roosevelt campaigned for the Democratic Party and travelled extensively, giving frequent lectures. In 1961, John F. Kennedy named her chair of the Presidential Commission on the Status of Women, a role she worked in until her death the next year.

"We must not be confused about what freedom is. Basic human rights are simple and easily understood: freedom of speech and a free press; freedom of religion and worship; freedom of assembly and the right of petition; the right of men to be secure in their homes and free from unreasonable search and seizure and from arbitrary arrest and punishment.

We must not be deluded by the efforts of the forces of reaction to prostitute the great words of our free tradition and thereby to confuse the struggle. Democracy, freedom, human rights have come to have a definite meaning to the people of the world which we must not allow any nation to so change that they are made synonymous with suppression and dictatorship."

Paris, France, 28th September 1948

Joseph McCarthy

ON THE PERILS OF COMMUNISM

On 9th February 1950, Joseph McCarthy (1908–57) made a speech to the Republican Women's Club of Wheeling, West Virginia, where he claimed that there were 205 'card-carrying' communists active in the State Department conspiring to subvert the USA. Many people, already anxious about the threat of communism, seized on McCarthy's words and he became the symbol of a campaign to preserve traditional American values. Despite having no proof for his claims, McCarthy's power grew – in 1952 he was named chairman of the Senate Committee on Government Operations, giving him licence to continue his crusade against communism. Hundreds of people faced government persecution for being involved in communist activities, often with little concrete evidence. McCarthy even attacked President Dwight D. Eisenhower and other senior political figures. Falling from grace in 1954, McCarthy hearings into communism in the US Army were televised, allowing the American people to see his bullying and blustering. Public support for him dropped, and that year he was formally censured by the Senate, putting an end to McCarthyism.

" Today we are engaged in a final, all-out battle between communistic atheism and Christianity. The modern champions of communism have selected this as the time, and ladies and gentlemen, the chips are down, they are truly down.

...Ladies and gentlemen, can there be anyone tonight who is so blind as to say that the war is not on? Can there by anyone who fails to realize that the Communist world has said the time is now... that this is the time for the show-down between the democratic Christian world and the communistic atheistic world?

...I have here in my hand a list... a list of names that were made known to the secretary of state as being members of the Communist Party and who nevertheless are still working and shaping policy in the State Department...

As you know, very recently the secretary of state proclaimed his loyalty to a man guilty of what has always been considered as the most abominable of all crimes, being a traitor to the people who gave him a position of great trust, high treason... He has lighted the spark which is resulting in a moral uprising and will end only when the whole sorry mess of twisted, warped thinkers are swept from the national scene so that we may have a new birth of honesty and decency in government. "

Wheeling, West Virginia, USA, 9th February 1950

Margaret Chase Smith

'I SPEAK AS AN AMERICAN'

A native of Maine, Margaret Chase Smith (1897–1995) was elected to the US House of Representatives in June 1940, taking the seat of her husband Clyde, who had died two months beforehand. She spent eight years representing her home state in the House, playing a major role in promoting legislation that allowed women to serve in the armed forces. In 1948, Smith successfully ran for the Senate. Always independent minded, on 1st June 1950, she became the first member of Congress to denounce the activities and methods of McCarthyism, which at the time had widespread support. In a speech on the Senate floor, she reminded the US public that they all had the right to criticize, protest and hold unpopular beliefs. Her stance against Joseph McCarthy was fully vindicated after his fall from power in 1954. Smith continued her career in the Senate, even running for the Republican presidential candidacy in 1964 (she finished fifth). Her political career ended in 1972 when, partly due to her age and rumours of ill health, she failed to win re-election to the Senate.

"I speak as briefly as possible because too much harm has already been done with irresponsible words of bitterness and selfish political opportunism. I speak as briefly as possible because the issue is too great to be obscured by eloquence. I speak simply and briefly in the hope that my words will be taken to heart. I speak as a Republican. I speak as a woman. I speak as a United States Senator. I speak as an American.

…The American people are sick and tired of being afraid to speak their minds lest they be politically smeared as Communists or Fascists by their opponents. Freedom of speech is not what it used to be in America. It has been so abused by some that it is not exercised by others.

…As an American, I am shocked at the way Republicans and Democrats alike are playing directly into the Communist design of confuse, divide and conquer. As an American, I don't want a Democratic Administration whitewash or cover-up any more than I want a Republican smear or witch hunt. As an American, I condemn a Republican Fascist just as much I condemn a Democratic Communist. I condemn a Democrat Fascist just as much as I condemn a Republican Communist. They are equally dangerous to you and me and to our country. As an American, I want to see our nation recapture the strength and unity it once had when we fought the enemy instead of ourselves."

Washington DC, USA, 1st June 1950

Robert Schuman

THE SCHUMAN DECLARATION

In the aftermath of World War II, much of Europe lay in ruins. To prevent such a damaging conflict happening again, many states moved towards reconciliation and partnership. In France, one of the leading proponents of international cooperation was Robert Schuman (1886–1963). Born in Luxembourg, in 1919 Schuman became a French citizen and was elected to the country's parliament. A senior official in the postwar French government, he became foreign minister in 1948. On 9th May 1950, he made a groundbreaking speech in which he proposed joining together French and West German coal and steel production, which would promote cooperation between the two countries and reduce the risk of conflict. Schuman's proposal led to the creation of the European Coal and Steel Community in 1952, which was joined by France, West Germany, the Netherlands, Belgium, Luxembourg and Italy. The organization proved to be the foundation stone of the European Union — to commemorate Schuman's role the date of his declaration is celebrated as Europe Day.

"World peace cannot be safeguarded without the making of creative efforts proportionate to the dangers that threaten it.

…Europe will not be made all at once, or according to a single plan. It will be built through concrete achievements that first create a de facto solidarity. The coming together of the nations of Europe requires the elimination of the age-old opposition of France and Germany. Any action taken must in the first place concern these two countries.

…With this aim in view, the French government proposes that action be taken immediately on one limited but decisive point. It proposes that Franco-German production of coal and steel as a whole be placed under a common high authority, within the framework of an organization open to the participation of the other countries of Europe… The solidarity in production thus established will make it plain that any war between France and Germany becomes not merely unthinkable, but materially impossible."

Paris, France, 9th May 1950

Eva Perón

SPEECH TO THE *DESCAMISADOS*

Juan Perón was elected president of Argentina in June 1946. A foundation of his rise to power was his wife Eva (1919–52), an actor and radio broadcaster affectionately nicknamed Evita ('Little Eva') by the people of Argentina. She was particularly popular with working-class Argentinians, or *descamisados*, meaning the 'shirtless ones'. As first lady, Perón did not hold an official government post, but she quickly became one of the most influential figures in the country. Working long hours, she established a charitable foundation that set up numerous hospitals, schools and orphanages, and was central to Argentinian women being given the right to vote in 1949. Such was Perón's popularity that, in 1951, her supporters urged her to be her husband's running mate in that year's presidential elections, although pressure from the army and the establishment forced her to decline. Despite suffering from cancer, Eva campaigned for her husband, making several rousing speeches, such as this one on 17th October, that paved the way to his re-election. Less than a year later Perón died – she was just 33 years old.

"What I say to Perón, who wanted to honour me with the highest distinction that could be granted a Peronist this evening, is that I will never cease repaying you and would give my life in gratitude for how good you have always been and are with me. Nothing I have, nothing I am, nothing I think is mine: it's Perón's. I will not tell you the usual lies. I won't tell you that I don't deserve this. Yes, I deserve this, my general. I deserve it for one thing alone, which is worth more than all the gold in the world. I deserve it for all I've done for the love of this people. I'm not important because of what I've done. I'm not important because of what I've renounced. I'm not important because of what I am or have. I have only one thing that matters, and I have it in my heart. It sets my soul aflame, it wounds my flesh and burns in my sinews: it's love for this people and for Perón. I gave you thanks, my general, for having taught me to know and love them. If this people asked me for my life I would joyfully give it, for the happiness of one *descamisado* is worth more than my entire life."

Buenos Aires, Argentina, 17th October 1951

Konrad Adenauer

'LET US ACT!'

In 1949, two nations were established in Germany: a one-party Soviet satellite state in the east and a parliamentary democracy in the west. That year elections were held in West Germany; the largest party was the Christian Democratic Union, whose leader, Konrad Adenauer (1876–1967), became chancellor. Before the war he had been the mayor of Cologne but was removed from office after Hitler came to power. As leader, he worked to rebuild his shattered country, helping lay the foundation for the *Wirtschaftswunder* (economic miracle) that saw West Germany achieve rapid growth. Under his leadership, West Germany became a member of the Council of Europe in 1950; the next year he addressed the body in Strasbourg, where he set out his country's commitment to building continental unity. He led West Germany into the European Coal and Steel Community in 1952 and NATO in 1955. In 1957, following the Treaty of Rome, West Germany became a founding member of the European Economic Community, the precursor to the European Union. Adenauer resigned in 1963 and is hailed as one of the greatest leaders in German history.

"It is of great significance for the political development of Europe that here, in the organs of the Council of Europe, we have a platform on which the representatives of Europe meet regularly, discuss their worries and anxieties, their desires and their hopes, a platform where they try to establish common criteria for evaluating their requirements, and where, in general, they cooperate with one another in a spirit of fairness and of good neighbourliness. In other words, here we find an expression of the European conscience. And it is also greatly significant that here, at any rate, there is a place where almost the whole of Europe gathers together, despite all the different shades of opinion that have shown themselves in our efforts to achieve closer organizational cooperation. European policy in every country will ultimately receive its impetus from the collective will of the European peoples. But nowhere is this so manifest as a collective will as it is in the Council of Europe.

...The whole German nation, with the exception of a tiny minority, acknowledges the values of Europe, and also is desirous that the unity of Europe should find its expression in some political form. Bitter and perilous experience has taught our people that all the forces available to sustain, develop and defend the civilization of the West must be exerted if this civilization is to survive. We are also profoundly conscious of the fact that the unity of Europe over wide areas of the social life of the participating nations, and not only in the sphere of civilization, has for long been a reality... There can be, for us, then, but one watchword: Let us act! Let us act quickly! Tomorrow it might be too late!"

Strasbourg, France, 10th December 1951

Fidel Castro

'HISTORY WILL ABSOLVE ME'

During the 1940s and 1950s, a US-backed military junta ruled Cuba, dominated by Colonel Fulgencio Batista, who declared himself president in 1952. In response, a clandestine movement to overthrow his authoritarian regime coalesced and was fronted by Fidel Castro (1926–2016), a lawyer who had previously taken part in left-wing rebellions in the Dominican Republic and Colombia. On 26th July 1953, Castro led an attack on the Moncada Barracks in the city of Santiago de Cuba; he hoped to seize weapons and spark a revolution. The plan failed. Castro was arrested and at his trial that October he passionately defended his actions but was sentenced to 15 years' imprisonment. Released early in 1955, he moved to Mexico and founded a revolutionary group dedicated to overthrowing Batista. Castro and his supporters returned to Cuba in 1956 and launched a guerrilla campaign that forced Batista to flee Cuba in 1959. Castro then assumed control of the country, establishing a one-party communist state. Despite facing constant opposition from the United States, Castro remained in power until 2008.

"Lacking even the most elementary revolutionary content, Batista's regime represents in every respect a 20-year regression for Cuba. Batista's regime has exacted a high price from all of us, but primarily from the humble classes, who are suffering hunger and misery. Meanwhile the dictatorship has laid waste the nation with commotion, ineptitude and anguish, and now engages in the most loathsome forms of ruthless politics, concocting formula after formula to perpetuate itself in power, even if over a stack of corpses and a sea of blood.

…Cuba is suffering from a cruel and base despotism.

You are well aware that resistance to despots is legitimate.

…The guilty continue at liberty and with weapons in their hands, weapons that continually threaten the lives of all citizens. If all the weight of the law does not fall upon the guilty because of cowardice or because of domination of the courts, and if then all the judges do not resign, I pity your honour. And I regret the unprecedented shame that will fall upon the judicial power.

I know that imprisonment will be harder for me than it has ever been for anyone, filled with cowardly threats and hideous cruelty. But I do not fear prison, as I do not fear the fury of the miserable tyrant who took the lives of 70 of my comrades. Condemn me. It does not matter. History will absolve me."

Santiago de Cuba, Cuba, 16th October 1953

Nikita Khrushchev

ON THE CULT OF PERSONALITY

When Joseph Stalin died in 1953, a power struggle ensued amongst senior figures in the ruling Communist Party, which ended with Nikita Khrushchev (1894–1971) becoming leader of the USSR. The son of a coal miner, Khrushchev had served in the Red Army during the Russian Civil War before rising through the ranks of Soviet government, surviving Stalin's purges and becoming one of his closest advisors. Khrushchev began to reverse many of his predecessor's policies, initiating a less repressive regime. Symbolic of this 'de-Stalinization' was a speech Khrushchev made to the Communist Party Congress in Moscow on 25th February 1956, in which he criticized Stalin for his violence and brutality towards suspected political enemies, and denounced the cult of personality that had built up around him. These words were shocking to many, as previously any criticism of Stalin had been forbidden. Following the speech there was a period of liberalization in the USSR, with a relaxation of censorship and the release of thousands of political prisoners at home, as well as a gradual improvement in relations with Western powers.

"After Stalin's death, the central committee began to implement a policy of explaining concisely and consistently that it is impermissible and foreign to the spirit of Marxism-Leninism to elevate one person, to transform him into a superman possessing supernatural characteristics, akin to those of a god. Such a man supposedly knows everything, sees everything, thinks for everyone, can do anything, is infallible in his behaviour. Such a belief about a man, and specifically about Stalin, was cultivated among us for many years.

…In practice, Stalin ignored the norms of party life and trampled on the Leninist principle of collective party leadership… Stalin had sanctioned in the name of the central committee of the All-Union Communist Party the most brutal violation of socialist legality, torture and oppression, which led as we have seen to the slandering and to the self-accusation of innocent people.

…You see what Stalin's mania for greatness led to. He completely lost consciousness of reality. He demonstrated his suspicion and haughtiness not only in relation to individuals in the USSR, but in relation to whole parties and nations… Comrades! The cult of the individual caused the employment of faulty principles in party work and in economic activity. It brought about rude violation of internal party and Soviet democracy, sterile administration, deviations of all sorts, cover-ups of shortcomings and varnishings of reality."

Moscow, former USSR, 25th February 1956

Gamal Abdel Nasser

ARAB NATIONALISM

Opened in 1869, the Suez Canal became a strategic waterway, contributing to the United Kingdom's occupation of Egypt in 1882. The British presence in Egypt ended in 1952, when a group of army officers seized power, among them Gamal Abdel Nasser (1918–70), who became prime minister in 1954 and president in 1956. One of his ambitions was to construct the Aswan High Dam, to modernize the Egyptian economy by generating hydroelectricity and improving irrigation. After pledging to finance the dam, both the British and American governments pulled out. Therefore, appealing to the nationalist spirit of his countrymen, on 26th July 1956, Nasser announced that he would nationalize the Suez Canal, using the tolls to fund the dam. Later that year France, the United Kingdom and Israel launched a joint attack on Egypt to regain control of the canal. Although they won a military victory, international pressure forced them to withdraw. Egypt retained ownership of the canal, enabling it to complete the Aswan High Dam (albeit with Soviet assistance). Nasser, a popular hero in the Arab world, remained president until his death in 1970.

"Today the Egyptian people are fully conscious of their sovereign rights and Arab nationalism is fully awakened to its new destiny.

…Those who attack Egypt will never leave Egypt alive.

We shall fight a regular war, a total war, a guerrilla war. Those who attack Egypt will soon realize they brought disaster upon themselves. He who attacks Egypt attacks the whole Arab world… They do not know how strong we really are. We believe in international law. But we will never submit. We shall show the world how a small country can stand in the face of great powers threatening with armed might. Egypt might be a small power but she is great inasmuch as she has faith in her power and convictions. I feel quite certain every Egyptian shares the same convictions as I do and believes in everything I am stressing now. We shall defend our freedom and independence to the last drop of our blood. This is the staunch feeling of every Egyptian. The whole Arab nation will stand by us in our common fight against aggression and domination. Free peoples, too, people who are really free will stand by us and support us against the forces of tyranny."

Alexandria, Egypt, 26th July 1956

Kwame Nkrumah

'LIBERATION OF AFRICA'

The leading light of Pan-Africanism in the mid-20th century was Kwame Nkrumah (1909–72), who believed that Africans must unite to bring an end to European colonial rule. Nkrumah had been born in a village in southern Ghana, at the time a British colony known as the Gold Coast, and in 1935 had moved to the United States to pursue his studies. Nkrumah returned to his homeland in 1947 and began agitating for self-government through nonviolent protest. He gained widespread support and his party won a majority in the 1952 legislative elections, leading to his installation as prime minister of the Gold Coast. On 6th March 1957, he proclaimed the independence of Ghana (the new name was taken from a powerful West African medieval empire) in Accra. Nkrumah buillt up Ghana's infrastructure and promoted African unity, but he grew increasingly authoritarian and the country faced corruption and economic upheaval. In 1966 a new regime seized power while Nkrumah was visiting China; he lived in exile in Guinea but died in Romania in 1972 while being treated for cancer.

"We must change our attitudes, our minds, we must realize that from now on, we are no more a colonial, but a free and independent people. But also, as I pointed out, that entails hard work. I am depending upon the millions of the country, and the chiefs and people, to help me to reshape the destiny of this country. We are prepared to pick it up and make it a nation that will be respected by every nation in the world. …We have awakened. We will not sleep anymore. Today, from now on, there is a new African in the world! That new African is ready to fight its own battles and show that after all, the black man is capable of managing his own affairs. We are going to demonstrate to the world, to the other nations, that we are prepared to lay our own foundation. …We have won the battle and we again re-dedicate ourselves… Our independence is meaningless unless it is linked up with the total liberation of Africa."

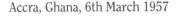

Accra, Ghana, 6th March 1957

Harold Macmillan

'WIND OF CHANGE'

After World War II, the British government initiated the process of dismantling parts of its overseas empire, although by 1960 it still retained control of many of its colonies, particularly in Africa. That year, Harold Macmillan (1894–1986), a Conservative statesman who had been prime minister for three years, embarked on a six-week tour of Africa, first visiting Ghana, Nigeria and the Federation of Rhodesia and Nyasaland (the later nations of Malawi, Zambia and Zimbabwe). He ended his trip in South Africa, addressing its parliament in Cape Town. In his speech, he recognized the rising force of African nationalism, signalling that the British government would speed up the process of granting its colonies in the continent independence, and also criticized the apartheid policies of the South African government. Macmillan was true to his words; the year of this speech Somalia and Nigeria both gained independence, and by the end of the decade the rest of Britain's former colonies in continental Africa had as well. Macmillan served as prime minister until his resignation in 1963, enjoying a long and politically active retirement until his death.

"In the 20th century, and especially since the end of the war, the processes which gave birth to the nation-states of Europe have been repeated all over the world. We have seen the awakening of national consciousness in peoples who have for centuries lived in dependence upon some other power... Today the same thing is happening in Africa, and the most striking of all the impressions that I have formed since I left London a month ago is of the strength of this African national consciousness. In different places it takes different forms, but it is happening everywhere. The wind of change is blowing through this continent and whether we like it or not, this growth of national consciousness is a political fact. And we must all accept it as a fact, and our national policies must take account of it.

...We must face the differences, but let us try to see a little beyond them down the long vista of the future. I hope, indeed I am confident, in another 50 years we shall look back on the differences that exist between us now as mere matters of historical interest, for as time passes and one generation yields to another, human problems change and fade. Let us remember these truths. Let us therefore resolve to build and not to destroy, and let us also remember that weakness comes from division, and in words familiar to you, strength from unity."

Cape Town, South Africa, 3rd February 1960

Patrice Émery Lumumba

'THE PRIDE OF AFRICA'

The territory that is now the Democratic Republic of the Congo fell under Belgian dominance in 1885, a cruel and repressive regime that focused on exploiting the territory's natural resources. During the 1950s, Patrice Lumumba (1925–61) led a growing demand for independence. In 1958, he helped to found the Congolese National Movement, a party that united pro-independence groups. In 1960, the Belgian government convened a conference in Brussels to discuss the future of the Congo and it was agreed the country would become independent that 30th June. Lumumba's party then won national elections, meaning he would lead what was to become the Republic of the Congo to independence. At the handover ceremony, Lumumba made a speech denouncing colonial rule, promising to build a new, fairer, nation. But the country descended into crisis. The UN would not help Lumumba stabilize the situation, so he requested assistance from the USSR. This further divided the Congo, and after months of uncertainty Lumumba was removed from power, arrested and, on 17th January 1961, murdered.

"We are deeply proud of our struggle, because it was just and noble and indispensable in putting an end to the humiliating bondage forced upon us. That was our lot for the 80 years of colonial rule and our wounds are too fresh and much too painful to be forgotten. We have experienced forced labour in exchange for pay that did not allow us to satisfy our hunger, to clothe ourselves, to have decent lodgings or to bring up our children as dearly loved ones. …The Republic of the Congo has been proclaimed and our beloved country's future is now in the hands of its own people. Brothers, let us commence together a new struggle, a sublime struggle that will lead our country to peace, prosperity and greatness. Together we shall establish social justice and ensure for every man a fair remuneration for his labour. We shall show the world what the black man can do when working in liberty, and we shall make the Congo the pride of Africa. We shall see to it that the lands of our native country truly benefit its children. We shall revise all the old laws and make them into new ones that will be just and noble. We shall stop the persecution of free thought. We shall see to it that all citizens enjoy to the fullest extent the basic freedoms provided for by the Declaration of Human Rights. We shall eradicate all discrimination, whatever its origin, and we shall ensure for everyone a station in life befitting his human dignity and worthy of his labour and his loyalty to the country. We shall institute in the country a peace resting not on guns and bayonets but on concord and goodwill."

Léopoldville (now Kinshasa),
Republic of the Congo, 30th June 1960

John F. Kennedy

INAUGURAL ADDRESS

Serving in the US Navy during World War II, John F. Kennedy (1917–63), who came from a wealthy Massachusetts family, was elected to the US House of Representatives in 1947 and the Senate in 1953. Distinguished by his youth, wit and energy, he became one of the leading Democrats in the country and, in 1960, won the party's nomination for president. He then defeated Richard M. Nixon in a tightly contested race, becoming the youngest person to be elected president, as well as the first Catholic. Kennedy was sworn in on 20th January 1961, before delivering his inaugural address to the assembled crowds – as well as a national television audience – from the Capitol Building in Washington DC. The Cold War with the former USSR was raging and Kennedy spoke of the duty that Americans had to deliver freedom and prosperity to their country and the world, whilst imploring his listeners to work together towards this common goal. Kennedy's vigour energized the nation, but tragically his presidency would be brutally cut short by his assassination in Dallas in 1963.

"In the long history of the world, only a few generations have been granted the role of defending freedom in its hour of maximum danger. I do not shrink from this responsibility, I welcome it. I do not believe that any of us would exchange places with any other people or any other generation. The energy, the faith, the devotion which we bring to this endeavour will light our country and all who serve it, and the glow from that fire can truly light the world.

And so, my fellow Americans: ask not what your country can do for you – ask what you can do for your country.

My fellow citizens of the world: ask not what America will do for you, but what together we can do for the freedom of man."

Washington, DC, USA, 20th January 1961

Yuri Gagarin

'THE MYSTERIES OF OUTER SPACE'

The Space Race saw the United States and the former USSR battle to master spaceflight. Initially the Soviets surged ahead, launching the first artificial satellite, Sputnik 1, into orbit in 1957, and sending the first human into outer space on 12th April 1961. The man who piloted the spacecraft, Vostok 1, was Yuri Gagarin (1934–68), who had been born in a village in western Russia and then joined the Soviet Air Forces before being selected to be a cosmonaut. Gagarin's flight was launched from Baikonur Cosmodrome in Kazakhstan – his capsule completed one orbit of Earth and then landed, the entire flight taking just 108 minutes. Two days later Gagarin addressed an adoring crowd at a celebration in Red Square, Moscow, and paid tribute to his colleagues and nation. He continued to work on the Soviet space programme, although the government forbade him to participate in any further spaceflights because they did not want to risk him dying. However, Gagarin's life ended prematurely in 1968, when he died in a fatal jet crash during a routine training flight.

" The genius and heroic work of our people created the spaceship Vostok, the most wonderful in the world, and its most ingenious, most reliable equipment. From the launching to the landing, I never doubted the successful outcome of the flight into outer space.

I should like to thank our scientists, engineers, technicians and all Soviet workers from the bottom of my heart for creating a vehicle like this that could confidently penetrate the mysteries of outer space. Allow me also to thank all my comrades and all those who took part in preparing me for my flight.

…We can state confidently that we shall fly our Soviet spaceships on more distant routes. I am boundlessly happy that my beloved Fatherland was the first in the world to penetrate into outer space. The first aeroplane, the first sputnik, the first spaceship and the first space flight are all landmarks on my country's great road towards mastery over the mysteries of nature. Our people are being confidently guided to this goal by our own Communist Party. "

Moscow, former USSR, 14th April 1961

John F. Kennedy

'ICH BIN EIN BERLINER'

As president, John F. Kennedy's first major foray into foreign policy was an embarrassing fiasco. In April 1961, he approved an invasion of Cuba that failed to overthrow Fidel Castro. To deter future invasions, Cuban leaders requested the former USSR install missile launch sites on their island. When American spy planes confirmed the presence of the missiles in October 1962, Kennedy ordered a naval blockade of Cuba, leading to tensions with the USSR that put the world on the brink of nuclear war. After 13 tense days, crisis was averted as the Soviets agreed to withdraw their missiles. A 'nuclear hotline' was installed between Washington and Moscow to enable better communication, and ten months later a nuclear test-ban treaty was signed. Elsewhere, Kennedy attempted to fight the spread of communism by sending aid to Latin America and escalating US involvement in Vietnam. In June 1963, he travelled to West Berlin, separated from the rest of the city by a recently constructed wall, and gave a speech where he emphasized US support for West Germany, reiterating his firm opposition to communism and his commitment to fighting it.

"Two thousand years ago, the proudest boast was *civis romanus sum*. Today, in the world of freedom, the proudest boast is *Ich bin ein Berliner*. …There are many people in the world who really don't understand, or say they don't, what is the great issue between the free world and the communist world. Let them come to Berlin. There are some who say that communism is the wave of the future. Let them come to Berlin. And there are some who say in Europe and elsewhere we can work with the communists. Let them come to Berlin. And there are even a few who say that it is true that communism is an evil system, but it permits us to make economic progress. *Lass sie nach Berlin kommen*. Let them come to Berlin.

…Freedom is indivisible, and when one man is enslaved, all are not free. When all are free, then we can look forward to that day when this city will be joined as one and this country and this great Continent of Europe in a peaceful and hopeful globe. When that day finally comes, as it will, the people of West Berlin can take sober satisfaction in the fact that they were in the front lines for almost two decades. All free men, wherever they may live, are citizens of Berlin, and therefore, as a free man, I take pride in the words *Ich bin ein Berliner*."

West Berlin, former West Germany, 26th June 1963

Martin Luther King, Jr

'I HAVE A DREAM'

Until the 1960s, racial segregation was the law in the Southern United States, and black people faced discrimination across the entire country. Civil rights campaigners struggled against this. From the mid-1950s, the leading activist was Dr Martin Luther King, Jr (1929–68), a Baptist minister from Atlanta. He rose to prominence when he led the Montgomery bus boycott of 1955, successfully challenging the segregation of public buses in the city. In spring 1963, King helped lead a series of peaceful protests in favour of integrating Birmingham, Alabama, which resulted in the desegregation of what had been amongst the most racially divided cities in the country. That August, the March on Washington for Jobs and Freedom took place. More than 250,000 gathered in support of equal civil and economic rights for African Americans. King addressed them from the Lincoln Memorial, ending his speech by sharing his dream of a nation where all enjoyed freedom and equality. King's leadership was central to the passing of the Civil Rights Act in July 1964, which outlawed discrimination, and he was awarded the Nobel Peace Prize that December.

"Five score years ago, a great American, in whose symbolic shadow we stand today, signed the Emancipation Proclamation. This momentous decree came as a great beacon light of hope to millions of Negro slaves who had been seared in the flames of withering injustice. It came as a joyous daybreak to end the long night of their captivity.

But one hundred years later, the Negro still is not free. One hundred years later, the life of the Negro is still sadly crippled by the manacles of segregation and the chains of discrimination. One hundred years later, the Negro lives on a lonely island of poverty in the midst of a vast ocean of material prosperity. One hundred years later, the Negro is still languished in the corners of American society and finds himself in exile in his own land.

…I say to you today, my friends, so even though we face the difficulties of today and tomorrow, I still have a dream. It is a dream deeply rooted in the American dream. I have a dream that one day this nation will rise up and live out the true meaning of its creed: We hold these truths to be self-evident, that all men are created equal. …I have a dream that my four little children will one day live in a nation where they will not be judged by the color of their skin but by the content of their character. I have a dream today.

…And when this happens, and when we allow freedom ring, when we let it ring from every village and every hamlet, from every state and every city, we will be able to speed up that day when all of God's children, black men and white men, Jews and Gentiles, Protestants and Catholics, will be able to join hands and sing in the words of the old Negro spiritual: Free at last! Free at last! Thank God Almighty, we are free at last!"

Washington, DC, USA, 28th August 1963

Malcolm X

'THE BALLOT OR THE BULLET'

Born in Nebraska, Malcolm Little (1925–65) grew up in Michigan, spending much of his childhood in foster homes. He became involved in criminal activity, and was imprisoned for robbery in 1946. While incarcerated, he joined the Nation of Islam (NOI), changing his name to Malcolm X. Released in 1952, he became a leading figure in the NOI, establishing new temples and founding the organization's newspaper. He was a charismatic speaker, advocating a radical alternative to mainstream civil rights campaigns and arguing black people should defend themselves 'by any means necessary'. In March 1964, Malcolm X left NOI after a dispute with its leadership. The next month, he gave a speech urging black people to exercise their power to vote, and stated that if their rights were ignored, violence would be inevitable. He then made a pilgrimage to Mecca, converting to Sunni Islam and adopting the name el-Hajj Malik el-Shabazz. Returning home, Malcolm X faced threats of violence from the NOI, and was assassinated by three of its members while lecturing in New York, in February 1965.

" If we don't do something real soon, I think you'll have to agree that we're going to be forced either to use the ballot or the bullet. It's one or the other in 1964. It isn't that time is running out, time has run out! 1964 threatens to be the most explosive year America has ever witnessed. The most explosive year. Why? It's also a political year. It's the year when all of the white politicians will be back in the so-called Negro community jiving you and me for some votes. The year when all of the white political crooks will be right back in your and my community with their false promises, building up our hopes for a letdown, with their trickery and their treachery, with their false promises which they don't intend to keep. As they nourish these dissatisfactions, it can only lead to one thing, an explosion. And now we have the type of black man on the scene in America today, I'm sorry, Brother Lomax, who just doesn't intend to turn the other cheek any longer.

...So it's time in 1964 to wake up. And when you see them coming up with that kind of conspiracy, let them know your eyes are open. And let them know you, something else that's wide open too. It's got to be the ballot or the bullet. The ballot or the bullet. If you're afraid to use an expression like that, you should get on out of the country. You should get back in the cotton patch. You should get back in the alley.

...Let the world know how bloody his hands are. Let the world know the hypocrisy that's practised over here. Let it be the ballot or the bullet. Let him know that it must be the ballot or the bullet. "

Cleveland, Ohio, 3rd April 1964

Nelson Mandela

'I AM PREPARED TO DIE'

The African National Congress (ANC) was founded in 1912 to campaign for voting rights for the black and mixed race population of South Africa. From the 1940s, it led the struggle against apartheid. In 1944, Nelson Mandela (1918–2013), the son of a clan chief, joined the organization. On 21st March 1960, the South African Police fired on demonstrators in Sharpeville, killing 69 people. In the aftermath of the massacre there were riots and strikes, leading the government to outlaw the ANC. Mandela, who had previously favoured nonviolent protest, became more militant, and supported acts of sabotage. He went underground, but was located and then arrested and imprisoned for five years in 1962. The next year he faced further punishment when authorities raided an ANC hideout at a farm in Rivonia, a suburb of Johannesburg, and found evidence of plans for armed struggle. Mandela and ten compatriots were tried for sabotage, treason and conspiracy in Pretoria. Facing execution, Mandela declared he was ready to die in the fight against tyranny. Although he escaped the death penalty, he was sentenced to life imprisonment.

"Above all, My Lord, we want equal political rights, because without them our disabilities will be permanent. I know this sounds revolutionary to the whites in this country, because the majority of voters will be Africans. This makes the white man fear democracy. …Our struggle is a truly national one. It is a struggle of the African people, inspired by our own suffering and our own experience. It is a struggle for the right to live. During my lifetime I have dedicated my life to this struggle of the African people. I have fought against white domination, and I have fought against black domination. I have cherished the ideal of a democratic and free society in which all persons will live together in harmony and with equal opportunities. It is an ideal for which I hope to live for and to see realized. But, My Lord, if it needs be, it is an ideal for which I am prepared to die."

Pretoria, South Africa, 20th April 1964

Che Guevara

'HOMELAND OR DEATH'

Born in Argentina, Che Guevara (1928–67) journeyed across South America while training to be a doctor. The scale of the poverty he witnessed was such that he became convinced that revolution was the only way to remedy the problems people faced. In 1955, Guevara met the exiled Cuban revolutionary Fidel Castro in Mexico. He joined Castro's movement to overthrow Fulgencio Batista, and the next year landed with Castro and his supporters in Cuba. Vital to the guerrilla campaign that dislodged Batista and installed Castro in 1959, Guevara became a leading figure in the new regime, often representing Cuba on the international stage. On 11th December 1964, wearing his trademark beret and military fatigues, he addressed the UN in New York, denouncing the lack of international action against state-sanctioned racism whilst calling for the masses of the world to rise up against their exploitation. Guevara did not rest, and continued to travel the world in support of revolutionary movements – in 1966, he travelled to Bolivia to join a guerrilla group but the next year was wounded and summarily executed in a clash with government troops.

"The final hour of colonialism has struck, and millions of inhabitants of Africa, Asia and Latin America rise to meet a new life and demand their unrestricted right to self-determination and to the independent development of their nations.

...Now, in the mountains and fields of America, on its flatlands and in its jungles, in the wilderness or in the traffic of cities, on the banks of its great oceans or rivers, this world is beginning to tremble. Anxious hands are stretched forth, ready to die for what is theirs, to win those rights that were laughed at by one and all for 500 years. Yes, now history will have to take the poor of America into account, the exploited and spurned of America, who have decided to begin writing their history for themselves for all time.

...For this great mass of humanity has said enough and has begun to march. And their march of giants will not be halted until they conquer true independence, for which they have vainly died more than once.

...All this, distinguished delegates, this new will of a whole continent, of Latin America, is made manifest in the cry proclaimed daily by our masses as the irrefutable expression of their decision to fight and to paralyse the armed hand of the invader. It is a cry that has the understanding and support of all the peoples of the world and especially of the socialist camp, headed by the Soviet Union.

That cry is: homeland or death!"

New York City, NY, USA, 11th December 1964

Lyndon B. Johnson

'WE SHALL OVERCOME'

After John F. Kennedy was assassinated in 1963, he was succeeded by his vice president, the Texan politician Lyndon B. Johnson (1908–73). Johnson invoked Kennedy's memory to garner support for his planned reforms, which had stalled in Congress – among them the Civil Rights Act, which prohibited segregation and racial discrimination. Johnson then ran for president, winning a landslide victory that November. Central to his campaign was the 'Great Society', a sweeping programme of domestic policies. Black people in the Southern states still faced discrimination and suppression of their voting rights. Using the phrase 'We Shall Overcome' (taken from a gospel song used by civil rights campaigners), Johnson addressed Congress calling on politicians to pass voting rights legislation. Five months later, he signed the Voting Rights Act into law. Despite such successes, Johnson's decision to escalate American involvement in Vietnam was increasingly costly and divisive. This decreased his popularity, leading him to decide not to run for re-election in 1968. He retired to his native Texas, where he died of a heart attack in 1973.

"This was the first nation in the history of the world to be founded with a purpose. The great phrases of that purpose still sound in every American heart, north and south: all men are created equal, government by consent of the governed, give me liberty or give me death. ...Those words are a promise to every citizen that he shall share in the dignity of man. This dignity cannot be found in a man's possessions. It cannot be found in his power, or in his position. It really rests on his right to be treated as a man equal in opportunity to all others. It says that he shall share in freedom, he shall choose his leaders, educate his children, and provide for his family according to his ability and his merits as a human being. To apply any other test, to deny a man his hopes because of his colour or race, his religion or the place of his birth, is not only to do injustice, it is to deny America and to dishonour the dead who gave their lives for American freedom... Because it is not just Negroes, but really it is all of us, who must overcome the crippling legacy of bigotry and injustice. And we shall overcome.

...The real hero of this struggle is the American Negro. His actions and protests, his courage to risk safety and even to risk his life, have awakened the conscience of this nation. His demonstrations have been designed to call attention to injustice, designed to provoke change, designed to stir reform. He has called upon us to make good the promise of America. And who among us can say that we would have made the same progress were it not for his persistent bravery, and his faith in American democracy."

Washington, DC, USA, 15th March 1965

Olof Palme

SPEECH ON IMMIGRATION

From the mid-20th century onwards, Sweden took on increasing numbers of immigrants, some of whom were refugees. Not everyone welcomed them, prompting Olof Palme (1927–86), a member of the ruling Social Democratic Workers' Party of Sweden and minister of communication, to make a speech on immigration on Christmas Day 1965. Signalling the multicultural policies that the country would eventually enact, he argued that Sweden must remain tolerant and always watchful of any signs of prejudice. In 1969, Palme became prime minister, championing sweeping social reforms that created a comprehensive system of welfare accessible to all. On the world stage, he campaigned for pacifism and criticized the policies of both the American and Soviet governments. In the midst of economic recession, Palme was defeated in the general elections of 1976 but returned to power in 1982. His life was tragically cut short in 1986, when he was murdered in Stockholm whilst walking home from the cinema with his wife; although someone was found guilty of the crime, the conviction was overturned and the crime remains unsolved.

"Crucial to the success of society's actions are the attitudes towards immigrants among individuals. Democracy is deeply rooted in our country. We respect the fundamental rights and freedoms. Turbid racial theories have never gained foothold. We like to see ourselves as open-minded and tolerant. But it's not that simple. Prejudice does not need to be rooted in some kind of execrable theory. Its origins are much more basic. Prejudice is always rooted in everyday life. It grows in the workplace and the neighbourhood. It gives vent to one's own failures and disappointments. Above all, it is an expression of ignorance and fear. Ignorance regarding other people's uniqueness. Fear of losing a position of social privilege, a prior right. Of course, skin-colour, race, language, and birthplace have nothing to do with human qualities. To grade people using such a yardstick is in glaring conflict with principles of human equality. But it is shamefully simple to make use of for the one who feels inferior in the workplace, in social life, in competition for a girl or a boy. Therefore, prejudice is always lurking even in an enlightened society. It can appear as a taunt, an insensible retort, a small turpitude. Maybe it is not meant to cause harm, but for the one at the receiving end, it can tear up wounds that will never be healed."

Broadcast from Stockholm, Sweden, 25th December 1965

Stokely Carmichael

'BLACK POWER'

Born in Trinidad, Stokely Carmichael (1941–98) immigrated to the United States in 1952, where he joined the civil rights movement. As a member of the Student Nonviolent Coordinating Committee (SNCC) campaigning group, he travelled to the Southern states to protest against segregation and enrol black voters.

In 1966, he became the chairman of the organization, but grew frustrated with the violence protestors were subjected to and the lack of progress in improving the lives of African Americans. He spoke out in favour of the right of black people to self-defence, calling for their unity and socio-economic autonomy, such as in this speech given in Berkeley, California. His slogan, 'Black Power', helped to inspire a major movement. The next year Carmichael stepped down as chair of the SNCC and joined the more radical Black Panthers. He left the United States in 1968, settling in Guinea the year after and changing his name to Kwame Ture.

"Now we are engaged in a psychological struggle in this country, and that is whether or not black people will have the right to use the words they want to use without white people giving their sanction to it, and that we maintain, whether they like it or not, we gonna use the word Black Power, and let them address themselves to that, but that we are not going to wait for white people to sanction Black Power. We're tired waiting. Every time black people move in this country, they're forced to defend their position before they move. It's time that the people who are supposed to be defending their position do that. That's white people. They ought to start defending themselves as to why they have oppressed and exploited us.

…We are on the move for our liberation. We have been tired of trying to prove things to white people. We are tired of trying to explain to white people that we're not going to hurt them. We are concerned with getting the things we want, the things that we have to have to be able to function. The question is, can white people allow for that in this country? The question is, will white people overcome their racism and allow for that to happen in this country? If that does not happen, brothers and sisters, we have no choice but to say very clearly, Move over, or we're going to move on over you."

Berkeley, California, USA, 29th October 1966

Martin Luther King, Jr

'I'VE BEEN TO THE MOUNTAINTOP'

Although the Civil Rights Act was passed in July 1964, Martin Luther King, Jr continued to campaign for equal rights for African Americans. In 1965, he participated in demonstrations in Selma, Alabama, to show the necessity for more protection from the federal government to allow black people to vote. This led to the Voting Rights Act prohibiting racial discrimination at the ballot box, but younger activists in the civil rights movement believed King's nonviolent methods were ineffective and his demands not radical enough. Perhaps as a response, King demanded more sweeping changes, declaring his opposition to the war in Vietnam in 1967 and launching his Poor People's Campaign in 1968, which sought to unify all races to fight poverty and unemployment.

On 3rd April, King spoke at a church in Memphis, Tennessee, in support of a strike by black sanitation workers in the city. As he ended his remarks, he mentioned the dangers his campaigning had subjected him to (including death threats and the bombing of his house). His words proved sadly prophetic – the next day King was assassinated, sparking riots across the country.

> " Well, I don't know what will happen now,
> we've got some difficult days ahead. But it
> really doesn't matter with me now, because
> I've been to the mountaintop. And I don't mind.
> Like anybody, I would like to live a long life –
> longevity has its place. But I'm not concerned
> about that now. I just want to do God's will.
> And He's allowed me to go up to the mountain.
> And I've looked over, and I've seen the Promised
> Land. I may not get there with you. But I want
> you to know tonight, that we, as a people, will
> get to the Promised Land. And so I'm happy
> tonight. I'm not worried about anything.
> I'm not fearing any man. Mine eyes have
> seen the glory of the coming of the Lord. "

Memphis, Tennessee, USA, 3rd April 1968

Pierre Trudeau

'A JUST SOCIETY'

In 1965, Pierre Elliott Trudeau (1919–2000), a professor of law at the University of Montreal, was elected to Canada's House of Commons as a member of the Liberal Party. Two years later, Prime Minister Lester Pearson appointed him attorney general and minister of justice. Trudeau introduced major legislation that, amongst other things, decriminalized homosexuality, imposed gun controls and legalized abortions. Pearson retired in December 1967, and Trudeau was elected prime minister the following April. His progressive ideas energized many in the country, particularly young people. He expanded the welfare system and implemented an official policy of multiculturalism that made English and French co-equal official languages. During the 1970s, Trudeau's popularity declined in the face of economic recession and he was voted out of office in 1979. He returned to power in 1980, overseeing reforms that led to the promulgation of a new national constitution. Trudeau retired from politics in 1984, and in 2015 his son Justin followed in his footsteps by winning election as Canada's prime minister.

"This is an extremely great honour that I have received from this great assembly of Liberals. An honour and a very heavy responsibility, and the only way in which I can show my appreciation for this honour will be to bear this responsibility with all my strength, and with all my energy.

Canada must be unified. Canada must be one. Canada must be progressive, and Canada must be a just society!"

Ottawa, Canada, 6th April 1968

Enoch Powell

RIVERS OF BLOOD

After 1945, there was a significant increase of immigration into the United Kingdom, mostly from the former British Empire. Many of these new arrivals, who helped rebuild a country devastated by war, came from the Indian subcontinent and the Caribbean, meaning there was a rapid rise in the non-white population of the country. There was a backlash from people who opposed migration, including from Conservative MP Enoch Powell (1912–98) a former classical scholar who had risen to senior rank in the British Army during World War II. On 20th April 1968, in opposition to proposed anti-racist legislation, Powell addressed a Conservative Party meeting in Birmingham. He claimed that migration had destabilized British society and would cause violence. His incendiary remarks made him a nationally known figure, incited several attacks on minorities and led to his sacking from the Shadow Cabinet. He remained an MP, although in 1974 he left the Conservatives and joined the Ulster Unionist Party, switching to represent the Northern Irish constituency of South Down.

"To be integrated into a population means to become for all practical purposes indistinguishable from its other members. Now, at all times, where there are marked physical differences, especially of colour, integration is difficult though, over a period, not impossible. There are among the Commonwealth immigrants who have come to live here in the last 15 years or so, many thousands whose wish and purpose is to be integrated and whose every thought and endeavour is bent in that direction. But to imagine that such a thing enters the heads of a great and growing majority of immigrants and their descendants is a ludicrous misconception, and a dangerous one.

We are on the verge here of a change. Hitherto it has been force of circumstance and of background which has rendered the very idea of integration inaccessible to the greater part of the immigrant population – that they never conceived or intended such a thing, and that their numbers and physical concentration meant the pressures towards integration which normally bear upon any small minority did not operate.

…For these dangerous and divisive elements the legislation proposed in the Race Relations Bill is the very pabulum they need to flourish. Here is the means of showing that the immigrant communities can organize to consolidate their members, to agitate and campaign against their fellow citizens, and to overawe and dominate the rest with the legal weapons which the ignorant and the ill-informed have provided. As I look ahead, I am filled with foreboding. Like the Roman, I seem to see the River Tiber foaming with much blood."

Birmingham, England, 20th April 1968

Gloria Steinem

ON THE EQUAL RIGHTS AMENDMENT

During the 1960s, there was a movement to address the subordinate status of American women by introducing a constitutional amendment that would guarantee equal rights to all, regardless of gender. In February 1970, under pressure from women's rights groups, the US Senate held hearings about this proposed Equal Rights Amendment. Amongst the speakers was Gloria Steinem (b. 1934), a feminist journalist and campaigner, who talked of the vital importance of changing the long-standing inequities suffered by women. Thanks to such testimony, and continuing protests, the Equal Rights Amendment was passed by Congress and approved by President Richard Nixon in 1972. However, for it to become part of the Constitution, it needed to be approved by three-quarters of state legislatures within seven years and this was not achieved, so the amendment was never formally ratified. Steinem continued her work to liberate women, cofounding the National Women's Political Caucus to support female candidates for elected offices, and in 2013 was awarded the Presidential Medal of Freedom.

"We have all been silent for too long.
But we won't be silent anymore.
...The truth is that all our problems stem from the same
sex-based myths. We may appear before you as white radicals or
the middle-aged middle class or black soul sisters, but we are
all sisters in fighting against these outdated myths.

...Women are not more moral than men.
We are only uncorrupted by power. But we do not want
to imitate men, to join this country as it is, and I think our
very participation will change it. Perhaps women elected
leaders – and there will be many more of them – will not
be so likely to dominate black people or yellow people
or men, anybody who looks different from us.
After all, we won't have our masculinity to prove."

Washington, DC, USA, 6th May 1970

Sheikh Mujibur Rahman

'STRUGGLE FOR INDEPENDENCE'

When it was created in 1947, Pakistan was comprised of two noncontiguous parts; West Pakistan dominated, whilst the Bengali population in the east was marginalized. In 1949, Bengali nationalists established their own party, the Awami League. One of its cofounders was Sheikh Mujibur Rahman (1920–75; known as 'Mujib'), who became party leader. On 7th March 1971, Mujib spoke to a mass gathering in Dhaka. Demanding independence for East Pakistan – to be renamed Bangladesh – he urged popular resistance to secure this. The Pakistani government responded with force, imposing martial law and killing thousands, whilst Mujib was arrested and imprisoned. The Bangladeshi people fought back and, with Indian support, defeated Pakistani forces that December. Mujib was freed and, in January 1972, he became prime minister of Bangladesh. Faced with growing opposition due to famine, economic strife and accusations of corruption, Mujib declared one-party rule in January 1975, but was assassinated seven months later during a military coup.

"With great sadness in my heart, I look back on the past 23 years of our history and see nothing but a history of the shedding of the blood of the Bengali people. Ours has been a history of continual lamentation, repeated bloodshed and innocent tears... The people of this land are facing elimination, so be on guard. If need be, we will bring everything to a total standstill.

...Collect your salaries on time. If the salaries are held up, if a single bullet is fired upon us henceforth, if the murder of my people does not cease, I call upon you to turn every home into a fortress against their onslaught. Use whatever you can put your hands on to confront this enemy. Every last road must be blocked.

We will deprive them of food, we will deprive them of water. Even if I am not around to give you the orders, and if my associates are also not to be found, I ask you to continue your movement without let-up. I say to them again, you are my brothers, return now to the barracks where you belong and no one will bear any hostility towards you. Only do not attempt to aim any more bullets at our hearts. It will not do you any good! ...And the seven million people of this land will not be cowed down by you or accept repression any more. The Bengali people have learned how to die for a cause and you will not be able to bring them under your yoke of oppression!

...Since we have given blood, we will give more of it. But, God willing, we will free the people of this land! The struggle this time is the struggle for emancipation! The struggle this time is the struggle for independence! Victory to Bangal!"

Dhaka, modern-day Bangladesh, 7th March 1971

Salvador Allende

FAREWELL TO THE NATION

A physician and a Marxist, Salvador Allende (1908–73) helped to found the Socialist Party of Chile in 1933 and served as minister for health from 1939–42. He ran for president three times, in 1952, 1958 and 1964, losing each time – but won in 1970, his fourth attempt. Allende introduced major reforms, including nationalizing many industries, raising the minimum wage and fixing prices. His agenda concerned traditionalists at home as well as foreign powers who had interests in Chile, particularly the United States, which cut off lines of credit and funded his opponents. In June 1973, army officers failed to overthrow Allende, but a military coup on 11th September proved more successful. Backed by the US government, it was led by Augusto Pinochet, the commander-in-chief of the Chilean Army. Facing defeat, Allende delivered a radio address to the nation, bidding the people farewell, but stating his faith in the future. He died later that day, although there are conflicting reports as to whether he committed suicide or was killed in the fighting. Pinochet then seized power, establishing a military dictatorship that lasted until 1990.

"The only thing left for me is to say to workers: I am not going to resign! Placed in a historic transition, I will pay for loyalty to the people with my life. And I say to them that I am certain that the seed that we have planted in the good conscience of thousands and thousands of Chileans will not be shrivelled forever. They have strength and will be able to dominate us, but social processes can be arrested neither by crime nor force. History is ours, and people make history. Workers of my country, I want to thank you for the loyalty that you always had, the confidence that you deposited in a man who was only an interpreter of great yearnings for justice, who gave his word that he would respect the constitution and the law and did just that.

…Workers of my country, I have faith in Chile and its destiny. Other men will overcome this dark and bitter moment when treason seeks to prevail. Go forward knowing that, sooner rather than later, the great avenues will open again where free men will walk to build a better society. Long live Chile! Long live the people! Long live the workers! These are my last words, and I am certain that my sacrifice will not be in vain, I am certain that, at the very least, it will be a moral lesson that will punish felony, cowardice and treason."

Santiago, Chile, 11th September 1973

Richard M. Nixon

RESIGNATION SPEECH

After serving in the US House of Representatives, then the Senate, Richard M. Nixon (1913–94) was Dwight D. Eisenhower's running mate in his run for presidency in 1952. Nixon himself lost narrowly to John F. Kennedy in the 1960 presidential elections, before being defeated in his bid to be governor of his native California in 1962. Although many speculated this would be the end of his political career, Nixon fought his way back and was elected president in 1968, winning a landslide second victory in 1972. As national leader, he improved relations with China and the former USSR, as well as withdrawing US troops from Vietnam. His downfall was the Watergate scandal, which erupted after it was revealed that he had attempted to cover up his administration's involvement in the burglary and wire-tapping of the Democratic Party's headquarters, and had obstructed further investigation into the matter. As more details of the illegal activities emerged, Nixon's impeachment became inevitable, but before this happened he announced his resignation to US citizens on 8th August 1974.

" I have never been a quitter. To leave office before my term is completed is abhorrent to every instinct in my body. But as president, I must put the interest of America first. America needs a full-time president and a full-time Congress, particularly at this time with problems we face at home and abroad.

To continue to fight through the months ahead for my personal vindication would almost totally absorb the time and attention of both the president and the Congress in a period when our entire focus should be on the great issues of peace abroad and prosperity without inflation at home. Therefore, I shall resign the presidency effective at noon tomorrow. Vice President Ford will be sworn in as president at that hour in this office.

…I regret deeply any injuries that may have been done in the course of the events that led to this decision. I would say only that if some of my judgments were wrong, and some were wrong, they were made in what I believed at the time to be the best interest of the nation. "

Washington, DC, USA, 8th August 1974

Muhammad Ali

'I'M BAD!'

On 25th February 1964, Cassius Clay (1942–2016) won the world heavyweight championship. Two days later he announced he was converting to Islam, eventually taking the name Muhammad Ali. His skill in the ring was matched by his eloquence and wit outside of it. A champion of black pride, Ali spoke out against racism and, on the grounds of religion, refused to be drafted into the US Army. As a result, in 1967, he was stripped of his titles and banned from fighting in the United States. Ali returned to boxing in 1970, but found it hard to regain his previous dominance. In 1974, he challenged undefeated heavyweight champion George Foreman for his belt in a fight that took place in Kinshasa, Zaire. Prior to the bout, Ali addressed the press in his usual indomitable style, saying he had been underestimated and that victory was assured. Watched by over one billion people worldwide, Ali upset the odds to triumph in the 'Rumble in the Jungle'. He continued fighting until 1981. After his retirement from boxing, and despite suffering from Parkinson's disease, Ali concentrated on humanitarian and charitable work until his death in 2016.

been choppin' trees. Done something new for
this fight. I done wrestled with an alligator.
That's right. I have wrestled with an alligator.
I done tussled with a whale. I done handcuffed
lightning, thrown thunder in jail. That's bad.
Only last week I murdered a rock, injured a stone,
hospitalized a brick, I'm so mean I make medicine sick.

Bad.

Fast. Fast. Fast! Last night I cut the light off in my
bedroom, hit the switch, was in the bed before the
room was dark. Fast!

And you, George Foreman, all of you chumps are
gonna bow when I whup him. All of you! I know you
got him. I know you got him picked, but the man's in
trouble. Imma show you how great I am. **"**

New York City, NY, USA, September 1974

Yasser Arafat

'DO NOT LET THE OLIVE BRANCH FALL'

The establishment of the State of Israel in 1948 led to the displacement of many Palestinian Arabs. In 1964, the Palestine Liberation Organization (PLO) was founded to campaign for their rights. Many Palestinian leaders advocated armed struggle against Israel, including Yasser Arafat (1929–2004), who became chairman of the PLO in 1969. Becoming more conciliatory, when he addressed the UN General Assembly in 1974, he stated he was open to diplomacy. The UN then granted the PLO observer status and recognized the right of the Palestinian people to self-determination. In 1988, Arafat announced the PLO's disavowal of terrorism and acknowledged Israel's right to exist, beginning negotiations with the Israeli government that culminated in the 1993 Oslo Accords. This led to the creation of a Palestinian National Authority, which would have limited self-government over the West Bank and Gaza Strip. The next year Arafat was awarded the Nobel Peace Prize alongside the Israeli prime minister Yitzhak Rabin. He was named the first president of the Palestinian National Authority, serving in the post until his death in 2004.

"Those who call us terrorists wish to prevent world public opinion from discovering the truth about us and from seeing the justice on our faces. They seek to hide the terrorism and tyranny of their acts, and our own posture of self-defence. …Why therefore should I not dream and hope? For is not revolution the making real of dreams and hopes? So let us work together that my dream may be fulfilled, that I may return with my people out of exile, there in Palestine to live with this Jewish freedom-fighter and his partners, with this Arab priest and his brothers, in one democratic State where Christian, Jew and Muslim live in justice, equality and fraternity.

…I appeal to you to aid our people's return to its homeland from an involuntary exile imposed upon it by force of arms, by tyranny, by oppression, so that we may regain our property, our land, and thereafter live in our national homeland, free and sovereign, enjoying all the privileges of nationhood. Only then can we pour all our resources into the mainstream of human civilization. Only then can Palestinian creativity be concentrated on the service of humanity. Only then will our Jerusalem resume its historic role as a peaceful shrine for all religions. I appeal to you to enable our people to establish national independent sovereignty over its own land. Today I have come bearing an olive branch and a freedom fighter's gun. Do not let the olive branch fall from my hand. I repeat: do not let the olive branch fall from my hand. War flares up in Palestine, and yet it is in Palestine that peace will be born."

New York City, NY, USA, 13th November 1974

Indira Gandhi

THE NEGLECT OF WOMEN'S EDUCATION

Jawaharlal Nehru, India's first post-independence prime minister, had only one child: Indira (1917–84), who in 1942 married Feroze Gandhi. In 1964, Indira was elected to the Indian parliament and named minister of information and broadcasting. Two years later, she was elected leader of the ruling Indian National Congress, meaning she became prime minister. An advocate for women's rights, in 1974, Gandhi spoke at the 50th anniversary of the founding of Indraprastha College for Women in Delhi, stating the necessity of gender equality in access to education. The next year, amidst accusations of violating electoral laws, Gandhi declared a state of emergency, arresting political opponents, censoring the press and suspending civil liberties. She lifted the restrictions in 1977, and was defeated in elections that year. In her second stint as leader, from 1980, Gandhi faced growing demands for autonomy by militant Sikh separatists in Punjab. In June 1984, she deployed the army against them, killing hundreds. Five months later, as an act of revenge, two of her Sikh bodyguards assassinated her in New Delhi.

"An ancient Sanskrit saying says, woman is the home and the home is the basis of society. It is as we build our homes that we can build our country. If the home is inadequate – either inadequate in material goods and necessities or inadequate in the sort of friendly, loving atmosphere that every child needs to grow and develop – then that country cannot have harmony and no country that does not have harmony can grow in any direction at all.

That is why women's education is almost more important than the education of boys and men. We, and by 'we' I do not mean only we in India but all the world, have neglected women's education.

…So, I hope that all of you who have this great advantage of education will not only do whatever work you are doing keeping the national interests in view, but you will make your own contribution to creating peace and harmony, to bringing beauty in the lives of our people and our country. I think this is the special responsibility of the women of India. We want to do a great deal for our country, but we have never regarded India as isolated from the rest of the world. What we want to do is to make a better world."

New Delhi, India, 23rd November 1974

Gough Whitlam

DISMISSAL SPEECH

In 1901, Australia became self-governing, with its own national parliament. The British monarch remained head of state with the ability to dismiss governments, which he or she could do via the governor-general, the monarch's representative appointed on the recommendation of the Australian prime minister. This 'reserve power' has only been used once to remove a national leader, in 1975. The prime minister at the time was Gough Whitlam (1916–2014) of the Labour Party, a reformer who had been in power for three years, but whose party had recently lost control of parliament. Whitlam refused to call new national elections, so to break the deadlock Governor-General Sir John Kerr dismissed him from office and appointed Malcolm Fraser, leader of the opposition Liberal Party, to head a caretaker government. Whitlam responded to his sacking in a speech on the steps of parliament in Canberra, and there were protests across Australia against the governor-general's actions. Despite this, Fraser won a landslide victory in the elections called that December, and remained prime minister for over seven years.

"Ladies and gentleman, well may we say God Save the Queen, because nothing will save the governor-general. The proclamation which you have just heard read by the governor-general's official secretary was countersigned 'Malcolm Fraser', who will undoubtedly go down in Australian history from Remembrance Day 1975 as Kerr's cur. They won't silence the outskirts of Parliament House, even if the inside has been silenced for the next few weeks.

…Maintain your rage and enthusiasm through the campaign for the election now to be held and until polling day."

Canberra, Australia, 11th November 1975

Barbara Jordan

'WE SHARE A COMMON DESTINY'

Born in Houston, Texas, lawyer and civil rights campaigner Barbara Jordan (1936–96) was the first black woman elected to Texas's state senate. In 1972, she won a seat in the US House of Representatives, and was named to the Judiciary Committee, giving the opening statement at the impeachment proceedings against Richard Nixon in 1974. Two years later, Jordan delivered the keynote address at the Democratic National Convention in New York, the first African-American woman to do so. She challenged the party to build a political platform that would inspire the American people and help the Democrats win that year's presidential election. Four months later, Jimmy Carter defeated Gerald Ford to win the presidency. Jordan remained in Congress until 1979, where she championed the rights of women, workers and minorities. She then taught at the University of Texas, although she remained highly active in political affairs, and again gave the keynote address at the 1992 Democratic National Convention, as well as being awarded the Presidential Medal of Freedom in 1994.

"We are a people in a quandary about the present. We are a people in search of our future. We are a people in search of a national community. We are a people trying not only to solve the problems of the present, unemployment, inflation, but we are attempting on a larger scale to fulfil the promise of America. We are attempting to fulfil our national purpose, to create and sustain a society in which all of us are equal.

…Let there be no illusions about the difficulty of forming this kind of a national community. It's tough, difficult, not easy. But a spirit of harmony will survive in America only if each of us remembers that we share a common destiny, if each of us remembers, when self-interest and bitterness seem to prevail, that we share a common destiny. I have confidence that we can form this kind of national community."

New York City, NY, USA, 12th July 1976

Anwar Sadat

ADDRESS TO THE KNESSET

When Abdel Nasser died in 1970, he was succeeded as president of Egypt by vice president Anwar Sadat (1918–81). The Sadat regime embarked on a 'Corrective Revolution' that saw Egypt distance itself from the USSR, enact economic reforms and imprison opposition groups. Initially Sadat sought to negotiate with Israel for the return of the Sinai Peninsula, which Israel had occupied in 1967. Talks proved unproductive, and on 6th October 1973, Sadat launched a surprise attack on Israel in conjunction with Syria. The resulting Yom Kippur War lasted until 25th October. Sadat then pursued peace with Israel. In 1977, he travelled to Jerusalem and spoke before the Knesset detailing his plans for harmony. The next year, with the help of US president Jimmy Carter, Sadat and the Israeli prime minister Menachem Begin signed the Camp David Accords, laying the groundwork for peace between their nations and the return of the Sinai Peninsula to Egypt. Despite this diplomatic triumph, at home Sadat faced economic problems and rising popular discontent, leading to his assassination by Muslim extremists in 1981.

"I come to you today on solid ground, to shape a new life, to establish peace. We all, on this land, the land of God, we all, Muslims, Christians and Jews, worship God and no one but God. God's teachings and commandments are love, sincerity, purity and peace.

…If I said that I wanted to save all the Arab People the horrors of shocking and destructive wars, I most sincerely declare before you that I have the same feelings and bear the same responsibility towards all and every man on earth, and certainly towards the Israeli People.

Any life lost in war is a human life, irrespective of its being that of an Israeli or an Arab. A wife who becomes a widow is a human being entitled to a happy family life, whether she be an Arab or an Israeli. Innocent children who are deprived of the care and compassion of their parents are ours, be they living on Arab or Israeli land. They command our top responsibility to afford them a comfortable life today and tomorrow.

…Yet, today I tell you, and declare it to the whole world, that we accept to live with you in permanent peace based on justice. We do not want to encircle you or be encircled ourselves by destructive missiles ready for launching, nor by the shells of grudges and hatred. I have announced on more than one occasion that Israel has become a fait accompli, recognized by the world, and that the two super powers have undertaken the responsibility of its security and the defence of its existence. As we really and truly seek peace, we really and truly welcome you to live among us in peace and security."

Jerusalem, Israel, 20th November 1977

Harvey Milk

'YOU HAVE TO GIVE PEOPLE HOPE'

In 1972, Harvey Milk (1930–78), a gay US Navy veteran and financial analyst, moved from New York to San Francisco, where he opened a camera shop. It was located in the Castro District, the neighbourhood at the centre of the city's LGBT community. In 1977, at his third attempt, Milk won a seat on San Francisco's Board of Supervisors (the body that ran the city), meaning he became one of the first openly gay elected officials in the United States. He set about establishing a programme of reforms including a bill that outlawed discrimination against homosexuals as well as day-care for single mothers and low-cost housing. On 25th June 1978, Milk spoke from the steps of City Hall at a rally to celebrate Gay Freedom Day, where he spoke of the hope his election brought to people who had previously considered themselves outsiders. He then helped defeat Proposition 6, a California referendum that would have banned gays and lesbians from working in the state's public schools. Milk's career was brutally cut short on 27th November when a disgruntled former city official assassinated him and George Moscone, the mayor of San Francisco.

"I can't forget the looks on faces of people who've lost hope. Be they gay, be they seniors, be they blacks looking for an almost impossible job, be they Latins trying to explain their problems and aspirations in a tongue that's foreign to them. I personally will never forget that people are more important than buildings. I use the word 'I' because I'm proud. I stand here tonight in front of my gay sisters, brothers and friends because I'm proud of you. I think it's time that we have many legislators who are gay and proud of that fact and do not have to remain in the closet.

…And you have to give them hope. Hope for a better world, hope for a better tomorrow, hope for a better place to come to if the pressures at home are too great. Hope that all will be all right. Without hope, not only gays, but the blacks, the seniors, the handicapped, the us'es, the us'es will give up. And if you help elect to the central committee and other offices, more gay people, that gives a green light to all who feel disenfranchised, a green light to move forward. It means hope to a nation that has given up, because if a gay person makes it, the doors are open to everyone.

So if there is a message I have to give, it is that I've found one overriding thing about my personal election, it's the fact that if a gay person can be elected, it's a green light. And you and you and you, you have to give people hope."

San Francisco, California, USA, 25th June 1978

Mother Teresa

'LOVE BEGINS AT HOME'

Agnes Gonxha Bojaxhiu (1910–97) was born in Skopje (now the capital of North Macedonia, then part of the Ottoman Empire), into a Catholic family of Albanian descent. In 1928, she left home for Ireland to join the Sisters of Loreto, a community of nuns devoted to teaching and missionary work. That year she was sent to India, and in 1931 took religious vows, taking the new name Teresa. She taught in Kolkata until 1948, when, moved by the poverty she had witnessed, she began to work with the residents of the city's slums. Teresa made it her mission to help the sick and poor that no one else would care for, and in 1950 gained permission from the papacy to start her own order, the Missionaries of Charity, which rapidly grew, opening centres all over India and eventually across the world. For her work combatting poverty, Teresa was awarded the Nobel Peace Prize in 1979, using her speech to extol the importance of love and charity, as well as to condemn the practice of abortion (which, along with her rejection of contraception, has made her a controversial figure). She died in 1997, and was canonized 19 years later.

"There is so much suffering, so much hatred, so much misery, and we with our prayer, with our sacrifice are beginning at home. Love begins at home, and it is not how much we do, but how much love we put in the action that we do. It is to God Almighty – how much we do it does not matter, because He is infinite, but how much love we put in that action. How much we do to Him in the person that we are serving. …And so here I am talking with you – I want you to find the poor here, right in your own home first. And begin love there. Be that good news to your own people."

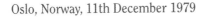

Oslo, Norway, 11th December 1979

Margaret Thatcher

'THE LADY'S NOT FOR TURNING'

In 1975, Margaret Thatcher (1925–2013), former secretary of state for education and science, challenged Edward Heath for leadership of the Conservative Party in the UK. She defeated him and, in 1979, won victory in the general election, to become prime minister. She oversaw reforms that shrank the role of government, limited the power of unions, cut taxes and reduced state spending, whilst privatizing and deregulating many sectors of the economy. Within the year, the country was mired in recession. In a speech at the Conservative Party Conference, Thatcher reacted to critics by stating her refusal to reverse her policies. The economy remained sluggish and Thatcher's popularity shrank until 1982, when victory in the Falklands War helped her to a landslide triumph in the general election the next year. Thatcher won a third term in 1987, but her decision to implement a poll tax two years later proved deeply unpopular, resulting in widespread discontent and a leadership challenge from within her own party. Thatcher resigned as prime minister in 1990, after 11 years in power, and died of a stroke in 2013.

> If our people feel that they are part of a great nation and they are prepared to will the means to keep it great, a great nation we shall be, and shall remain. So, what can stop us from achieving this? What then stands in our way? The prospect of another winter of discontent? I suppose it might. But I prefer to believe that certain lessons have been learnt from experience, that we are coming, slowly, painfully, to an autumn of understanding. And I hope that it will be followed by a winter of common sense.
> …To those waiting with bated breath for that favourite media catchphrase, the U turn, I have only one thing to say. You turn if you want to. The lady's not for turning.
> …So let us resist the blandishments of the faint hearts. Let us ignore the howls and threats of the extremists. Let us stand together and do our duty, and we shall not fail.

Brighton, England, 10th October 1980

Lech Wałęsa

NOBEL PRIZE ACCEPTANCE SPEECH

In 1980, there were protests against rising food prices across Poland, at the time under single-party communist rule. The largest protest took place in Gdansk, where 17,000 shipyard workers went on strike, led by the electrician Lech Wałęsa (b. 1943). On 31st August, the government gave workers the right to unionize freely. Millions of Poles joined unions, which federated into a national organization called Solidarity, with Wałęsa as its chairman. Alarmed, the government declared Solidarity illegal and arrested its leaders, including Wałęsa, who was incarcerated for nearly a year. He was awarded the Nobel Prize at the end of the year – fearing he would not be allowed to return to his country, Wałęsa did not travel to Oslo to accept the prize in person. Instead, a speech made on his behalf conveyed the great honour of receiving the award, and the resolve and inspiration it would bring those fighting for liberty in his country. In 1989, when communist regimes across the Eastern Bloc were overthrown, elections held in Poland saw Solidarity emerge as the dominant party. The next year Wałęsa was elected president, serving in the office until 1995.

"Let my words convey to you the joy and the never extinguished hope of the millions of my brothers, the millions of working people in factories and offices, associated in the union whose very name expresses one of the noblest aspirations of humanity. Today all of them, like myself, feel greatly honoured by the prize. With deep sorrow I think of those who paid with their lives for the loyalty to Solidarity, of those who are behind prison bars and who are victims of repressions. I think of all those with whom I have travelled the same road and with whom I shared the trials and tribulations of our time.

…We desire peace, and that is why we have never resorted to physical force. We crave for justice, and that is why we are so persistent in the struggle for our rights. We seek freedom of convictions, and that is why we have never attempted to enslave man's conscience nor shall we ever attempt to do so. We are fighting for the right of the working people to association and for the dignity of human labour. We respect the dignity and the rights of every man and every nation. The path to a brighter future of the world leads through honest reconciliation of the conflicting interests and not through hatred and bloodshed. To follow that path means to enhance the moral power of the all-embracing idea of human solidarity."

Oslo, Norway, 11th December 1983

Geraldine Ferraro

'IF WE CAN DO THIS, WE CAN DO ANYTHING'

The daughter of Italian immigrants, Geraldine Ferraro (1935–2011) worked as a teacher before practising law in New York. In 1974, she took a position as an assistant district attorney, rising to head the Special Victims Bureau that dealt with serious cases such as rape and domestic violence and earning a reputation as a tough prosecutor. Ferraro first won political office in 1978, when she was elected to the House of Representatives as a Democrat. Her ability to appeal to conservative voters whilst speaking out for progressive policies and women's rights won her the position of Walter Mondale's running mate in the 1984 presidential elections. Ferraro, the first woman (and Italian-American) to appear on a major party's ticket, accepted the nomination in her speech at the Democratic National Convention in San Francisco. Mondale lost in a landslide to the incumbent Ronald Reagan. Ferraro, who had given up her seat in the House of Representatives, was twice unsuccessful in running for the Senate and died in 2011 after a long battle with cancer.

"My name is Geraldine Ferraro.
I stand before you to proclaim tonight:
America is the land where dreams
can come true for all of us.
…By choosing a woman to run for
our nation's second highest office,
you send a powerful signal to all Americans:
There are no doors we cannot unlock.
We will place no limits on achievement.
If we can do this, we can do anything."

San Francisco, California, USA, 19th July 1984

Thomas Sankara

'DOWN WITH PUPPETISM'

The West African nation of Upper Volta gained full independence from France in 1960, after which it experienced great political instability. In 1983, a group of radical army officers gained control of government, setting up a National Revolutionary Council headed by Thomas Sankara (1949–87), a 33-year-old communist and soldier who had won fame for his valour and bravery in battle. As president, Sankara sought a radical reform of the country, symbolizing this by renaming it Burkina Faso, which means 'Land of Incorruptible People'. Sankara fought corruption, encouraged vaccination and education, embarked on building and environmental programmes, nationalized many industries and promoted women's rights. In October 1984, Sankara addressed the UN in New York, stating the necessity of his revolutionary policies to bring progress and prosperity to Burkina Faso. Despite his achievements, Sankara faced economic upheaval and opposition from conservatives. On 15th October 1987, he was overthrown in a military coup and assassinated.

"We swear that in future in Burkina Faso, nothing will be done without the participation of the people of Burkina Faso themselves, nothing that has not been decided by us, that has not been prepared by us. There shall be no more attacks on our honour and dignity. Strengthened by this conviction we want our words to cover all those who suffer all those whose dignity has been crushed by a minority or a system. Let me say to those who are listening to me now that I speak not only on behalf of Burkina Faso, my country which I love so much, but also on behalf all those who suffer, wherever they may be. I speak on behalf of those millions of human beings who are in ghettos because their skin is black, or because they have a different kind of culture, those whose status is hardly higher than that of an animal. …Down with international reaction! Down with imperialism! Down with neo-colonialism! Down with puppetism! Eternal glory to the peoples who are struggling for their freedom! Eternal glory to the peoples who stand shoulder to shoulder to defend their dignity! Eternal victory to the peoples of Africa, Latin America and Asia in their struggle! Fatherland or death! We shall triumph."

New York City, NY, USA, 4th October 1984

Neil Kinnock

'DELIVER THE BRITISH PEOPLE FROM EVIL'

After the UK Labour Party suffered a crushing electoral defeat at the hands of Margaret Thatcher's Conservatives in 1983, its members selected Welshman Neil Kinnock (b. 1942) as their new leader. He was charged with rescuing a party that was haemorrhaging votes and riven by internal disputes. To regain public support, he shifted Labour closer to the political centre, and worked to remove the influence of Militant, a Trotskyist faction that had infiltrated the party. Two years into his leadership, Kinnock delivered a speech at the Labour Party conference in Bournemouth, where he criticized Militant-dominated Liverpool City Council, which had refused to set a budget in protest against government spending cuts, leading to a financial crisis in the city. He denounced those who refused to adapt to reflect public opinion, signalling that he would not be tied to hard-left dogma. Labour lost the general election in 1987, but its results improved and Kinnock remained leader; however, he resigned after suffering another defeat in 1992. Retiring from Parliament in 1995, he served on the European Commission until 2004.

"There are some who will say that power and principle are somehow in conflict. Those people who think that power and principle are in conflict only demonstrate the superficiality, the shallowness, of their own socialist convictions. For whilst they are bold enough to preach those convictions in little coteries, they do not have the depth of conviction to subject those convictions, those beliefs, that analysis, to the real test of putting them into operation in power.

There is no collision between principle and power. For us as democratic socialists the two must go together, like a rich vein that passes through everything that we believe in, everything that we try to do, everything that we will implement. Principle and power, conviction and accomplishment, going together. We know that power without principle is ruthless and vicious, and hollow and sour. We know that principle without power is naive, idle sterility. That is useless – useless to us, useless to the British people to overcome their travails, useless for our purpose of changing society as democratic socialists. I tell you that now. It is what I have always said, it is what I shall go on saying, because it is what I said to you at the very moment that I was elected leader.

…We will get that victory with our policies, our principles, intact. I know it can be done. Reason tells me it can be done. The people throughout this movement, who I know in huge majority share all these perceptions and visions and want to give all their energies, they know it can be done. Realism tells me it can be done, and the plain realities and needs of our country tell me it must be done. We have got to win, not for our sakes, but really, truly to deliver the British people from evil."

Bournemouth, England, 11th October 1985

Corazon Aquino

'WE ARE FREE AGAIN'

In 1965, the Philippines fell under the dictatorial rule of Ferdinand Marcos, whose rivals faced intimidation. In 1983, Marcos had opposition politician Benigno Aquino Jr., assassinated, stirring action against him. The figurehead of the movement was Aquino's widow Corazon (1933–2009). When Marcos was forced to hold presidential elections on 7th February 1986, Aquino stood against him. Marcos claimed to have won the poll, but it became clear he had practised electoral fraud and voter intimidation, and he lost the support of many, including leading military and religious figures. A mass movement, the People Power Revolution, emerged and through peaceful protest forced Marcos to flee into exile. On 25th February, Aquino was inaugurated as president, and hailed the protesters who had returned their country to freedom. She then rolled back her predecessor's corrupt administration and enacted a new constitution. Aquino weathered many coup attempts and her popularity declined as a result of political infighting, natural disasters and economic problems. She did not run for re-election after her term ended in 1992.

"People power shattered the dictatorship, protected those in the military that chose freedom, and today has established a government dedicated to this protection and meaningful fulfilment of our rights and liberties. We became exiles, we Filipinos who are at home only in freedom, when Marcos destroyed the Republic 14 years ago. Now, by God's grace and the power of the people, we are free again."

San Juan, Manila, Philippines, 25th February 1986

Ronald Reagan

'TEAR DOWN THIS WALL'

Having risen to fame as a movie actor, Ronald Reagan (1911–2004) entered politics and served as governor of California from 1967–75. Running as the Republican candidate for president in 1980, he defeated Jimmy Carter in the elections held later that year. Reagan was an avowed anti-communist, publicly denouncing the former USSR as an 'evil empire'. Re-elected in 1984, he softened his tone and began to work with the reform-minded Soviet leader, Mikhail Gorbachev, concluding a treaty that saw both states reduce their nuclear capabilities. When Reagan visited Berlin in 1987, for the 750th anniversary of the city's founding, he delivered a speech at the Brandenburg Gate, demanding Gorbachev continue his reforms and urging him to tear down the Berlin Wall. In 1989, the communist regimes that dominated much of Eastern and Central Europe began to collapse, and in 1991 the USSR split apart. Although by this time Reagan was out of office, his administration played a fundamental role in ensuring the Cold War was won by the American-led Western Bloc.

> Standing before the Brandenburg Gate, every man is a German separated from his fellow men. Every man is a Berliner, forced to look upon a scar. …Yet, I do not come here to lament. For I find in Berlin a message of hope, even in the shadow of this wall, a message of triumph.

> …There is one sign the Soviets can make that would be unmistakable, that would advance dramatically the cause of freedom and peace. General Secretary Gorbachev, if you seek peace, if you seek prosperity for the Soviet Union and Eastern Europe, if you seek liberalization, come here to this gate. Mr. Gorbachev, open this gate. Mr. Gorbachev, Mr. Gorbachev, tear down this wall!

> …Yes, across Europe, this wall will fall, for it cannot withstand faith; it cannot withstand truth. The wall cannot withstand freedom. "

West Berlin, former West Germany, 12th June 1987

Mikhail Gorbachev

'FREEDOM OF CHOICE'

By the early 1980s, the former USSR was struggling with a stagnant economy, an inefficient bureaucracy and war in Afghanistan. There was also a rapid turnover of leaders. The latest ruler was Mikhail Gorbachev (b. 1931), who aimed to transform the USSR through two policies: *glasnost* (openness), aimed at making the government more transparent, and *perestroika* (restructuring), which introduced democracy and some free-market reforms. In December 1988, he spoke at the UN General Assembly in New York, where he hailed the importance of freedom of choice. That month, constitutional changes created a partially elected parliament for the USSR. Gorbachev achieved better relations with the West, withdrew from Afghanistan and did not intervene when Eastern Bloc nations overthrew their communist leaders in 1989–90. In recognition of the last, he was awarded the Nobel Peace Prize. At home, Gorbachev struggled to hold the USSR together in the face of nationalist movements in its constituent republics, and on 25th December 1991, he resigned as leader of the USSR, which was dissolved the next day.

" The compelling necessity of the principle of freedom of choice is also clear to us. The failure to recognize this, to recognize it, is fraught with very dire consequences, consequences for world peace. Denying that right to the peoples, no matter what the pretext, no matter what the words are used to conceal it, means infringing upon even the unstable balance that is, has been possible to achieve. Freedom of choice is a universal principle to which there should be no exceptions. "

New York City, NY, USA, 7th December 1988

Slobodan Milošević

GAZIMESTAN SPEECH

In 1389, an Ottoman army fought a Serbian-led force at the Battle of Kosovo. Neither could claim victory. However, in the years after the battle the Ottomans conquered much Serbian territory. Six hundred years later Slobodan Milošević (1941–2006), the leader of Serbia, at the time part of Yugoslavia, spoke to a huge crowd at Gazimestan, a monument close to the site of the battlefield. He claimed Serbia had sacrificed itself to defend Europe and that it would retain control of Kosovo, a region with a largely ethnically Albanian Muslim population. Such language prefigured the nationalist sentiment that contributed to the break-up of Yugoslavia in 1991–92, leading to years of warfare accompanied by numerous atrocities. Milošević emerged as president of the new republic of Serbia and Montenegro and, in 1998, brutally attacked rebels who wanted independence for Kosovo. NATO intervened, forcing Milošević to withdraw, and he was voted out of office two years later. The next June, he stood trial for war crimes committed during the Yugoslav Wars, but died of a heart attack in 2006, before a verdict was reached.

"Through the play of history and life, it seems as if Serbia has, precisely in this year, in 1989, regained its state and its dignity and thus has celebrated an event of the distant past that has a great historical and symbolic significance for its future.

…Six centuries ago, Serbia heroically defended itself in the field of Kosovo, but it also defended Europe. Serbia was at that time the bastion that defended the European culture, religion and European society in general. Therefore today it appears not only unjust but even unhistorical and completely absurd to talk about Serbia's belonging to Europe. Serbia has been a part of Europe incessantly, now just as much as it was in the past, of course, in its own way, but in a way that in the historical sense never deprived it of dignity. In this spirit we now endeavour to build a society, rich and democratic, and thus to contribute to the prosperity of this beautiful country, this unjustly suffering country, but also to contribute to the efforts of all the progressive people of our age that they make for a better and happier world.

Let the memory of Kosovo heroism live forever!
Long live Serbia! Long live Yugoslavia! Long live peace and brotherhood among peoples!"

Pristina, Kosovo, 28th June 1989

Nicolae Ceaușescu

FINAL SPEECH

A single-party communist state since 1947, Romania was led by Nicolae Ceaușescu (1918–89) from 1965. He oversaw a highly centralized regime, used secret police to crush opponents and created a cult of personality that presented him as an infallible man of genius. His closest ally was his wife Elena, portrayed as 'mother of the nation' and named deputy prime minister in 1980. During the 1980s, Romania suffered severe economic problems and food shortages when Ceaușescu imposed harsh austerity measures to pay off the country's mounting international debts. This led to anti-government demonstrations and unrest spreading across the country in 1989. That December, Ceaușescu addressed crowds gathered in Bucharest's main square. Despite attempts to stage-manage the event, the audience grew restless, chanting against Ceaușescu and leaving the square. Ceaușescu's inability to stop them symbolized the collapse of his authority; the next day he and Elena fled Bucharest, but were both captured by the army, tried before a military tribunal and shot. Romania then transitioned from communism to democracy.

"Dear comrades and friends, citizens of the capital of Socialist Romania. First, I desire to address you, participants of this great popular meeting, to all residents of the Bucharest Municipality, warm revolutionary greetings, along with best wishes for success in all fields!

I also wish to thank the initiators and organizers of this great demonstration in Bucharest, considering it as a... ...Comrades! Stay quiet! Comrades..."

Bucharest, Romania, 21st December 1989

Václav Havel

NEW YEAR'S ADDRESS

A satellite state of the former USSR, Czechoslovakia experienced the Prague Spring in 1968, which saw a new, liberalized regime emerge. But a Soviet-led invasion and occupation soon put this down. Unrest returned in 1989, the year revolutions occurred across the Eastern Bloc. Protests swept across the nation after student demonstrations in Prague were met with violence. The subsequent Velvet Revolution culminated in the communist leadership giving up power. The leading opposition group was the Civic Forum, which had been founded by Václav Havel (1936–2011), a political dissident and playwright who had been imprisoned several times. On 29th December, he was named the interim president, and on New Year's Day 1990 spoke to the country about his hopes for the future. He was elected president after free elections held that July, but due to his opposition to the 'Velvet Divorce', the peaceful split of the country into the Czech Republic and Slovakia, he resigned in 1992. Havel was elected the Czech Republic's first president in 1993 and served in the post for a decade, dying in 2011.

"This moment holds within itself the hope that in the future we will no longer suffer from the complex of those who must always express their gratitude to somebody. It now depends only on us whether this hope will be realized and whether our civic, national and political self-confidence will be awakened in a historically new way. Self-confidence is not pride. Just the contrary. Only a person or a nation that is self-confident, in the best sense of the word, is capable of listening to others, accepting them as equals, forgiving its enemies and regretting its own guilt. Let us try to introduce this kind of self-confidence into the life of our community and, as nations, into our behavior on the international stage. Only thus can we restore our self-respect and our respect for one another as well as the respect of other nations.

…You may ask what kind of republic I dream of. Let me reply. I dream of a republic independent, free and democratic, of a republic economically prosperous and yet socially just, in short, of a humane republic that serves the individual and that therefore holds the hope that the individual will serve it in turn. Of a republic of well-rounded people, because without such people it is impossible to solve any of our problems – human, economic, ecological, social or political."

Prague, former Czechoslovakia, 1st January 1990

Mary Fisher

'AFRAID TO SAY THE WORD AIDS'

During the 1980s, US scientists reported and identified a lethal new disease that interfered with the immune system. It became known as acquired immunodeficiency syndrome (AIDS), and was caused by infection with the human immunodeficiency virus (HIV). Initially, the virus appeared to be concentrated amongst gay men, leading to much prejudice, even when it became clear that it could infect anyone, regardless of sexual orientation. Government officials in the United States, and across the world, were ineffective in the face of the mounting crisis of the AIDS epidemic. Either they failed to address the seriousness of the disease or spread false or misleading information about it. In 1992 Mary Fisher (b. 1944), a 44-year-old heterosexual woman who had contracted HIV through her second husband, spoke to the Republican Convention in Houston. She challenged the party's members and politicians to end their silence about AIDS, and to fight it with compassion and openness. Since then, Fisher has been active in speaking out on issues surrounding HIV/AIDS, establishing support groups and serving on government commissions.

"I have come tonight to bring our silence to an end.
I bear a message of challenge, not self-congratulation.
I want your attention, not your applause.
…We must lift our shroud of silence, making it safe for you
to reach out for compassion. It is our task to seek safety for
our children, not in quiet denial, but in effective action.
…I ask no more of you than I ask of myself or of my children.
To the millions of you who are grieving, who are frightened, who have
suffered the ravages of AIDS firsthand: have courage, and you will
find support. To the millions who are strong, I issue the plea: set aside
prejudice and politics to make room for compassion and sound policy.
…To all within the sound of my voice, I appeal: learn with me
the lessons of history and of grace, so my children will not be
afraid to say the word AIDS when I am gone. Then, their
children and yours may not need to whisper it at all."

Houston, Texas, USA, 19th August 1992

Nelson Mandela

'LET FREEDOM REIGN'

On 12th June 1964, Nelson Mandela (1918–2013) was sentenced to life imprisonment for his campaigning against apartheid. While he was in prison, opposition to South Africa's racist policies mounted. The rising tide of protest at home and abroad forced the government to begin negotiations that would end apartheid. In 1990, Mandela was released and the ban on his party, the African National Congress (ANC), was lifted. Mandela led further talks with the government that, in April 1994, culminated in the first elections in which all South African citizens, regardless of race, could vote. Led by Mandela, the ANC triumphed and the next month he was sworn in as president. In his inauguration speech, which was broadcast across the world, Mandela promised peace and justice for all. As national leader, he enacted a new democratic constitution and established a Truth and Reconciliation Commission to investigate human rights abuses that had occurred under apartheid. Mandela only served one term. Retiring from politics in 1999, he continued to be an influential, celebrated and beloved figure until his death in 2013.

"We are both humbled and elevated by the honour and privilege that you, the people of South Africa, have bestowed on us, as the first president of a united, democratic, non-racial and non-sexist South Africa, to lead our country out of the valley of darkness.

We understand it still that there is no easy road to freedom.

We know it well that none of us acting alone can achieve success.

We must therefore act together as a united people, for national reconciliation, for nation building, for the birth of a new world.

Let there be justice for all.

Let there be peace for all.

Let there be work, bread, water and salt for all.

Let each know that for each the body, the mind and the soul have been freed to fulfil themselves.

Never, never and never again shall it be that this beautiful land will again experience the oppression of one by another and suffer the indignity of being the skunk of the world.

Let freedom reign."

Pretoria, South Africa, 10th May 1994

Benazir Bhutto

'WE ARE A PLANET IN CRISIS'

The Bhutto family is one of the most powerful in Pakistan. Zulfikar Ali Bhutto founded the Pakistan People's Party (PPP) in 1967 and was elected prime minister in 1973. Four years later, he was deposed in a military coup led by Muhammad Zia-ul-Haq and executed. His daughter, Benazir Bhutto (1953–2007), led the democratic opposition to the Zia regime. Zia died in an aeroplane crash in 1988 and elections were held in Pakistan. Leading the PPP to a majority, Bhutto became prime minister but faced dismissal after less than two years, amidst rumours of corruption. She returned to power after winning elections in 1993 and the next year travelled to Cairo for a major international conference on population and development. She called for global cooperation to guarantee dignity and prosperity for all. Just over two years later she was removed for a second time following reports of misconduct. Facing criminal charges, Bhutto went into exile in 1999 and returned home in 2007 after agreeing an amnesty deal with the government. Her life was cut short when she was assassinated while campaigning for a third term as prime minister.

"I dream of a Pakistan, of an Asia, of a world
not undermined by ethical divisions brought upon by
population growth, starvation, crime and anarchy.
I dream of a Pakistan, of an Asia, of a world, where we can
commit our social resources to the development of human life
and not to its destruction. That dream is far from the
reality we endure. We are a planet in crisis, a planet out
of control, a planet moving towards catastrophe.
…What we need is a global partnership for improving
the human condition. We must concentrate on that which
unites us. We should not examine issues that divide us.
…Our destiny does not lie in our stars. It lies within us.
Our destiny beckons us. Let us have the strength to grasp it."

Cairo, Egypt, 7th September 1994

Aung San Suu Kyi

'THE SHACKLES OF INTOLERANCE'

In January 1947, nationalist leader Aung San secured the British government's agreement that Burma (now Myanmar) would gain independence within 12 months. Before this happened, however, Aung San was assassinated by political rivals. By the time his daughter Aung San Suu Kyi (b. 1945) entered politics, in 1988, the Burma Socialist Programme Party (BSPP) was ruling the country as a military dictatorship. As leader of the National League for Democracy (NDP), Suu Kyi was repeatedly placed under house arrest. Even when free, her movements were so restricted that she had to deliver this keynote address at the UN World Conference on Women in Beijing via videotape. By the time of her final release, in 2010, democracy had been restored in Myanmar, and Suu Kyi won a seat in parliament. Her party was victorious in the 2016 elections and Suu Kyi became head of government. As leader, she has worked to build the country's economy and further open it to foreign investment, but has also drawn criticism for her inaction in the face of the violent persecution of the Muslim Rohingya people.

"Last month I was released from almost six years of house arrest. The regaining of my freedom has in turn imposed a duty on me to work for the freedom of other women and men in my country who have suffered far more, and who continue to suffer far more, than I have. It is this duty that prevents me from joining you today. Even sending this message to you has not been without difficulties. But the help of those who believe in international cooperation and freedom of expression has enabled me to overcome the obstacles. They made it possible for me to make a small contribution to this great celebration of the struggle of women to mould their own destiny and to influence the fate of our global village.

...As we strive to teach others, we must have the humility to acknowledge that we, too, still have much to learn. And we must have the flexibility to adapt to the changing needs of the world around us. Women who have been taught that modesty and pliancy are among the prized virtues of our gender are marvellously equipped for the learning process. But they must be given the opportunity to turn these often merely passive virtues into positive assets for the society in which they live.

These, then, are our common hopes that unite us. As the shackles of prejudice and intolerance fall from our own limbs, we can together strive to identify and remove the impediments to human development everywhere."

Beijing, China, 31st August 1995

Hillary Clinton

'WOMEN'S RIGHTS ARE HUMAN RIGHTS'

When Bill Clinton became president of the United States in 1993, his wife Hillary (b. 1947) became the first lady. She had been a prominent lawyer, advocate for children and families, campaigner for health-care reform and supporter of women's rights. As first lady, Clinton did not shy away from publicly addressing these issues, despite facing pressure to be less outspoken. In September 1995, she travelled to Beijing to speak at the UN World Conference on Women. In her speech, she challenged sexist and misogynist attitudes and reminded the world that women and girls were more likely to live in poverty, be illiterate or be excluded from political life. Although her refrain, 'women's rights are human rights', dated back to the 19th century, the phrase became indelibly linked to Clinton and the continuing battle for gender equality.

Clinton was a senator from 2001–09 and served as Secretary of State from 2009–13. Although she was defeated in her bid to be elected president in 2016, her political impact is undoubted.

"If there is one message that echoes forth from this conference, let it be that human rights are women's rights... And women's rights are human rights, once and for all. ...As long as discrimination and inequities remain so commonplace everywhere in the world, as long as girls and women are valued less, fed less, fed last, overworked, underpaid, not schooled, subjected to violence in and out of their homes, the potential of the human family to create a peaceful, prosperous world will not be realized. Let this conference be our – and the world's – call to action. Let us heed the call so that we can create a world in which every woman is treated with respect and dignity, every boy and girl is loved and cared for equally, and every family has the hope of a strong and stable future."

Beijing, China, 5th September 1995

Yitzhak Rabin

FINAL SPEECH

Yitzhak Rabin (1922–95) was chief of staff of Israel's armed forces during the 1967 Six-Day War. The conflict had seen Israel defeat neighbouring Arab states to win control of the Sinai Peninsula, Gaza Strip, West Bank and Golan Heights. In the years that followed, Rabin embarked on a political career that saw him serve twice as Israel's prime minister, as leader of the Labour Party.

Rabin's second term was dominated by his conviction that Israel should negotiate with Palestine to shape a lasting settlement between the two countries. In 1993, he signed the Oslo Accords with the Palestine Liberation Organization (PLO), and subsequently agreed a peace treaty with Jordan, in 1994. On 4th November 1995 Rabin spoke at an anti-violence rally held in Tel Aviv in support of the peace process. Following his speech, a Jewish extremist assassinated the prime minister, claiming to oppose the concessions that Rabin had made in pursuit of harmonious relations with the Palestinians.

"Today I believe that there are prospects for peace, great prospects. We must take advantage of this for the sake of those standing here, and for the sake of those who do not stand here. And they are many among our people. I have always believed that the majority of the people want peace, are prepared to take risks for peace. And you here, by coming to this rally, along with the many who did not make it here, prove that the people truly want peace and oppose violence.

…Peace exists first and foremost in our prayers, but not only in prayers. Peace is what the Jewish people aspire to, a true aspiration. Peace entails difficulties, even pain. Israel knows no path devoid of pain."

Tel Aviv, Israel, 4th November 1995

Bill Clinton

'SOLDIERS HAVE LEFT THE STREETS OF BELFAST'

Governor of Arkansas, USA, from 1979–81 and 1983–92, Bill Clinton (b. 1946) won the 1992 presidential elections and served two successive terms. Although he failed to pass major health-care reforms, he presided over strong economic growth. Overseas, he worked to end the violent sectarian conflict that had dogged Northern Ireland since the 1960s. A peace process that started in the late 1980s really began to take shape in 1994, when paramilitary groups declared a ceasefire. In 1995, Clinton visited Belfast, denouncing violence in a speech at a metal plant with Catholic and Protestant workers. He then played a key role in talks that culminated in the 1998 Good Friday Agreement, which set out a framework for multi-party, devolved government for Northern Ireland. Clinton was beset by scandal; amidst investigations into alleged misconduct, it was discovered he had attempted to hide an affair with White House intern, Monica Lewinsky. Seven months after the Good Friday Agreement he was impeached by Congress for perjury and obstruction of justice. He was acquitted, however, allowing him to continue as president until 2001.

"Peace, once a distant dream, is now making a real difference in everyday life in this land. Soldiers have left the streets of Belfast. Many have gone home. People can go to the pub or the store without the burden of a search or the threat of a bomb. As barriers disappear along the border, families and communities, divided for decades, are becoming whole once more.

…There will always be those who define the work of their lives not by who they are but by who they aren't, not by what they're for but by what they are against. They will never escape the dead-end street of violence. But you, the vast majority, Protestant and Catholic alike, must not allow the ship of peace to sink on the rocks of old habits and hard grudges. You must stand firm against terror. You must say to those who still would use violence for political objectives, you are the past, your day is over, violence has no place at the table of democracy and no role in the future of this land. By the same token, you must always be willing to say to those who renounce violence and who do take their own risks for peace, that they are entitled to be full participants in the democratic process. Those who do show the courage to break with the past are entitled to their stake in the future."

Belfast, Northern Ireland, UK, 30th November 1995

Thabo Mbeki

'I AM AN AFRICAN'

The anti-apartheid African National Congress (ANC) was banned in South Africa in 1960, forcing many of its members to flee the country. One of them, Thabo Mbeki (b. 1942), escaped to England in 1962. After completing his university studies there, he spent time in the former USSR before returning to Africa to continue working for the ANC, living in Zambia, Botswana, Swaziland and Zimbabwe. Mbeki played a major role in the talks between the South African government and the ANC that led to the end of apartheid, allowing him finally to return to his home country in 1990. When Mandela won the presidency four years later, Mbeki was named one of his deputies. A new constitution was passed in 1996 and Mbeki made a speech in Cape Town to mark the event, stating his pride to be an African, his love for the continent and his hopes for its future. Mbeki succeeded Mandela as president in 1999 and served in the office until 2008. As leader he oversaw economic growth but has been criticized for his lack of action in combating HIV/AIDS.

"I am an African. I owe my being to the hills and the valleys, the mountains and the glades, the rivers, the deserts, the trees, the flowers, the seas and the ever-changing seasons that define the face of our native land.

…I have experience of the situation in which race and colour is used to enrich some and impoverish the rest. I have seen the corruption of minds and souls as a result of the pursuit of an ignoble effort to perpetrate a veritable crime against humanity. I have seen concrete expression of the denial of the dignity of a human being emanating from the conscious, systemic and systematic oppressive and repressive activities of other human beings.

…I am an African. I am born of the peoples of the continent of Africa. The pain of the violent conflict that the peoples of Liberia, and of Somalia, of the Sudan, of Burundi and Algeria is a pain I also bear. The dismal shame of poverty, suffering and human degradation of my continent is a blight that we share. The blight on our happiness that derives from this and from our drift to the periphery of the ordering of human affairs leaves us in a persistent shadow of despair.

This is a savage road to which nobody should be condemned.

The evolution of humanity says that Africa reaffirms that she is continuing her rise from the ashes. Whatever the setbacks of the moment, nothing can stop us now! Whatever the difficulties, Africa shall be at peace!"

Cape Town, South Africa, 8th May 1996

Tony Blair

GENERAL ELECTION VICTORY SPEECH

When Tony Blair (b. 1953) became leader of the UK Labour Party in 1994, it had been out of power for over 15 years. He moved the party closer to the political centre, reinventing it as 'New Labour'. This proved successful in gaining wider public support and Labour won the 1997 general election by a landslide. The next day Blair officially became prime minister, and spoke from the steps of London's 10 Downing Street, signalling the plans of his administration, prioritizing education and health. Blair would remain national leader for just over a decade, achieving two more general election victories, and overseeing increases in public spending, a national minimum wage and devolved power for Wales and Scotland. He also played a central role in the Northern Irish peace process. However, Blair's decision to involve the United Kingdom in the 2003 invasion of Iraq proved controversial, both in his own party and amongst the wider public. Since standing down as prime minister in June 2007, Blair's main focus has been on diplomatic work in the Middle East.

I know well what this country has voted for today. It is a mandate for New Labour and I say to the people of this country, we ran for office as New Labour, we will govern as New Labour. This is not a mandate for dogma or for doctrine, or for a return to the past, but it is a mandate to get those things done in our country that desperately need doing for the future. …Above all, we have secured a mandate to bring this nation together, to unite us. One Britain, one nation in which our ambition for ourselves is matched by our sense of compassion and decency and duty towards other people. Simple values, but the right ones. For 18 years, for 18 long years, my party has been in opposition. It could only say, it could not do. Today we are charged with the deep responsibility of government. Today, enough of talking. It is time now to do. **"**

London, England, 2nd May 1997

Elie Wiesel

'INDIFFERENCE IS A PUNISHMENT'

Born into a Jewish family in Romania, Elie Wiesel (1928–2016) was deported to Auschwitz in 1944, and forced to join a death march to Buchenwald, a concentration camp in Germany, in 1945. Following the liberation of Buchenwald by Allied troops in April 1945, the 16-year-old Wiesel resettled in France, where he attended the Sorbonne and worked as a journalist. Wiesel moved to New York in 1956 and two years later published *La Nuit*, a memoir of his experiences in the Holocaust. Living in the United States, Wiesel wrote dozens more books and spoke out against the oppression suffered not just by Jews, but by all victims of prejudice. In 1986, he was awarded the Nobel Peace Prize, and that year he founded the Elie Wiesel Foundation for Humanity with his wife Marion, an organization that works to foster understanding, equality and peace between peoples. Central to Wiesel's mission was educating young people about the dangers of intolerance. In 1999 he gave a lecture at the White House where he spoke of the perils of indifference in the face of suffering and violence. He continued his work and activism until his death aged 87, in 2016.

"We are on the threshold of a new century, a new millennium. What will the legacy of this vanishing century be? How will it be remembered in the new millennium? Surely it will be judged, and judged severely, in both moral and metaphysical terms. These failures have cast a dark shadow over humanity: two world wars, countless civil wars, the senseless chain of assassinations – Gandhi, the Kennedys, Martin Luther King, Sadat, Rabin – bloodbaths in Cambodia and Nigeria, India and Pakistan, Ireland and Rwanda, Eritrea and Ethiopia, Sarajevo and Kosovo; the inhumanity in the gulag and the tragedy of Hiroshima. And, on a different level, of course, Auschwitz and Treblinka. So much violence, so much indifference.

What is indifference? Etymologically, the word means 'no difference'. A strange and unnatural state in which the lines blur between light and darkness, dusk and dawn, crime and punishment, cruelty and compassion, good and evil.

...Of course, indifference can be tempting – more than that, seductive. It is so much easier to look away from victims. It is so much easier to avoid such rude interruptions to our work, our dreams, our hopes. It is, after all, awkward, troublesome, to be involved in another person's pain and despair.

...Indifference, then, is not only a sin, it is a punishment. And this is one of the most important lessons of this outgoing century's wide-ranging experiments in good and evil."

Washington, DC, USA, 12th April 1999

Pope John Paul II

SPEECH AT YAD VASHEM

In 1978, Pope John Paul I died after just 33 days in office. Elected successor was the Archbishop of Kraków, Karol Wojtyła (1920–2005). Taking the regnal name John Paul II, at just 58 years of age he was the youngest pope in over a century and was also the first non-Italian elected to the office since 1522. A vigorous and outspoken leader, he visited 129 countries during his papacy, speaking with world leaders and often preaching to crowds that numbered in the millions. He was unafraid to speak out on political matters, particularly in his native Poland, where he encouraged resistance to the ruling communist regime. John Paul II also worked to improve relations between the Catholic Church and Judaism, and in 2000 travelled to Jerusalem to visit Yad Vashem, Israel's memorial to the Holocaust. In his speech, he spoke of the Catholic Church's grief regarding the suffering and violence the Jewish people had been subjected to, and also rejected any form of racism. After years of worsening health, John Paul II died in 2005 – he was canonized nine years later.

"As bishop of Rome and successor of the Apostle Peter, I assure the Jewish people that the Catholic Church, motivated by the Gospel law of truth and love, and by no political considerations, is deeply saddened by the hatred, acts of persecution and displays of anti-Semitism directed against the Jews by Christians at any time and in any place. The Church rejects racism in any form as a denial of the image of the Creator inherent in every human being. In this place of solemn remembrance, I fervently pray that our sorrow for the tragedy that the Jewish people suffered in the 20th century will lead to a new relationship between Christians and Jews. Let us build a new future in which there will be no more anti-Jewish feeling among Christians or anti-Christian feeling among Jews, but rather the mutual respect required of those who adore the one Creator and Lord, and look to Abraham as our common father in faith."

Jerusalem, Israel, 23rd March 2000

George W. Bush

'AXIS OF EVIL'

On 11th September 2001, al-Qaeda crashed hijacked airplanes into the World Trade Center and the Pentagon, killing nearly 3,000 people. President George W. Bush (b. 1946), responded by launching a 'War on Terror' against terrorists and the governments that supported them. His first target was the Taliban regime in Afghanistan, which had been harbouring Osama bin Laden, the founder of al-Qaeda. On 7th October, American and allied forces invaded Afghanistan, toppling the Taliban. On 29th January 2002, Bush delivered his State of the Union address, in which he denounced Iran, Iraq and North Korea for their sponsoring of terrorism and plans to develop 'weapons of mass destruction', terming them an 'axis of evil'. In March 2003, an American-led coalition attacked Iraq, overthrowing Saddam Hussein. Bush was re-elected in 2004, serving as president until 2009. His administration has been criticized for its handling of the wars in Afghanistan and Iraq, but won praise for launching the President's Emergency Plan For AIDS Relief, an international campaign to fight the disease that has saved over a million lives.

"Iraq continues to flaunt its hostility toward America and to support terror. The Iraqi regime has plotted to develop anthrax, and nerve gas, and nuclear weapons for over a decade. This is a regime that has already used poison gas to murder thousands of its own citizens, leaving the bodies of mothers huddled over their dead children. This is a regime that agreed to international inspections, then kicked out the inspectors. This is a regime that has something to hide from the civilized world.

States like these, and their terrorist allies, constitute an axis of evil, arming to threaten the peace of the world. By seeking weapons of mass destruction, these regimes pose a grave and growing danger. They could provide these arms to terrorists, giving them the means to match their hatred. They could attack our allies or attempt to blackmail the United States. In any of these cases, the price of indifference would be catastrophic.

...We'll be deliberate, yet time is not on our side. I will not wait on events, while dangers gather. I will not stand by, as peril draws closer and closer. The United States of America will not permit the world's most dangerous regimes to threaten us with the world's most destructive weapons.

Our war on terror is well begun, but it is only begun. This campaign may not be finished on our watch, yet it must be and it will be waged on our watch. We can't stop short. If we stop now, leaving terror camps intact and terror states unchecked, our sense of security would be false and temporary.

History has called America and our allies to action, and it is both our responsibility and our privilege to fight freedom's fight."

Washington, DC, USA, 29th January 2002

Saddam Hussein

SPEECH AT THE START OF THE IRAQ WAR

In 1968, the Ba'ath Party seized power in Iraq. One of its leading figures was Saddam Hussein (1937–2006), who became president in 1979. He crushed internal dissent to his dictatorial rule, brutally and violently targeting Shi'a Muslims and the Kurdish ethnic group, even using chemical warfare. In 1980, Hussein led Iraq into conflict with neighbouring Iran. Lasting until 1988, the war proved costly and in an attempt to shore up his government's finances, Hussain invaded and annexed Kuwait in 1990, aiming to exploit its oil reserves. This led to the Gulf War, where an international coalition led by the United States forced Iraqi troops out of Kuwait. Hussein remained in power, but faced strict sanctions as part of the ceasefire. His failure to fully cooperate with UN weapons inspections led to an American-led coalition invading Iraq on 20th March 2003. Hussein remained defiant, and four days later vowed to fight off the attack – however, his forces crumbled and Baghdad was taken on 9th April. His regime over, Hussein went into hiding but was captured by the end of the year. He was executed in 2006 after being found guilty of crimes against humanity.

"Now we are living through decisive days in which fighters
and the great Iraqi people are doing exceptionally well and for which
they deserve victory and satisfaction from God, as He promised
the true faithful against the enemies of God and humanity.
It is our right, nay our duty, to be proud as fighting believers
who are patient in this epic war.
…The enemy is trapped in the sacred land of Iraq,
which is being defended by its great people and army.
O brave fighters, hit your enemy with all your strength. O Iraqis,
fight with the strength of the spirit of jihad, which you carry in you
and push them to the point where they cannot go on.
You will reap stability and dignity with victory. For our martyrs the prize of
heaven and for you the prize of honour that satisfies God and that will be
recorded by history. The lesson you teach the enemy will make them think twice,
and even be incapable, of attacking you, your nation and humanity again.
Hit them so that good and its people may reign and evil evicted back to its place.
Mothers, daughters, fathers and sons, together with all the faithful and good,
will sleep in comfort after being terrified by aggression. Your struggle will
dishearten the aggressor. Oh Arabs, oh faithful of the world, oh those who
support justice and oppose evil, we herald the victory that God has promised
us in the conflict against the lowlifes and enemies of humanity."

Baghdad, Iraq, 24th March 2003

Wangari Maathai

'RISE UP AND WALK!'

In 1971, the Kenyan Wangari Maathai (1940–2011) became the first woman from East Africa to obtain a PhD; she then lectured at the University of Nairobi and served on Kenya's National Council of Women. Her political work exposed her to the environmental problems facing the country – particularly the drying up of streams and deforestation. In 1977, she founded the Green Belt Movement to encourage villagers to plant trees. Under her leadership it grew into a major international nongovernmental organization that aims to conserve the world's natural resources whilst giving power to local communities, particularly women. Maathai also campaigned for greater democratic rights and state accountability, as well as for the cancellation of the huge debts amassed by many African nations. For her work, she was awarded the Nobel Peace Prize in 2004, the first African woman to win it. The next year she delivered the annual Nelson Mandela lecture in Johannesburg and, using Mandela's 'Madiba' title of respect, called on Africa to rise up and free itself from poverty. Maathai is regarded a champion of the environment.

"Often, those in power invent excuses to justify the exclusion and other injustices against those perceived to be weak and vulnerable. But when resources are scarce, so degraded that they can no longer sustain livelihoods, or when they are not equitably distributed, conflicts will invariably ensue. Equitable distribution of resources cannot be effected unless there is democratic space, which respects the rule of law and human rights. Such democratic space gives citizens an enabling environment to be creative and productive. What is clear is that there is a close linkage between sustainable management of resources and equitable distribution of the same on the one hand and democratic governance and peace on the other. These are the pillars of any stable and secure state. Such a state has the enabling environment for development. People who are denied the three pillars eventually become angry and frustrated, and undermine peace and security in their neighbourhoods and beyond. For that reason, we need to manage our resources sustainably, accountably and responsibly. We need to share those resources equitably. Otherwise, we shall continue to invest in wars and conflicts, fighting crime and domestic instability, rather than promoting development and thereby eliminating poverty. …Madiba, I know this is the dream you have for Africa. An Africa free of poverty. An Africa with economic and political freedom. An empowered Africa. So my fellow Africans. Let's heed the call of Madiba: Rise Up and Walk!"

Johannesburg, South Africa, 19th July 2005

Hugo Chávez

'THE DEVIL IS RIGHT AT HOME'

In Venezuela in 1982, and disillusioned with the country's traditional ruling parties, an army officer called Hugo Chávez (1954–2013) founded a left-wing group called the Revolutionary Bolivarian Movement-200, which unsuccessfully tried to seize power ten years later. Despite his coup's failure, Chávez grew in popularity and was elected president in December 1998. After taking office in February 1999, he pursued a populist socialist agenda, spending oil revenue on government programmes and nationalizing many industries whilst introducing a new constitution that gave him sweeping new powers. Re-elected in 2000, his increasingly authoritarian rule led to a mass rally marching on his palace in 2002. The army responded by removing Chávez from power but he was restored within a few days. Chávez was a vocal critic of the United States's 'imperialist' foreign policy. In a September 2006 speech at the UN, he denounced George W. Bush as the 'devil'. Despite facing increasing internal dissent, Chávez was re-elected president that December and won a fourth term in 2012, but died of cancer in 2013 before he could be sworn in again.

"The devil is right at home. The devil, the devil himself, is right in the house. And the devil came here yesterday. Yesterday the devil came here. Right here. And it smells of sulfur still today. Yesterday, ladies and gentlemen, from this rostrum, the president of the United States, the gentleman to whom I refer as the devil, came here, talking as if he owned the world. Truly. As the owner of the world.

…I have the feeling, dear world dictator, that you are going to live the rest of your days as a nightmare because the rest of us are standing up, all those of us who are rising up against American imperialism, who are shouting for equality, for respect, for the sovereignty of nations. Yes, you can call us extremists, but we are rising up against the empire, against the model of domination."

New York City, NY, USA, 20th September 2006

Barack Obama

'YES WE CAN'

Born in Hawaii in 1961, Barack Obama graduated from Harvard Law School at the age of 30 and moved to Chicago. Practising as a civil rights attorney, he became active in Democratic Party politics, winning election to the Illinois state senate in 1996. National fame followed his delivery of the keynote address at the Democratic National Convention in 2004, and later that year he was elected to the US Senate. His powerful oratory and message of change saw him win the Democrat nomination for the presidency and on 4th November 2008, he became the first African-American president of the United States. That evening he gave a victory speech in Chicago, acknowledging his hopes for the future. Obama won a second term in 2012. Although he failed to meet his promise to close the detention camp at Guantanamo Bay and oversaw the escalating use of drone strikes against enemy targets overseas, amongst Obama's achievements as leader were guiding the United States through its recovery from the Global Financial Crisis, landmark health-care legislation, and the normalization of relations with Cuba.

"If there is anyone out there who still doubts that America is a place where all things are possible, who still wonders if the dream of our founders is alive in our time, who still questions the power of our democracy, tonight is your answer. …It's the answer spoken by young and old, rich and poor, Democrat and Republican, black, white, Latino, Asian, Native American, gay, straight, disabled and not disabled – Americans who sent a message to the world that we have never been a collection of Red States and Blue States: we are, and always will be, the United States of America. …This is our moment. This is our time. To put our people back to work and open doors of opportunity for our kids. To restore prosperity and promote the cause of peace. To reclaim the American Dream and reaffirm that fundamental truth that out of many, we are one, that while we breathe, we hope, and where we are met with cynicism, and doubt, and those who tell us that we can't, we will respond with that timeless creed that sums up the spirit of a people: Yes We Can."

Chicago, Illinois, USA, 4th November 2008

Evo Morales

IN DEFENCE OF MOTHER EARTH

The first indigenous person to serve as president of Bolivia is Evo Morales (b. 1959), a member of the Aymara people. Before entering politics he was a farmer; one of his crops was coca, which is used to make cocaine but has many other medicinal uses and has been cultivated in the Andes for millennia. Becoming involved in trade union activism, Morales led a campaign against the government suppression of coca farming. In 1997, he was elected to the Bolivian legislature as a member of the Movement Towards Socialism party. He finished second in the 2002 presidential elections, before winning a majority victory in 2005. Taking office on 22nd January 2006, Morales introduced reforms including greater recognition of indigenous rights, land redistribution and nationalization of some industries. One of his main priorities was to protect the environment – in September 2009 he addressed the UN's General Assembly, stating that respect and good stewardship of Mother Earth was essential to the future of humanity. That December Morales was re-elected for a second term as president, and he won a third term in 2014.

"There exists an ongoing debate about the financial crisis, climate change and democracy. We cannot forget the food and energy crises. I applaud the addresses that focus on the origins of the crisis. However, the majority of the speeches only speak of effects, never the cause. I came here today to speak plainly with you all. The origin of this crisis is the exaggerated accumulation of capital in far too few hands. It is the permanent removal of natural resources and the commercialization of Mother Earth.

...I've concluded that in this new 21st century, defending Mother Earth will be more important than defending human rights. If we do not defend the rights of Mother Earth, there is no use in defending human rights. I am willing to debate this concept, but now or later it will be proven that the rights of Mother Earth supersede the rights of human beings. We must protect what gives us life."

New York City, NY, USA, 23rd September 2009

Tawakkol Karman

NOBEL LECTURE

The Arab Spring involved a series of popular uprisings that swept through North Africa and the Middle East from 2010–12. There were mass protests against corruption, unemployment and political repression, leading to the overthrow of authoritarian regimes in many countries. At the time, the Republic of Yemen had been ruled by President Ali Abdullah Saleh for over two decades. One of his most vocal opponents was Tawakkol Karman (b. 1979), a journalist and advocate for women's rights and democratic reform. When she was arrested in January 2011 for organizing protests against Saleh, it triggered larger demonstrations. Karman was quickly released, and became a leading figure in the campaign for political change in Yemen, despite facing threats of death and imprisonment. That October, Karman was awarded the Nobel Peace Prize. In her acceptance speech, she emphasized her commitment to nonviolence and human rights. Saleh was forced to resign in February 2012, but this did not bring stability to Yemen, which since 2015 has been torn apart by civil war.

> " The Arab people who are revolting in a peaceful and civilized manner have, for so many decades, been oppressed and suppressed by the regimes of authoritarian tyrants who have indulged themselves deeply in corruption and in looting the wealth of their people. They have gone too far in depriving their people of freedom and of the natural right to a dignified life. They have gone too far in depriving them of the right to participate in the management of their personal affairs and the affairs of their communities. These regimes have totally disregarded the Arab people as a people with a legitimate human existence, and have let poverty and unemployment flourish among them in order to secure that the rulers and their family members after them will have full control over the people. Allow me to say that our oppressed people have revolted declaring the emergence of a new dawn, in which the sovereignty of the people, and their invincible will, will prevail. "

Oslo, Norway, 10th December 2011

Vladimir Putin

ON THE REUNIFICATION OF CRIMEA

After the dissolution of the former USSR in 1991, the newly created Russian Federation experienced economic depression, rising levels of poverty and internal conflict. The first president, Boris Yeltsin, earmarked as his political heir Vladimir Putin (b. 1952), a former KGB officer and deputy mayor of St Petersburg. After Yeltsin resigned in 1999, Putin served as acting leader and then won a majority in the presidential elections held the following year. He provided firm and decisive leadership, gaining popularity for his rebuilding of the economy and winning re-election in 2004. Although Putin stepped down as president in 2008, his successor and ally Dmitry Medvedev named him as prime minister, meaning he retained a high level of influence. Amidst reports of vote rigging, Putin won a third term as president in 2012. In 2014, he sent troops into Ukraine and annexed Crimea from them – on 18th March he stated in a speech that that the peninsula had always been a part of Russia. Putin was re-elected in 2018 but has attracted criticism for his growing authoritarianism and interventions into the affairs of other states.

"In people's hearts and minds, Crimea has always been an inseparable part of Russia. This firm conviction is based on truth and justice and was passed from generation to generation, over time, under any circumstances, despite all the dramatic changes our country went through during the entire 20th century.

…Like a mirror, the situation in Ukraine reflects what is going on and what has been happening in the world over the past several decades. After the dissolution of bipolarity on the planet, we no longer have stability. Key international institutions are not getting any stronger. On the contrary, in many cases, they are sadly degrading.

Our Western partners, led by the United States of America, prefer not to be guided by international law in their practical policies, but by the rule of the gun. They have come to believe in their exclusivity and exceptionalism, that they can decide the destinies of world, that only they can ever be right. They act as they please. Here and there, they use force against sovereign states, building coalitions based on the principle: if you are not with us, you are against us."

Moscow, Russia, 18th March 2014

Pope Francis

'THE DUNG OF THE DEVIL'

Born in Buenos Aires in 1936, into an Italian immigrant family, Jorge Mario Bergoglio was ordained a Catholic priest in 1969. After working and teaching at a seminary and undertaking further studies in theology in Germany, Bergoglio was appointed auxiliary bishop of Buenos Aires in 1992. He became archbishop of the city in 1998 and was consecrated as a cardinal in 2001, winning a reputation for his humble lifestyle and work with the poor. After Benedict XVI resigned in 2013, Bergoglio travelled to Rome to attend the papal conclave and was elected pope on the fifth ballot. Taking the regnal name Francis, in honour of St Francis of Assisi, he was the first pope from the Americas and the first Jesuit. He sought to rebuild a Church that had struggled with scandal and declining membership, spreading a message of spiritual renewal. One of Francis's chief concerns has been to address the issues of climate change and global poverty, which he summed up in his 2015 speech to the World Meeting of Popular Movements, an event held in Bolivia to bring together grass-roots activists and religious leaders.

"Time, my brothers and sisters, seems to be running out. We are not yet tearing one another apart, but we are tearing apart our common home. Today, the scientific community realizes what the poor have long told us: harm, perhaps irreversible harm, is being done to the ecosystem. The earth, entire peoples and individual persons are being brutally punished... An unfettered pursuit of money rules. This is the dung of the devil. The service of the common good is left behind. Once capital becomes an idol and guides people's decisions, once greed for money presides over the entire socioeconomic system, it ruins society, it condemns and enslaves men and women, it destroys human fraternity, it sets people against one another and, as we clearly see, it even puts at risk our common home, sister and mother earth. ...The future of humanity does not lie solely in the hands of great leaders, the great powers and the elites. It is fundamentally in the hands of peoples and in their ability to organize. It is in their hands, which can guide with humility and conviction this process of change. I am with you. Each of us, let repeat from the heart: no family without lodging, no rural worker without land, no labourer without rights, no people without sovereignty, no individual without dignity, no child without childhood, no young person without a future, no elderly person without a venerable old age. Keep up your struggle and, please, take great care of Mother Earth."

Santa Cruz de la Sierra, Bolivia, 9th July 2015

Nadia Murad

ON HUMAN TRAFFICKING

The Yazidi people of northern Mesopotamia follow a faith that combines elements of ancient Iranian religions, Judaism, Christianity and Islam. Since 2014, the Islamic State of Iraq and the Levant (ISIL) has been carrying out a genocidal campaign against them. Thousands of Yazidi have been killed or forced to convert to Islam, whilst women and girls have been forced into sexual slavery. They include Nadia Murad (b. 1993), who was captured from her home village of Kocho in northern Iraq at the age of 21 and held in brutal conditions for three months before escaping in November 2014. She fled to Europe and resettled in Germany. On 16th December 2015, Murad briefed the UN Security Council on human trafficking. She spoke of the indignities suffered by women and children who, like her, were sold into sexual slavery. The next year she founded Nadia's Initiative, an organization that supports victims of sexual violence and rebuilds communities that have suffered as a result of violence. In 2018, Murad was awarded the Nobel Peace Prize.

"It is with great sadness, gratitude and hope that I stand before you today as one of the few survivors of one of the world's oldest ethnic and religious groups now threatened by extinction. I am here today to speak on the way the so-called Islamic State trafficked us, transformed the Yazidi women into sex slaves and the way IS committed a genocide against my people. I am here to tell you what happened to me and my community, which lost hope and headed into the unknown, I am here also to speak on behalf of those who remain in captivity. I am here to speak about a global terrorist organization that came to end our existence, culture and freedom, to speak about the nightmare that changed life for a community overnight. ...The Islamic State didn't come to kill the women and girls, but to use us as spoils of war, as objects to be sold with little or to be gifted for free. Their cruelty was not merely opportunistic. The IS soldiers came with a pre-established policy to commit such crimes. ...Bring an end to ISIL, I have seen them, I have lived the pain they caused. We have to bring all human traffickers, criminals and those who committed genocide to justice so that the women and children in Nigeria, Syria, Somalia and everywhere in the world can live in peace. These crimes against women and their freedom shall stop now."

New York, NY, USA, 16th December 2015

Angela Merkel

NEW YEAR'S EVE SPEECH 2016

The daughter of a Lutheran pastor, Angela Merkel (b. 1954) grew up in East Germany, working as a research scientist and gaining a doctorate in quantum chemistry in 1986. After the fall of the Berlin Wall in 1989, she embarked on a political career and, in 1990, was elected to the Bundestag as a member of the Christian Democratic Union (CDU) in the first elections to be held following German reunification. Merkel rose through the ranks of government and was elected leader of the CDU in 2000. In 2005, she was appointed chancellor of Germany, becoming the first woman ever to hold the position. She proved to be a popular and effective leader, winning re-election in 2009 and 2013. Perhaps Merkel's most challenging year was 2016, when Germany faced several deadly terrorist attacks that led to a nationalist backlash against migrants. In her New Year's Eve speech that year, she asked the public not to give in to hate and to continue to welcome new arrivals. Merkel, who has become one of the most influential world leaders, won a fourth term as chancellor in 2017.

"My fellow citizens, 2016 has been a year of difficult trials… but I would like to speak about why I am confident in Germany in spite of everything, and why I am so very convinced of the strengths of our country and its people.

…Where Europe is challenged as a whole, as it is in global competition, in the protection of our external borders or regarding migration, it must find a response as a whole, however painstaking and tough this may be. And we Germans have every interest in playing a leading role in this.

…Cohesion, openness, our democracy and a strong economy that serves the well-being of all, these are the things that make me confident in our future here in Germany."

Berlin, Germany, 31st December 2016

Donald Trump

INAUGURAL ADDRESS

Born in New York City in 1946, Donald J. Trump worked for his father's real estate business after graduating from university, and was appointed its president in 1971. He renamed the company the Trump Organization and expanded its operations, moving into casinos, golf courses, hotels, skyscrapers and even an airline. During the 1990s, financial troubles forced many of Trump's enterprises into bankruptcy and he increasingly relied on his celebrity status to gain publicity and credence for his forays into political commentary, licensing his name to many products and becoming a television personality. He became involved in politics and, in 2015, announced he was seeking to be the Republican candidate for the US presidency. Despite being the subject of numerous scandals, including allegations of sexual misconduct, he secured the nomination and then, in November 2016, defeated Hillary Clinton to win the presidency. Trump was inaugurated in Washington, DC, on 20th January 2017, and in his address promised to live up to his campaign pledge to 'make America great again'.

"The oath of office I take today is an oath of allegiance to all Americans. For many decades, we've enriched foreign industry at the expense of American industry, subsidized the armies of other countries while allowing for the very sad depletion of our military, we've defended other nation's borders while refusing to defend our own, and spent trillions of dollars overseas while America's infrastructure has fallen into disrepair and decay. We've made other countries rich while the wealth, strength and confidence of our country has disappeared over the horizon. One by one, the factories shuttered and left our shores, with not even a thought about the millions upon millions of American workers left behind. The wealth of our middle class has been ripped from their homes and then redistributed across the entire world. But that is the past. And now we are looking only to the future. We assembled here today are issuing a new decree to be heard in every city, in every foreign capital and in every hall of power. From this day forward, a new vision will govern our land. From this moment on, it's going to be America first. …Together, we will make America strong again. We will make America wealthy again. We will make America proud again. We will make America safe again.

And, yes, together, we will make America great again. Thank you, God bless you, and God bless America."

Washington, DC, USA, 20th January 2017

Oprah Winfrey

SPEECH AT THE GOLDEN GLOBES

Growing up in poverty in rural Mississippi, Oprah Winfrey (b. 1954) found national fame hosting her eponymous talk show, which aired for 25 years. She pursued a range of other activities, including acting, film and television production, and publishing, and founded her own television network. Amassing a huge fortune, Winfrey became the first black female billionaire in 2003. Always active in charity work, she has raised and donated millions of dollars, and has become increasingly involved in politics, endorsing Barack Obama's presidential campaign.

In 2017, the film producer Harvey Weinstein was accused of sexual abuse against dozens of women, sparking the 'Me Too' movement. Women across the world shared their experiences of assault and harassment, making it clear just how pervasive it was and breaking a decades-long silence. Winfrey vocally supported this struggle. When she won the Cecil B. DeMille Award for lifetime achievement in motion pictures at the Golden Globes in 2018, she made a passionate speech calling for gender (and racial) equality.

"I want all the girls watching here, now, to know that a new day is on the horizon! And when that new day finally dawns, it will be because of a lot of magnificent women, many of whom are right here in this room tonight, and some pretty phenomenal men, are fighting hard to make sure that they become the leaders who take us to the time when nobody ever has to say 'me too' again."

Los Angeles, California, USA, 7th January 2018

Jacinda Ardern

'WHAT WORDS...?'

On 1st August 2017, just seven weeks before a general election, Jacinda Ardern (b. 1980), a member of the New Zealand Parliament for nine years, became leader of the opposition Labour Party, which had been steadily losing public support. Her charismatic leadership and progressive agenda reinvigorated the party's fortunes, and in the elections that September it won enough votes to form a coalition government. Ardern assumed office the next month, becoming prime minister at just 37 years of age. New Zealand, and Ardern, faced one of their darkest days on 15th March 2019, when a far-right white-supremacist terrorist attacked two mosques in the city of Christchurch, killing 51 people and injuring 50 more. Ardern won national and international renown for her compassionate and forceful response to the attacks. Comforting the shocked community, she condemned extremism and initiated legislation that banned the types of firearms used in the attacks. Two weeks later, Ardern addressed a memorial service for the victims, where she called on the nation to reject hatred and embrace diversity.

"What words adequately express the pain and suffering of 50 men, women and children lost, and so many injured? What words capture the anguish of our Muslim community being the target of hatred and violence? What words express the grief of a city that has already known so much pain? I thought there were none. And then I came here and was met with this simple greeting.

Asalamu Aleykum. Peace be upon you.

They were simple words, repeated by community leaders who witnessed the loss of their friends and loved ones. Simple words, whispered by the injured from their hospital beds. Simple words, spoken by the bereaved and everyone I met who has been affected by this attack. *Asalamu Aleykum*. Peace be upon you.

…Over the past two weeks we have heard the stories of those impacted by this terrorist attack. They were stories of bravery. They were stories of those who were born here, grew up here, or who had made New Zealand their home. Who had sought refuge, or sought a better life for themselves or their families. These stories, they now form part of our collective memories. They will remain with us forever. They are us. But with that memory comes a responsibility.

A responsibility to be the place that we wish to be. A place that is diverse, that is welcoming, that is kind and compassionate. Those values represent the very best of us.

But even the ugliest of viruses can exist in places they are not welcome. Racism exists, but it is not welcome here. An assault on the freedom of any one of us who practises their faith or religion, is not welcome here. Violence, and extremism in all its forms, is not welcome here."

Christchurch, New Zealand, 29th March 2019

Key lines

Speakers

Key themes